Cookies For Dummies®

T0065718

Top Tips for Baking Cookies

- ✔ Set aside enough time to enjoy the cookie-baking experience.
- ✔ Read through each recipe thoroughly so you know what to do.
- ✔ Check to make sure that you have all the ingredients needed to make the recipes you choose.
- ✔ Prepare the ingredients by measuring them and doing other steps that may be needed, such as chopping nuts or grinding spices.
- ✔ Assemble the necessary equipment.
- ✔ Make sure that your workspace is clean and organized.
- ✔ Preheat the oven before baking.
- ✔ Leave space between cookies on the cookie sheet so that they have room to spread as they bake.
- ✔ Don't forget to set the timer when the cookies are in the oven.
- ✔ Let the cookies cool completely before storing them.
- ✔ Taste to make sure that you're satisfied with the results of your baking efforts.

Cookies to Dazzle Your Friends

For Dummies: Bestselling Book Series for Beginners

BESTSELLING
BOOK SERIES

Cookies For Dummies®

Cheat Sheet

Measurement Equivalents

Butter

1 tablespoon butter	=	½ ounce				
1 stick butter	=	8 tablespoons	=	½ cup	=	4 ounces
2 sticks butter	=	16 tablespoons	=	1 cup	=	½ pound
4 sticks butter	=	32 tablespoons	=	2 cups	=	1 pound

Liquids

1 cup	=	16 tablespoons	=	8 fluid ounces
1 pint	=	2 cups	=	16 fluid ounces

Other measurements

1 tablespoon	=	3 teaspoons
2 tablespoons	=	⅛ cup
4 tablespoons	=	¼ cup
8 tablespoons	=	½ cup

See Appendix C for metric conversions.

Ingredient Substitutions

In place of	Use
1 cup light brown sugar	1 cup sugar plus 3 tablespoons molasses OR ½ cup sugar plus ½ cup dark brown sugar
1 cup dark brown sugar	1 cup sugar plus ¼ cup molasses
1 cup sugar	1 cup superfine sugar OR 2 cups powdered sugar OR 1 cup firmly packed light brown sugar
1 cup confectioners' sugar	½ cup plus 1 tablespoon sugar
1 cup all-purpose flour	1 cup plus 2 tablespoons cake flour
1 cup cake flour	1 cup minus 2 tablespoons all-purpose flour
1 teaspoon baking powder	½ teaspoon cream of tartar plus ¼ teaspoon baking soda
1 ounce unsweetened baking chocolate	3 tablespoons cocoa powder plus 1 tablespoon butter
1 ounce semisweet chocolate	½ ounce unsweetened chocolate plus 1 tablespoon sugar
1 cup light corn syrup	1¼ cups sugar OR firmly packed brown sugar and ⅓ cup water boiled together until the sugar dissolves
1 cup dark corn syrup	¾ cup light corn syrup plus ¼ cup molasses
1 cup milk	½ cup evaporated milk plus ½ cup water

Wiley, the Wiley Publishing logo, For Dummies, the Dummies Man logo, the For Dummies Bestselling Book Series logo and related trade dress are trademarks or registered trademarks of John Wiley & Sons, Inc. and/or its affiliates in the United States and other countries and may not be used without written permission. All other trademarks are the property of their respective owners. Wiley Publishing, Inc., is not associated with any product or vendor mentioned in this book.

For Dummies: Bestselling Book Series for Beginners

Praise for Cookies For Dummies

"If you want to learn the fundamentals of cookie making, this book should be first on your list. Carole supplies you with everything you need — delicious tasting recipes for all kinds of cookies, straightforward technical advice (including how to figure out when something goes wrong), storage tips, and even how to 'dress up' cookies with chocolate embellishments and icing. With this book, everyone can easily become a master cookie baker and have fun doing it."

> — Emily Luchetti, cookbook author, Executive Pastry Chef, Farallon Restaurant

"If you want to make the jump from Cookie Monster to ace Cookie Maker, here's the guide you need. Carole Bloom's wise tips and techniques, her clearly written instructions and her expert advice guarantee that each time you make one of her recipes you'll turn out great cookies and have great fun doing it."

> — Dorie Greenspan, author of *Baking with Julia*

"Cookies are the friendliest desserts you can make, and Carole Bloom streamlines the process for you. Her recipes, which are easy to understand and follow, include all types. Keep this book and your baking pans at the ready to satisfy all your cookie whims."

> — Flo Braker, author of *The Simple Art of Perfect Baking* and *Sweet Miniatures*

"*Cookies For Dummies* is another Carole Bloom winner. I'm always on the lookout for teachers willing to pass wisdom and knowledge from one generation to the next. Carole's clear instructions, superb recipes, and 'secret' tips will transform both beginners and seasoned cookie veterans into cookie masters."

> — Peter Reinhart, author of *The Bread Baker's Apprentice*

"*Cookies For Dummies* is loaded with enticing recipes and superlative instructions that will have you mixing and baking cookies that are guaranteed not to crumble."

> — Marcel Desaulniers, author of *Death by Chocolate*

"Every book that Carole Bloom crafts promises delicious things from your kitchen and this new cookie book is no exception. You don't have to be a novice baker to appreciate the clearly written, easy-to-follow, foolproof recipes that will make you glad that you are baking with Carole at your side."

> — Lora Brody, author of *Basic Baking*

Cookies

FOR

DUMMIES®

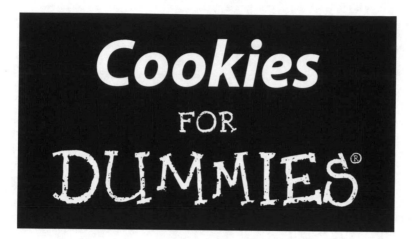

by Carole Bloom

Wiley Publishing, Inc.

Cookies For Dummies®

Published by
Wiley Publishing, Inc.
111 River St.
Hoboken, NJ 07030-5774
www.wiley.com

Copyright © 2001 by Wiley Publishing, Inc., Indianapolis, Indiana

Published by Wiley Publishing, Inc., Indianapolis, Indiana

Published simultaneously in Canada

For general information on our other products and services, please contact our Customer Care Department within the U.S. at 877-762-2974, outside the U.S. at 317-572-3993, or fax 317-572-4002.

For technical support, please visit www.wiley.com/techsupport.

Wiley also publishes its books in a variety of electronic formats. Some content that appears in print may not be available in electronic books.

Library of Congress Control Number: 2001092751

ISBN-13: 978-0-7645-5390-5

10 9 8 7 6 5 4 3 2 1

About the Author

Carole Bloom, CCP, is a European-trained pastry chef and confectioner, cookbook author, food writer, media chef, cooking instructor, and spokesperson. In addition to having professional experience in world-class hotels and restaurants in Europe and the United States, Carole has taught her art for over 20 years at cooking schools throughout the United States. She has also worked as a consultant for both new and established culinary enterprises.

Carole is the author of five cookbooks. Her most recent is *All About Chocolate: The Ultimate Resource for the World's Favorite Food* (Macmillan/IDG), winner of Best Chocolate Book 1999 at Eurochocolate. Carole's other books include *Truffles, Candies, and Confections* (Crossing Press), *The International Dictionary of Desserts, Pastries, and Confections* (Morrow), *The Candy Cookbook* (Chronicle Books), and *Sugar and Spice* (HP Books). She also contributed to the candy chapter for the newly revised edition of the American culinary classic *Joy of Cooking* (Scribner). Carole's food articles appear regularly in national magazines, including *Bon Appétit, Fine Cooking, Food & Wine,and Gourmet.* She is often on television for cooking demonstrations and interviews, with appearances on the *Today Show, ABC World News This Morning,* CNN, and Better Homes and Gardens Television. Carole speaks frequently at national and international conferences and is one of the chefs who make annual appearances at the Chef's Holidays in Yosemite, California. She has been the national spokesperson for the American Boxed Chocolate Manufacturers Group.

Dedication

With love to my husband, Jerry, a true cookie monster.

Author's Acknowledgments

For moral support and tasting lots of cookies, I thank my mother, Florence Bloom, and good friends Terrie Chrones, Susie Hostetter, and April Stinis (ice skating buddies extraordinaire), and Suzy Semanick-Schurman. Special thanks to Kitty Morse for being such a supportive and understanding friend. Thanks to my agent, Jane Dystel, for her savvy and for always being there when I need her. Thanks to acquisitions editor Linda Ingroia for breathing new life into this book. Project editor Suzanne Snyder did a masterful job and was a real pleasure to work with. Many thanks to my husband, Jerry, my premiere cookie taster, dish washer, computer guru, resident comedian, and travel planner. Without his unwavering support and help I would not have been able to complete this project.

Publisher's Acknowledgments

We're proud of this book; please send us your comments through our Dummies online registration form located at www.dummies.com/register/.

Some of the people who helped bring this book to market include the following:

Acquisitions, Editorial, and Media Development

Project Editor: Suzanne Snyder

Senior Acquisitions Editor: Linda Ingroia

Senior Copy Editor: Tina Sims

Assistant Acquisitions Editor: Erin Connell

Technical Editor and Recipe Tester: Emily Nolan

Nutritional Analyst: Patty Santelli

Editorial Manager: Pam Mourouzis

Editorial Assistant: Carol Strickland

Composition Services

Project Coordinator: Nancee Reeves

Layout and Graphics: Amy Adrian, LeAndra Johnson, Jackie Nicholas, Barry Offringa, Jacque Schneider, Betty Schulte, Joyce Haughey

Proofreaders: Aptara, Marianne Santy, Rob Springer

Indexer: Aptara

Illustrator: Liz Kurtzman

Art Director: Michele Laseau

Cover: David Bishop, photographer; Brett Kurzweil, food stylist; Donna Larsen, prop stylist

Publishing and Editorial for Consumer Dummies

Diane Graves Steele, Vice President and Publisher, Consumer Dummies

Joyce Pepple, Acquisitions Director, Consumer Dummies

Kristin Ferguson-Wagstaffe, Product Development Director, Consumer Dummies

Ensley Eikenburg, Associate and Publisher, Travel

Kelly Regan, Editorial Director, Travel

Publishing for Technology Dummies

Andy Cummings, Vice President and Publisher, Dummies Technology/General User

Composition Services

Debbie Stailey, Director of Composition Services

Contents at a Glance

Cartoons at a Glance

By Rich Tennant

"I couldn't find any rose petals, but I figured brownies make more sense in a milk bath anyway."

page 111

"We're making hand-formed cookies, why?"

page 153

"...because I'm more comfortable using my own tools. Now, how much longer do you want me to sand the cookie batter?"

page 287

"Why do I sense you're upset? Because you're piping that cookie with hand grenades instead of rosettes."

page 267

YOUR CHILDS FANTASY RESTAURANT

I'll start with the Rugelach, Pinolate, and Walnut Mandelbrot medley. For an entree I'll have Kourambiedes on a bed of crushed Biscochitos.

VERY GOOD SIR.

page 193

"This is chocolate chip cookie dough ice cream, Oscar. That's why they're not holding their shape in the oven."

page 7

"Folks around here really go for giant drop cookie exchanges. Just fill 'em with dough and heave ho."

page 73

Cartoon Information:
Fax: 978-546-7747
E-Mail: richtennant@the5thwave.com
World Wide Web: www.the5thwave.com

Recipes at a Glance

International Cookies

Molded Cookies

Nut Cookies

Pressed Cookies

Refrigerator Cookies

Table of Contents

Chapter 4: Foolproof Techniques for Outstanding Cookies 57

Introduction

*E*veryone seems to like cookies and has a favorite cookie or two or three. Maybe for you it's one of the old standards, like oatmeal, chocolate chip, or peanut butter. Or maybe it's a cookie with ethnic origins that your mother or grandmother made. Actually, I like just about every cookie. I especially like homemade cookies fresh out of the oven. With milk, coffee, or tea, or just plain as a snack, cookies seem to fit in nicely whenever and wherever.

This book goes much further than simply showing you how to make great cookies. It tells you how to make cookies easily, quickly, and with flair. It gives you all the necessary tips and tricks so that you can streamline the process and avoid any pitfalls. By following the guidelines in this book, you'll quickly be a pro at making drop, rolled, refrigerator, shaped, bar, and sandwich cookies. This book is a fail-safe guide to making great cookies. You get all the necessary information to guide you to success, from what equipment and ingredients to have on hand to how to show off your cookie creations. The book is loaded with easy techniques to help you be successful every time you make cookies. I offer more than 100 cookie recipes, many with variations. These are the best of the best cookies.

How to Use This Book

You don't need to read everything in this book before you start baking your first batch of cookies. However, you should look over all of the non-recipe chapters to see what's in them. When you come across something that you're unfamiliar with or something that you want to find out a little more about, stop and read that section. Then move on to whatever else you think you need to bone up on. My hunch is that you will end up reading most of the book before you begin to make your first batch of cookies. But it wouldn't be nice of me to tell you to read every word first before making some of these yummy cookies.

For very first-time cookie makers, I do suggest that you read through all of the sections prior to making any recipes. You can discover a lot about the whole world of cookie making, especially some important techniques. You'll also gain some confidence from taking in all that cookie-making knowledge.

Every recipe in this book has been tested, so you can be sure that they all work. And each recipe has a nutritional analysis provided so that you know exactly how many calories you're eating, along with how they're distributed. For people watching their weight, I include reduced-fat cookies and tips for lowering fat in regular cookies. For people with kids, I offer a chapter on how to get the kids involved in cookie baking, complete with kid-friendly recipes. Check out the chapters on holiday cookies and international specialties if you want to search out a cookie that may be a particular favorite or try many others that may become your favorites. I also include chapters on decorating cookies, including chocolate decorative touches, and I offer tips on storing, presenting, and transporting your cookies.

My objective in writing this book is to show everyone how easy it is to make great cookies — those that make your mouth water just thinking about them and those that your family and friends want you to make for them. Just dive in, and in short order, you'll be smelling the wonderful aroma of baking cookies. Soon thereafter you'll be saying, "Which one shall I do next?"

Conventions Used in This Book

All the recipes in this book include preparation and baking times so that you know what to expect when choosing a recipe. If you need specialty tools or equipment, I provide that information. The following details hold true throughout the whole book but are not repeated for each recipe.

- All eggs should be large.
- Eggs should be at room temperature.
- All brown sugar should be firmly packed.
- Use only *pure* vanilla extract.
- All oven temperatures are Fahrenheit.
- Always use the middle shelf of the oven unless a recipe indicates otherwise.

Foolish Assumptions

I don't expect the reader of this book to own every little piece of baking equipment necessary to make every recipe in this book. For equipment and tools that you're not familiar with, please see Chapter 2, where I discuss them in depth. For those pieces of equipment and tools that you would like to obtain, see Appendix B for a list of sources. You can learn how to use the equipment by looking at the various chapters that deal with certain individual types of cookies.

How This Book Is Organized

This book is organized by parts, with several chapters in each part. Each part has a major theme, and the chapters in the parts offer more specific information on the theme. In this section, I explain what each part includes.

Part 1: Ready, Set, Let's Bake Cookies

Part I gives you information on how to get started making your own cookies, including information on how to organize your space, the equipment and tools you will need, and the basic ingredients that you'll want to have on hand. You also find out how to get the most out of your equipment and tools and how to measure your ingredients so your cookies turn out just right.

Part II: Popular Types of Cookies

Drop, rolled, and refrigerator cookies are staples in most households. These are the types of cookies that people most often make and eat. In Part II, you find a variety of cookie recipes, such as Oatmeal Raisin Walnut Cookies, Almond Butter Cookies, and Butterscotch Coins. I provide a lot of techniques and tips to help you easily and quickly make these cookies. For very first-time cookies makers, this is a good place to start.

Part III: Stylish Cookies

Part III takes cookies to a slightly higher level. To reach this level, bar, sandwich, and filled cookies require a little more effort. They're not difficult, but some recipes require an extra task to finish off the cookies. Several creative techniques are presented in Part III, including how to use a pastry bag and how to make a parchment paper pastry cone. When you see how great these cookies look and taste, you'll be glad you tried them.

Part IV: Shaping Up Your Cookies

Part IV is where you can really get artistic with your cookies with a limited amount of effort. Pressed, hand-formed, and molded cookies can be made in a variety of sizes and shapes. Here you discover how to make these types of cookies using a cookie press and cookie molds. I also provide some helpful hints on hand forming cookies. In this part, you can practice making cookies look uniform and making them look free-form.

Part V: Cookies of Distinction

In Part V, you get a chance to make several different types of cookies using a wide variety of methods. Here you can find international cookies, such as Chinese Almond Cookies, and holiday cookies, such as Moravian Molasses Spice Cookies. I also include chapters on chocolate cookies, oversize cookies, and reduced-fat cookies, for those of you watching your calorie intake. Many tips and techniques are presented throughout Part V. If you enjoy exploration, this part will take you on a very rewarding journey — one where you'll discover a lot and want to return time and time again.

Part VI: Dressing Up Your Cookies

Part VI is where you find out how to make your cookies look the very, very best they can. Here you find out how to use chocolate in a variety of ways to give your cookies a better look and taste. I cover how to handle chocolate as well as how to write with chocolate using a paper pastry cone. Decorating with fruit and nuts and tips on cookie painting are also covered. You can read about several techniques to help you make your cookies beautiful.

Part VII: The Part of Tens

This part is a mixed bag of helpful information. The troubleshooting tips can save a batch of cookies from disaster. Part VII also provides you some great ideas on ways to share your cookies, including hosting a cookie exchange. I also talk about the best ways to package cookies and send them all over the world.

Appendixes

Appendix A is a glossary of cookie and cookie-related terms. You'll find some enlightening information there to help you become a cookie-making aficionado.

Appendix B has a list of sources for supplies and ingredients. Where applicable, I also supply the Web site. You can get just about everything you need for cookie baking through these sources.

Appendix C is a metric equivalents chart that can come in pretty handy in case you need to translate any measurements.

Web site

For ways to display and otherwise show off your cookies, please go to our Web site at www.dummies.com/bonus/cookies.

Icons Used in This Book

The following icons appear throughout the book to feature specific points you'll want to be sure not to miss.

This icon highlights extra advice and hints to make cookie baking easier and more hassle free.

When you see this icon, pay special attention. I'm giving you a warning about what to avoid or do so that you don't make mistakes.

This icon points out information that you don't want to forget. You may have read it before in this book, but I want to remind you once again.

This icon lets you know that I'm providing a fact or some trivia about cookies or cookie baking that may be of special interest to you.

Smaller icons appear at the beginning of each recipe heading. They represent the recipe's level of difficulty, as follows:

This "E" stands for "easy." Look for this icon if you want to whip up a batch of cookies at a moment's notice, or if you are a beginner and want to gain experience in making cookies. Recipes marked with this icon present great opportunities for children to participate in the cookie-making process as well.

This "I" stands for "intermediate." Recipes marked with an "I" are a bit more involved than the "easy" recipes. To make these cookies, you may have to use techniques such as rolling — or special equipment, such as cookie cutters.

This "A" stands for "advanced." Recipes at this level often involve more steps than do the recipes from the other two levels. They also may require more ingredients and be more time-consuming to prepare.

Part I
Ready, Set, Let's Bake Cookies

The 5th Wave   By Rich Tennant

"This is chocolate chip cookie dough ice cream, Oscar. That's why they're not holding their shape in the oven."

In this part . . .

This part sets the stage for making cookies. It covers how to organize your space with emphasis on having plenty of elbow room, all the neat equipment and tools that you will be using, and the basic ingredients that you want to have on hand. By having the right equipment and ingredients, your cookie-making experience will be quick, easy, and fun.

This part further discusses how to make friends with your tools and equipment and how to get the most out of them. You will also learn that measuring ingredients can be a little tricky, so you want to pay close attention to the methods for this. Techniques are at the core of success. By following the techniques presented here, everything will go smoothly.

Chapter 1

How to Get Started as a Great Cookie Baker

In This Chapter

▶ Discovering the joy of homemade cookies

▶ Being prepared makes cookie baking easy

▶ Organizing your kitchen

▶ Taking your first steps to becoming a cookie master

*W*hen it comes to cookies, it doesn't take too much to get people excited. All you need to say is, "Would you like a cookie?" and the response will most often be, "Yes, please!" Most people don't even ask what type of cookie they're getting, because they simply like cookies. This is the way I am. Of course, I do have some favorites, but I'm like most people — when it comes to cookies, they're all good.

Why do most people like cookies so much? First and foremost, people like the taste. For those who like sweet foods, cookies satisfy that craving. Cookies also come in a range of interesting flavors, so many, in fact, that it's almost easier to make a list of flavors that you *can't* get in cookies. Cookies also leave a wonderful aftertaste — the kind that makes your taste buds tingle and makes you say, "I'll have another one, please." People who are around when the cookies are baking also appreciate the aroma of cookies — nothing can beat the smell of freshly baked cookies! The texture of cookies, ranging from crunchy to smooth to everything in between, is also part of the appeal of cookies.

Cookies have a close connection with your memory. This is what makes them so magical. Just the smell of freshly baked cookies can transport you back to fun times in the kitchen, baking cookies with Mom or Grandma. Cookies can also take you, if only for a moment, out of the hustle and bustle of daily life. Baking cookies is a type of stress reliever. And cookies are a great way to share and make friends. Nothing conveys your feelings better than, "Would you like a cookie? I made them myself."

The Benefits of Making Your Own Cookies

Cookies that are store-bought are okay, but cookies that are homemade are wonderful. "Store-bought" conveys the impression of being mass produced and stale. "Homemade," on the other hand, means that the cookies contain someone's personal touch and are fresh. So why don't more people always make their own cookies at home? Mainly because they mistakenly believe that baking takes too much time and because they worry about whether they can do a good job.

Time doesn't have to be a problem. Some cookie recipes have only a few ingredients and a few steps and — voilà! — they're in and out of the oven. It's possible to whip up a couple of batches, bake 'em, and eat 'em in about a half hour. (I know this from experience.) And what about making a batch of bad cookies? Not possible, unless you really, really, really mess up. Your worst enemy here is the oven; either the heat is too high, or the cookies stay too long in the oven (see Chapter 22). Don't worry; just remember to set that timer. But when you're anticipating the result, you will most likely be checking the progress. And you'll surely smell the aroma, so you probably won't be able to forget about them.

At first you may feel a little uneasy about baking cookies. But I can assure you that you'll gain confidence quickly because success comes very easily. It doesn't take a rocket scientist to bake great cookies, although I bet a lot of rocket scientists *do* bake cookies. I'm at least certain that they *eat* them!

Most of the ingredients you need to make cookies are probably already in your kitchen, so you won't need to buy much. Yes, you need to get certain recipe ingredients, but that won't be any hassle because everything you need is sold in the same supermarkets where you buy your other groceries. But what about the skills needed to bake cookies? That's the easy part. Most cookies are so easy to make that, well, even a little kid could do it — with a little adult supervision, of course. For more on baking cookies with children, see Chapter 18.

Getting started is the simple part. First you need to tell yourself, "No more store-bought cookies; I'm making my own." Then you have to decide what equipment, tools, and ingredients you need. After you get everything you need together, you have to organize your space — a topic that is covered in the following sections. For more information about tools, ingredients, and techniques, see Chapters 2, 3, and 4, respectively. If you've already chosen a particular cookie to bake, you can go directly to the recipe to determine the necessary ingredients.

The word cookie comes from the Dutch word *koekje*, meaning small cakes.

A Good Cookie Maker Is Always Prepared

Like a good scout, cookie bakers need to be prepared. By being well prepared, you make your work a whole lot easier. There's nothing more frustrating than being in the middle of making a batch of cookies and finding that you have to stop and search for something or, worse, discovering that you're missing a key ingredient.

Preparation is a broad area and consists of more than simply checking to see whether you have all the ingredients. It involves setting aside time, selecting your recipe, reading the recipe to make sure that you understand what needs to be done, and getting the ingredients ready to be used, among other things. Although preparation is important, don't spend all your time getting ready and not have time to enjoy the process. My motto when baking cookies is simple: "Ready, set, bake!"

First things first: Select and review your recipe

Choose an appropriate recipe. Do you want to bake holiday cookies? Or do you want to bake cookies with young children? Maybe you want cookies for a tea party or for a picnic. Pick the cookie recipe that best fits your need. There are so many types of cookies from which to choose that one is bound to be perfect. Once you've decided which cookies to bake, read through the recipe.

Again, make sure that the cookie recipe you pick is appropriate for the occasion. If you bake delicate cookies for a picnic, they'll probably be crumbled and broken by the time you're ready to eat them.

Whether you're a first-time cookie baker or have been baking cookies for a long time, reading the recipe through to be sure that you understand what needs to be done is always a good idea. If something isn't clear, read the recipe again to see whether it can be clarified. If the recipe contains a word or term you don't understand, most likely you can find its definition in Appendix A of this book.

You may be wondering how many cookies you need to make. The answer depends, of course, on your household's demand. Bake as many batches as you feel you have time for. Don't make cookie baking an obligation — it should be fun. I like to use my cookie baking time as a way to relax and escape life's everyday pressures.

Assemble the ingredients

When I'm ready to bake cookies, one of the first things I do is take all the ingredients I need out of the pantry. If I notice that I don't have an ingredient, I can go to the store and buy it, or I can pick an appropriate substitute (or choose another recipe). This way, I'm not in for any surprises while I'm in the middle of mixing the dough.

Make a list of the ingredients you need, along with the quantity needed, before going to the store. Your shopping trip will be quicker and more efficient, enabling you to return to the kitchen and start baking sooner. A grocery list helps you remember to buy necessary items and may deter you from buying items you don't really need.

Review the equipment

As you read a recipe, notice the specialty tools and equipment you need and check to make sure that you have everything. Take what you need out of the cabinet and place it within easy reach (see Figure 1-1). It's no fun to be digging around in the back of cabinets or drawers when you're in the middle of preparing a batch of dough. If any equipment needs washing, this is a good time to do it. If you find that you're low on wax paper or parchment paper, write the item on your shopping list so that you can replace it before your next cookie-baking session.

Figure 1-1: Gathering together the equipment you will need.

Prepare the ingredients

Take a tip from professional pastry chefs and spend a few minutes preparing the ingredients, such as measuring flour and sugar, toasting and chopping nuts, and softening butter, before starting to mix the dough. If the ingredients are ready, mixing the batter or dough goes quicker, and you can get your cookies in the oven even faster.

Preheat the oven

Cookies baked in a cold oven won't bake properly. Always preheat the oven to the temperature called for in a recipe before starting to mix the dough. Doing so gives the oven time to heat up and be ready when the cookies are ready to bake. Preheating an oven takes 8 to 10 minutes.

Keep an oven thermometer in your oven and check it occasionally to be sure that your oven is heating and maintaining the correct heat. The wrong oven temperature can spell disaster for your cookies.

Be Organized

Before baking cookies, organize your ingredients, equipment, and work space so that you can get the job done as efficiently as possible and don't have to work in a cluttered environment. Make space available for the tasks you're doing and have everything you need close at hand.

Give me some space!

Finding that you need to set something down but don't have any place to put it can be annoying, especially in the kitchen. For example, have you ever removed cookie sheets from the oven and then wondered where you were going to put them? You don't have worry about such an occurrence if you plan your work space efficiently.

First, think about what you'll be using, including equipment, tools, ingredient containers, bowls, and cookie sheets. Try to allow as much space as possible for these. A good idea is to have a station for mixing, another for shaping, and a third for the cookie sheets. Be as liberal with space as you can; the more space, the better.

Set the equipment and ingredients out before actually making the cookies so that you know whether you'll have enough space when you start the work for real — kind of a mock-up of your cookie making operation.

Have racks set up and ready for cooling the cookies. If you don't have such a place in the kitchen, use a breakfast room or dining room table.

If a cooling rack isn't available when you first remove the cookie sheets from the oven, use the top of your stove temporarily to hold the cookie sheets. Be careful, though, because the stovetop may be hot from the oven use, even if the burners haven't been on.

The kitchen sink can become a real mess if you're not careful during cookie making. Try not to haphazardly pile things up, because the stack of dirty dishes can grow surprisingly tall rather quickly. The best bet is to stack items next to the sink for washing later. This way, you won't always be bumping into them when you wash your hands or rinse out a dish. Better yet, put things directly into the dishwasher as you finish with them. If space is at a premium in your kitchen, take a break now and then to wash the dirty stuff, dry it, and put it away. Yes, you must dry the dishes and put them away, or they'll continue to take up valuable space.

If you have a small kitchen, don't despair. You have to be a little more efficient, but baking cookies is definitely doable. You may have to make only one batch at a time, eat them or store them (less fun), and then make another batch, eat them . . . you get the idea.

One primary reason to keep some table and counter space clear of clutter is so that you can keep the flow going. Having to stop and search for space can be a real drag. Once you get used to making space, you'll find that you actually have more space around the kitchen than you thought.

Clean up as you go

As a beginning cookie baker, you may find yourself using every bowl and utensil in the kitchen to make a batch of cookies. It's hard to work in a kitchen that's cluttered with dirty bowls and utensils. Baking is easier when the surroundings are tidy.

Clean up items as you go. Once you're done with bowls, fill them with water so that they'll be easy to wash later. If you use a dry measuring cup for flour and will need it again for another ingredient, wipe it out with a paper towel. Wipe down countertops often. Keep your hands clean to prevent getting other things dirty, such as the oven door. If you follow these suggestions, you'll have more counter space to use for rolling out dough and cooling cookies and less to clean up at the end.

Place everything within easy reach

You probably can't redesign your kitchen so that everything is just a step away. But if you take a little time to organize your countertops, cabinets, and drawers, you can really save yourself a lot of extra steps and reaching. You need to set up your cookie kitchen only once.

First, think about what you'll be using, the order in which you'll be using these items, and how often you'll use them. Although your answers may vary depending on which cookies you bake, recipe steps generally follow the same order.

More than likely, you don't want to go to the trouble and expense of moving the stove, fridge, or kitchen sink, so you have to work around them. But you can definitely organize your countertops, drawers, and cabinets.

✔ Keep your equipment, including your stand mixer and food processor, close to each other on the countertop so that transferring ingredients from or to them will be easy. Store mixing bowls, flat beaters, wire whips, and cutting blades for this equipment nearby. Try storing them in cabinets directly under the counter where the equipment is stored. If possible, keep your mixer and food processor close to the stove in case you need to transfer a food that has been heated. If you store dry ingredients in canisters, keep these at the back of the counter so that you can pull them forward when you need them. Keep only those appliances that you use most often on the countertop and put the others away so that you have enough work space. Too many appliances on the counter clutter up your work space.

Keep your food processor and stand mixer on your countertop so they're readily available to use. If you have to dig in the cabinet to find them, you won't use them.

✔ Use tins or tall jars to hold often-used utensils, such as wooden spoons and rubber spatulas, so that they're within easy reach on the countertop.

✔ Use a knife block to store your knives. That way, they're in one place that's easy to reach, and they're less likely to be damaged by other equipment. If you have more drawer space than counter space, find a knife rack that fits inside a drawer or one that attaches to the side of the countertop.

✔ Drawer organization is simple. Just stack up everything that you could possibly use, such as rubber spatulas, and keep them all in adjacent drawers. Keep your measuring cups and spoons together in one drawer. Place bowl scrapers in another drawer, and pastry bags and tips in yet another drawer. Keeping a separate drawer for each category of utensils helps you more easily find them when you need them. If you don't have enough drawers to keep each item separate, use drawer separators, available in different shapes and sizes.

✔ Organizing cabinets is a little more difficult because some items are large. Definitely keep all the bowls together, including small ones. Stack the cookie sheets together and place cooling racks on top of them. Keep other baking pans near the cookie sheets. Store all these items within easy reach. If you have to stand on a step stool to reach them, you probably won't bother. If you don't have cabinet space, you can store these items in the oven. Just be sure to remove them before you turn the oven on.

Hanging things, including bowls, can work in some kitchens. But be careful to hang them securely and out of the way of your cookie baking area — and your head.

If you bake cookies regularly, you may want to get some racks on wheels. These are useful for holding cookie sheets before they go into the oven and as they cool. Racks can be found at professional kitchen supply stores and through some mail order catalogs (see Appendix B). They're available in different sizes, making it easy to find one that fits your kitchen.

More storage ideas

Wherever you store your dry goods (maybe you're lucky enough to have a walk-in pantry), they need to be organized and labeled clearly. If you have transferred items to special storage containers, label the contents of each container and the date it was purchased. Keep similar items together and place the ones you use most often right up front. This same rule also applies to storage in the fridge. For example, keep dairy items on the top shelf and nuts on the door rack.

Aprons, dish towels, hand towels, and the broom and dustpan should be as close to the action as possible. The same advice holds true for other cleanup paraphernalia. It's maddening to need a sponge, for example, and have to hunt for it if your hands are dirty and the kitchen is cluttered with your baking gear.

I usually keep a hand towel tucked on one side of my apron belt and a dish towel on the other side. If you don't like to wear aprons, keep a few old shirts handy to wear over your clothes — like an artist's smock — when baking. Then you can rub your dirty hands on your shirt and not worry about ruining your good clothes.

Having two of some kitchen tools is very useful. For example, if you have two mixer bowls, you don't need stop to wash and dry the bowl every time you need to mix up another batch of dough. If you have the room and the budget, duplicates of some kitchen accessories can make your cookie kitchen the envy of other cookie bakers.

Making the Cookies

Following cookie recipes is simply a matter of working through the steps. Mix, stir, whip, and form as directed, and then place the dough on the cookie sheet and bake. Yes, you'll probably want to become proficient in some baking techniques, which are covered mostly in Chapter 4. These techniques will take a little time to refine, but the only way to improve those skills is to bake cookies.

Timing is everything

Set aside enough time to relax and enjoy the experience of baking cookies. It's a fun activity, so don't rush it. Although each recipe has the preparation time listed, this is only a guideline. People work at their own pace. If you're a novice cookie baker, you'll need more time than someone who has been baking cookies for years.

After your cookies are in the oven, set a timer for the recommended baking time. You may think that you'll remember how long they've been baking, but you won't. I've burned too many cookies to ever think I can bake without using a timer. Your baking experience will be a lot more fun if you don't have to worry about remembering to check the oven. Make sure that you have a reliable timer and that it's working properly when you set it. Always set the timer for the least amount of baking time recommended in a recipe and begin to check for doneness early. You can always add a few more minutes, but you can't do anything if the cookies have baked too long.

Jot down those notes!

Keep a pad and pencil handy just in case you want to jot down a note or two as you're making cookies. You may want to remind yourself about something that you want to look up in this book a little later. Perhaps you want to remember a new way of doing something that you discovered, or maybe you came up with an idea for a new cookie. You may also want to write the date you made the recipe and any comments in the margins. Record the response from cookie testers — did they love it or just like it? Was it fun to make or too much work? Your notes will make for amusing reading at a later date.

Chapter 2
The Cookie Baker's Toolbox

*H*aving the right tools makes a job much easier, whether it's baking cookies or assembling airplanes. If you're just starting out as a cookie baker, walking into a cookware shop or the cookware section of a department store can be overwhelming. These places are stocked from floor to ceiling (at least it seems that way) with a huge variety of cookware and utensils. If you don't know what you're looking for, figuring out where to begin can be a daunting project. Fortunately, cookie baking requires relatively few tools and utensils to get started. You can always add to your stock as you become more proficient and more interested.

I always recommend buying the best quality equipment you can afford. That way, you won't have to go back and replace it after a short time. Equipment of inferior quality may even fail as you're using it, which can be frustrating. Many tools and utensils will last a lifetime if you buy good quality. You don't have to invest in professional-quality equipment, available through catalogs, specialty supply companies, and some cookware shops, unless you choose to. Much of the equipment made for home use is excellent.

This chapter describes the most important cookie-making equipment and utensils. You don't have to own every cookie tool in the store. Simply choose those pieces that you need to bake the cookies you like.

Before buying, research the items you think you want. What are their functions and features? What are the best brands? What's a good price?

Take Your Measure

In general cooking, you can usually safely add a pinch of this and some of that and still come out with something tasty at the end. Cookie baking, on the other hand, demands more precise measurements to ensure success. Each cookie recipe has been developed so that the ingredients work together like a well-tuned orchestra.

Measuring is near the top of my list with respect to importance in cookie baking. Too much of one ingredient can quickly spell disaster. Guessing doesn't work. Ingredients need to be accurately measured. In order to do this, you need to use the correct tools and pay close attention. For information on how to use the various measuring tools presented in this section, please see Chapter 4.

Have both measuring cups and spoons on hand for cookie baking. I have several sets of each so that I don't have to wash them in between each use.

Measuring cups

There are two types of measuring cups: dry measures and wet measures (see Figure 2-1).

✔ Dry measuring cups are used for ingredients such as flour and sugar, and for solid fats. They come in sets of nested and graduated cups ranging in size from ¼ cup to 1 cup. They're available in plastic, aluminum, and stainless steel. These types of measuring cups are filled to their tops, so you can use any of these materials and easily see the quantity.

✔ Liquid measuring cups are for — surprise! — liquids, such as water or cooking oil. They have a small pour spout and handle on the side. They come in 1-, 2-, and 4-cup sizes and are marked on the sides with lines indicating the quantity. Some have markings for both metric and U.S. measurements. They're available in glass, plastic, and metal. These measuring cups have extra room above the top measurement line to allow room for liquids to move around. I prefer to use clear plastic or glass liquid measuring cups so that I can clearly see the quantity I'm measuring.

Measuring spoons

Measuring spoons, shown in Figure 2-2, are used for measuring small amounts of both dry and liquid ingredients. They usually come in nested sizes of ¼ teaspoon, ½ teaspoon, 1 teaspoon, and 1 tablespoon. Some sets also have ⅛ teaspoon and/or 1½ tablespoon measures. Sets of measuring spoons are available in metal and plastic.

Figure 2-1: Liquid and dry measuring cups.

liquid measure cup   dry measure cups

Detach measuring spoons from the metal or plastic ring holding them together and arrange them in a kitchen drawer by size. That way, finding the measuring spoon you need is easy. In addition, the measuring spoons you don't need, especially if you've been measuring liquid ingredients, don't get in the way.

Don't use the teaspoons and tablespoons from your silverware drawer to measure ingredients. These spoons don't hold the same amount as measuring spoons, so using them rather than measuring spoons can lead to a cookie-baking disaster. You can use these spoons, however, to spoon out cookie batter when called for because the batter isn't measured to a specific amount for each cookie.

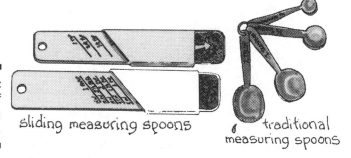

Figure 2-2: Varieties of measuring spoons.

sliding measuring spoons   traditional measuring spoons

Oven thermometer

All cookie recipes give a temperature for baking. Most home ovens are off by as much as 25 degrees. If your oven isn't accurate, your cookies will be either underbaked or overbaked. The best way to ensure that your oven is accurate is to buy a good-quality mercury oven thermometer. Keep it in the oven at all times, check it often, and adjust the oven temperature as needed. This tool isn't expensive and will save you both money and time. Actually, it's a good idea to keep two oven thermometers in your oven. You can be sure that your oven temperature is really accurate if both thermometers register the same heat.

Scales

A scale is a useful tool for weighing ingredients called for in recipes. There are three types of scales, shown in Figure 2-3: spring, balance, and electronic. A spring scale is the preferred type for the home baker. It's easy to use and can be set to zero for each new ingredient added while other ingredients are on the platform. Spring scales measure up to 4½ pounds. They're usually made of plastic and have a bowl that fits over the platform to act as a cover when the scale isn't in use. I keep my kitchen scale on the countertop so it's easy to find and to use. Electronic scales display a digital readout of the weight of the ingredient. They're battery operated and extremely accurate and can weigh amounts up to 10 pounds.

Scales come in very handy for weighing ingredients such as chocolate, butter, cream cheese, dried fruit, and, sometimes, nuts and flour.

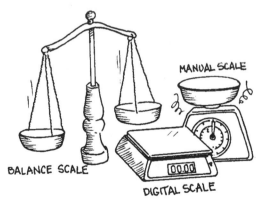

Figure 2-3:
The three types of scales: balance, electronic (or digital), and spring (or manual).

Timer

You can't bake without a timer to remind you when the cookies are done, especially if you're baking more than one batch at a time. Keep a timer near the oven and set it for the minimum time called for in a recipe. You can always add a few extra minutes of baking time, but you can't do anything about overbaked cookies. I like to use a timer that has three different channels to time three things. It's available at many cookware shops and through catalogs.

Many other kinds of timers are available. Some people prefer the windup type, while others like the electronic ones. Whichever one you choose, be sure that you're comfortable with it so you'll use it.

Heavy Equipment

What I call "heavy equipment" includes mixers, mixing bowls, and food processors. Some cookies can be mixed by hand, but most are best accomplished with a mixer. A good-quality mixer will be one of your biggest and most important kitchen investments. Shop around and choose the best-quality mixer you can afford. It will last the better part of a lifetime.

Mixing bowls are essential not only for mixing but also for holding other ingredients after they've been measured or weighed. Mixing bowls are easily used with a hand-held mixer when preparing cookie dough and batter. Although a food processor is used for mixing cookie dough in some recipes, it is different than a mixer and can't really be substituted for one.

Mixers

There are two main types of mixers — stand and hand-held. I prefer a stand mixer, shown in Figure 2-4, because it leaves my hands free for other tasks (such as measuring ingredients) while the dough is mixing.

Stand mixers have a solid base that sits on a countertop. The best-quality mixers have a heavy-duty motor and several adjustable speeds. They mix ingredients more quickly than a hand-held mixer. This type of mixer is available in different sizes that hold varying capacities, such as 4½- and 5-quart. I've had a KitchenAid mixer for 20 years that has never skipped a beat. I would be lost without it. Most mixers come with at least one bowl and attachments, such as a flat beater and a wire whip. Extra bowls and attachments can be purchased. Have two bowls and two sets of attachments so that you don't have to wash them midway through cookie making for each use.

Hand-held mixers, such as the one shown in Figure 2-5, have two removable beaters set into a housing that holds a motor. Some heavy-duty models come with different attachments. These mixers are good for small quantities, and their portability is a plus. Hand-held mixers generally have three speeds. Compared to a stand mixer, mixing the same ingredients with a hand-held mixer takes a little longer.

Figure 2-4:
Stand mixer.

Figure 2-5:
Hand-held
mixer.

Mixing bowls

Keep a supply of a few different sizes and types of mixing bowls. I like stainless steel, glass, and ceramic bowls. Mixing bowls come in a wide variety of sizes, ranging from 1 cup up to 17 quarts. Leave extra room in the bowl for mixing or tossing ingredients.

Food processors

A food processor, shown in Figure 2-6, is one of my most treasured kitchen tools. I don't think I could live without it. A food processor makes great cookie dough, chops and grinds nuts, and purées mixtures. Most food processors come with a few blades, but the most valuable is the metal blade.

Extra bowls and blades can be purchased, if needed. Several sizes of food processors are available, ranging from mini to extra large. Choose the one that fits your style of baking.

Let the food processor take care of some mundane jobs so that you have more time to be creative. Use the pulse button to chop and blend. Use the on button for final mixing chores.

Look for a food processor that's heavy enough to stay in place and not move around the countertop while it works. Look for one that also has a pulse button. Buy a good-quality food processor so that it will last many years.

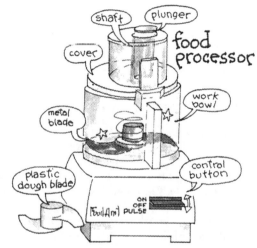

Figure 2-6:
Food processors are extremely useful in cookie making.

Pots, Pans, Sheets, and Racks

Baking cookies would be impossible without pots, pans, cookie sheets and wire racks. The following sections explain some of this equipment in more detail.

Double boilers

Double boilers insulate and provide a consistent source of heat for evenly melting ingredients such as chocolate and butter, and for holding them at a constant temperature without burning. A double boiler is made of two pots that fit snugly together or a bowl that fits over a pan, as shown in Figure 2-7. The bottom pot, which is slightly larger than the top pot or bowl, holds a small amount of water. The two pieces of the double boiler should fit snugly together so that no water or steam escapes and mixes with the ingredients in the top pot.

You can make your own double boiler with a heatproof bowl that fits tightly over a pot. Glass or stainless steel are good choices for the top bowl. The bowl will be hot when removed from the pot, so handle it with care.

Figure 2-7:
A double
boiler.

double boiler

Baking pans

Baking pans are used when making bar cookies and brownies. The most popular sizes of baking pans for cookies are 8 x 8 x 2 inches and 9 x 13 x 2 inches. I prefer to use heavy-gauge aluminum pans with square corners. Using these sizes of pans makes it easy to get squares and bars of the same size because they can easily be divided into equal squares and rectangles. Using glass pans is okay, but turn the oven temperature down 25 degrees and check the cookies for doneness at least 5 minutes early. Glass conducts heat faster than aluminum, so the cookies will bake quicker.

If you like to make specialty items, keep these pans on hand:

- **Ladyfinger pan:** A flat, rectangular, tinned-steel pan with ten 3-inch-long shallow indentations to form the spongy, finger-shaped cookies called ladyfingers.

- **Madeleine pan:** This pan, also called a madeleine plaque or sheet, is a special flat, rectangular pan made of tinned steel or aluminum with shell-shaped indentations. See Chapter 13 for more information on how to make madeleines.

Cookie sheets

The best cookie sheets are made of heavy-gauge aluminum. (See Figure 2-8.) They have a shiny surface and a flat rim. Baking sheets are also used for baking cookies. They are made of the same material as cookie sheets but have a very low rolled rim. Thin cookie sheets buckle in the oven and result in unevenly baked cookies. Measure the inside of your oven and buy cookie sheets that allow for at least 2 inches of space around them so that air can circulate well during baking.

Keep at least four cookie sheets on hand so that you don't have to wait for one batch to come out of the oven before arranging the next. Place unbaked cookies on cool cookie sheets. If the cookie sheets are hot, the cookies will spread before you put them in the oven.

Jelly roll pans, shown in Figure 2-8, are slightly larger than cookie sheets. They have a 1-inch-high rolled rim on all sides that's made to hold batter for cakes or big batches of bar cookies.

You can easily substitute jelly roll pans for cookie sheets. That's what I often do. If you have several batches of cookies going, enlist jelly roll pans to fill in and get the job done. This way, you don't have to wait for each pan to cool between batches, and you can keep the cookie baking process going.

Figure 2-8:
Jelly roll
pan and
cookie
sheets.

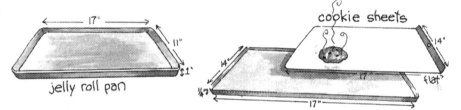

Here are some other types of cookie sheets that are available. Be aware, though, that each has certain drawbacks.

- ✔ **Cookie sheets that sandwich a layer of air between two pieces of metal (also called insulated baking sheets):** They're fine to use if the bottoms of cookies are browning too much, but using them results in soft cookies.

- ✔ **Nonstick cookie sheets:** These have a coating that causes cookies that need to bake on an ungreased surface to spread too much. Uncoated cookie sheets are a better choice for these kinds of cookies.

    Don't grease nonstick cookie sheets. The nonstick surface takes the place of greasing. If you grease them, the cookies spread too much, and the cookie dough may even slide off the pan while in the oven.

- ✔ **Dark cookie sheets:** These aren't a good choice, because they absorb more heat and bake cookies too quickly, causing them to be too dark and dry.

Making wise buys on baking equipment

After you get started baking cookies, you'll most likely want to add to your equipment inventory. Follow these tips to be sure that you make the best use of your equipment dollars. Buy only what you know you'll use. There's no use having kitchen tools around if they're only gathering dust and taking up space.

✔ Start slow and build your equipment inventory over time.

✔ Buy during sales but know what you want before you shop.

✔ Check mail order catalogs and online stores for good deals.

✔ Buy quality so that you get equipment that lasts.

✔ Store your equipment correctly to keep it in good condition.

Cooling racks

This kitchen utensil, used to cool baked cookies, is made of closely spaced parallel metal wires that rest on ½-inch-high feet. A cooling rack allows air to circulate around the cookie sheet or cookies as they cool so that steam doesn't build up and cause them to become soggy on the bottom. Cooling racks come in several shapes: round, square, and rectangle. Buy sturdy ones so that they won't collapse. Have several of them on hand, especially when you're baking a lot of cookies.

Basic Tools

Cookie baking doesn't require a lot of fancy equipment. However, you do need some basic tools to make cookie baking easy and fun and to ensure success. These tools will make baking easier, without draining your bank account.

Chef's knife

A *chef's knife,* an important tool to have, is useful for cutting, chopping, and slicing. Choose a knife by how it feels in your hand and how it will be used. Let the weight of the knife do the work instead of wearing yourself out and flapping your arms like you're trying to fly.

Choose a knife of good quality so that it will last a long time. A blade made of high-carbon stainless steel won't rust and is soft enough to be sharpened easily. Keep your knife razor sharp. There's less chance of making mistakes with a sharp knife than a dull one. Knives should be washed and dried immediately after use. Store knives in a slotted wood block or in a drawer on a magnetic bar to protect the blades.

Never wash knives in the dishwasher. Doing so ruins the handles and dulls the blades.

Dough scraper

A *dough scraper* is a thin, flat, flexible piece of plastic or nylon shaped like a half-moon that fits in the palm of the hand. A dough scraper is useful for scraping out bowls, cutting dough, and cleaning work surfaces. Some dough scrapers have a metal blade that fits into a wood handle. I prefer to use the plastic dough scrapers because they're more pliant.

Dredger

A *dredger* looks like a large salt shaker, about 3½ inches high and 2½ inches round with a handle on the side. The top is either flat metal with holes, or an arched mesh screen, depending on the material the dredger is made of. A dredger is used to dust powdered sugar or cocoa powder when garnishing cookies or to dust flour when rolling out cookie dough.

Flexible-blade spatula

A *flexible-blade spatula* has a long, narrow, stainless steel blade with a rounded end and straight sides, set into a wooden handle. The blade is flexible, but not wobbly. Flexible-blade spatulas come in a variety of sizes, from a 3-inch-long blade to a 14-inch-long blade. The shorter blades are most useful in the cookie kitchen and are great for transferring cookies from one place to another.

Nutmeg grater and grinder

Freshly grated or ground spices are so much more flavorful than preground, and preparing them right before use is quick and easy. A *nutmeg grater* is specifically designed for grating a whole nutmeg. A grater is about 4 inches long and 2 inches wide. The back side is flat, and the top is a tapered half-moon shape with fine mesh for grating the nutmeg. Some nutmeg graters have a compartment where the whole nutmeg can be stored; the compartment has a cap on top that clamps shut.

A *nutmeg grinder,* sometimes called a *nutmeg mill,* is a short, 3-inch-round, stocky-shaped mill with a hand crank on top. A whole nutmeg is held in place inside the mill in a small shaft. A plate with tiny prongs on one side holds the nutmeg in place while it's being ground. A clear cover for storing whole nutmegs surrounds the top portion of the grinder. A nutmeg grinder makes fine shavings rather than the powder made with a grater.

To prevent hurting your fingers when using a nutmeg grater, grasp the nutmeg securely at the end that is farthest away from the teeth. As the nutmeg wears down, hold your fingertips flat to keep them out of the way of the teeth.

Pastry brushes

Pastry brushes, such as the one shown in Figure 2-9, are used to brush excess flour off cookies, to butter the inside of pans and molds, and to brush the tops of cookies with glazes or chocolate before and after baking. Hand wash pastry brushes in warm, soapy water soon after use and dry them with the bristles up. All types of pastry brushes can be found in most places where baking supplies are sold, such as catalogs, Web sites, department stores, and specialty shops.

Generally speaking, there are two types of pastry brushes:

- **Bristle pastry brushes** look like paintbrushes. Use the ones with natural bristles, not nylon bristles, because nylon bristles tear the dough and melt when they come in contact with heat. These brushes have wooden handles and come in a variety of sizes, ranging from ½ inch to 2½ inches wide. Keep a few sizes on hand.

- **Goosefeather pastry brushes** have several feathers sewn together and attached by their quills. They're used for glazing delicate cookies and for applying egg washes. Goosefeather pastry brushes have a soft texture and won't scratch or otherwise disturb the surface of foods.

Figure 2-9:
A bristle pastry brush.

Potholders

Potholders are essential for removing hot cookie sheets from the oven or hot pans from the stovetop. I keep several sets of potholders in the drawer closest to the oven. You may also want to keep some on a hook for quicker access.

Rolling pin

A rolling pin is used to roll out cookie dough before it's cut into shapes. Many types of rolling pins are available. My favorite is a long, solid, hardwood cylinder with no handles. It's easy to manipulate, and I don't have to worry about the handles making marks in the dough. I can place my hands anywhere on the rolling pin, so it's comfortable for me to use. I recommend using a heavy-weight rolling pin because the weight allows the rolling pin to do most of the work. Wipe or hand wash your rolling pin after each use and never wash it in the dishwasher.

Rubber spatulas

Rubber spatulas, such as the one shown in Figure 2-10, have a thin, flat, flexible, rectangular solid rubber or plastic blade attached to a handle. I keep long-handled and short-handled rubber spatulas in my kitchen. The long-handled spatulas are invaluable for scraping out bowls and mixing dough and batters. The short-handled spatulas come in very handy for stirring chocolate and other delicate ingredients as they melt and for scraping out food processors and other small bowls.

The new heat-resistant rubber spatulas can withstand very high temperatures without melting. They're great to use for stirring chocolate as it melts and sugar syrups. They come in a variety of colors, which makes it easy to tell them apart from rubber spatulas that are not heat resistant.

Figure 2-10: Rubber spatula.

Ruler

A ruler may sound like a strange item to have in the kitchen, but in fact, a ruler is an essential kitchen tool. I use a ruler to measure the size of dough as I'm rolling it out and to measure even squares and rectangles when cutting bar cookies. I keep a ruler in the kitchen drawer with spatulas and turners. Plastic rulers are easier to clean than wooden ones.

Scissors

Keep a pair of sturdy, good-quality scissors in a kitchen drawer. They come in handy for many jobs, such as trimming parchment paper, snipping the point off paper pastry cones, opening plastic bags, trimming cookie dough, and chopping dried fruits.

Scoops

A stainless steel ice cream scoop with a squeeze handle is the easiest way to portion out drop cookie batter uniformly. It also keeps your hands clean and results in less waste than using a spoon because you get less dough on your fingers that you may be tempted to taste. I use a small scoop for regular size cookies and a larger one for giant cookies.

Sifters and strainers

Sifters and strainers are very useful tools for aerating dry ingredients, such as flour, powdered sugar, and cocoa powder, and for mixing dry ingredients together. Sifters (see Figure 2-11) are either manually operated or battery powered. I like to use a large, shallow sifter called a drum sieve because it's easy to push the ingredients through by hand.

Figure 2-11:
A sifter.

Strainers are often used for sifting small quantities of ingredients. They are also useful for straining purées and glazes. I prefer strainers with plastic rims and mesh because they can be washed in the dishwasher. Keep a few different sizes of strainers on hand.

Turners

Turners are ideal for removing warm cookies from cookie sheets and transferring them to cooling racks. A turner has a solid, flat, square or rectangular metal blade attached to a wooden or plastic handle. A turner allows you to keep your hands away from hot surfaces.

Whisk

This teardrop-shaped hand-held kitchen utensil is made of several thin stainless steel looped wires attached to a wooden or stainless steel handle. Whisks are useful for whipping air into ingredients such as eggs and cream and for stirring hot mixtures as they cook.

Wooden spoons

Several sizes of wooden spoons are useful in the cookie kitchen. These are great for hand mixing ingredients and stirring mixtures as they cook. I like wooden spoons with long handles because they keep my hands far away from hot mixtures. Wash wooden spoons by hand in warm, soapy water and dry immediately.

Zester

A *zester,* shown in Figure 2-12, is designed to remove the aromatic outer rind or zest from citrus fruits, without also removing the bitter white pith. A zester is about 6 inches long. It has five small sharp holes in the end of a short metal strip attached to a wooden or plastic handle. The holes of the zester are pressed against a citrus fruit and pulled from top to bottom, removing the zest in thin threads.

Figure 2-12:
A zester.

Specialty Tools

Some cookie recipes require specialized tools. You don't have to buy all the tools at once. Instead, you can acquire them over time as you try new and exciting recipes. If a recipe in this book requires a specialty tool, the tool is mentioned in the "Specialty tools" line (directly above the "Preparation time" line) above the ingredients.

Cookie cutters

Cookie cutters come in a huge variety of shapes and sizes. Don't feel that you have to run out and buy every one in sight. I've been collecting cookie cutters for many years and still don't have them all. Buy a few basic cookie cutters to get started and add to your collection when the mood strikes you. Plenty of holiday and special-occasion cookie cutters are available and fun to collect in anticipation of those events.

I use 1½-inch star cutters and 2- and 2½-inch round fluted cutters the most. I also like to use a nested set of cutters of varying sizes. Cookie cutters come in metal and plastic — both work equally well. I like to store my cookie cutters in colorful tins and clear glass jars.

Oval cookie cutters are hard to find. Make your own by taking a round, thin aluminum cookie cutter and bending it into an oval.

Cookie molds

Cookie molds, shown in Figure 2-13, shape cookie dough before it's baked. Some molds also hold the batter or dough as it bakes; others arc uscd to shape the dough before it is released and then baked. Cookie molds are made of metal, wood, or ceramic.

Here are some specific kinds of cookie molds:

- **Shortbread molds:** Ceramic shortbread molds are available as round or square shallow plates. The dough is pressed into the molds, baked, and then cut into wedges or squares while warm. When turned out of the molds, the cookies hold the impressions of the mold. Molds are available in different designs, such as flowers or fruits. You also can find some round shortbread molds designed to make individual cookies.

- **Springerle molds:** These elaborately carved wooden molds are pressed into rolled-out dough to shape their designs. The cookies are air-dried before baking so they hold the impressions of the mold. Springerle molds often become collectors' items because of their shapes and designs. Some springerle molds qualify as antiques. See Chapter 13 for more information on making springerle cookies.

- **Speculaas molds:** These molds of holiday figures are used to form cookies that are popular in Holland and Belgium. Some molds are very tall, as high as 2 feet. Dough for these cookies is rolled or pressed into the molds and then released before baking. Ceramic cookie molds, similar to speculaas molds, are available in a large variety of shapes. See Chapter 13 for more information on making speculaas cookies.

Figure 2-13: The center mold is for shortbread; the other two can be used for both springerle and speculaas cookies.

COOKIE MOLDS

Cookie press

Sometimes called a cookie gun, a *cookie press* has a cylindrical barrel with several different round templates or nozzles that fit at one end. At the other end is a trigger or plunger mechanism that forces the soft cookie dough out through the template, forming different shapes. You can use the same cookie dough to make a huge variety of cookie shapes. All you have to do is change the template on the end of the cookie press. Once you get the hang of working with a cookie press, you'll really pop them out in no time.

Keep the templates for your cookie press in a clear jar or canister so that you can see what you have and keep them all together.

Cookie stamps

Made of glass, ceramic, plastic, or wood, *cookie stamps,* shown in Figure 2-14, are used to press a small ball of unbaked cookie dough flat, giving the cookie its shape and imprinting the design into the dough. A cookie stamp is usually round or square and only a few inches in diameter. It has a small knob handle on top and a design etched into the underside. Cookie stamps are available in many different designs.

COOKIE STAMPS

Figure 2-14:
Cookie
stamps.

To keep a cookie stamp from sticking to the dough, dip it in flour between each pressing.

Pastry bags and tips

A cone-shaped pastry bag fitted with a decorative tip, shown in Figure 2-15, is used to shape batter and dough and to fill and decorate cookies after they're baked. I prefer to use cloth pastry bags that can be washed and reused many times. I recommend using 12- or 14-inch pastry bags because they can hold a sufficient amount of batter without overfilling. These sizes are easy to handle and don't need to be refilled as often.

Pastry tips are made of plastic or metal, which is the most popular. The large pastry tubes that are 2 inches long are easier to use. For cookies, you need a tube with a ½-inch round opening and an open star tip. You can make disposable pastry bags from parchment paper (see Chapter 9). These disposable bags are especially handy when you're doing small decorating tasks with icing or chocolate or when piping jam filling into cookies.

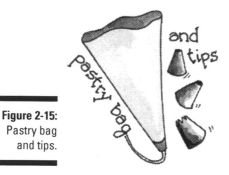

Figure 2-15:
Pastry bag
and tips.

Pizzelle iron

A *pizzelle iron* is a specialized piece of equipment used to make pizzelle cookies. It is made of two round cast-aluminum plates that are hinged together. Each plate is engraved with intricate designs and has a handle. Pizzelle batter is placed in the center of one of the plates, the handles are brought together to spread the batter, and the iron is placed over a stove burner to cook the batter. Pizzelle irons are also available in electric models that look similar to waffle irons. The standard-size electric pizzelle irons make two 5-inch round pizzelles at a time. Miniature pizzelle irons that make four at a time are also available. See Chapter 14 for more information on making pizzelles.

Cookie Storage Containers

Myriad types of cookie jars are available. Be sure the one you choose has a snug-fitting lid, or air will seep in and cause your cookies to turn stale quickly. Tins are a good way to store cookies. Line them with aluminum foil or wax paper to keep the cookies from tasting like the metal. Plastic containers are also good for storing cookies. Choose those that are airtight, if possible.

Paper Goods and Wrappings

Aluminum foil is a great kitchen staple. It's excellent for lining cookie sheets, especially for delicate meringue cookies, because the cookies won't stick to the foil. Aluminum foil is also invaluable for covering trays of cookies that are held at room temperature. It can also be used to line baking pans when baking bar cookies and brownies. Using foil makes it easy to lift the cookies out of the pan so they can be cut on a board rather than in the pan.

Greaseproof nonstick parchment paper is handy for lining cookie sheets and baking pans so that the baked goods won't stick. I always line cookie sheets with parchment paper. This technique eliminates the need to grease and flour pans, making cleanup a lot easier. You can also use parchment paper to make pastry cones for piping out batters and for doing decorative work. Parchment paper comes in sheets, rolls, or triangles.

A nonstick silicone baking mat or pan liner works the same way as parchment paper, except that it's reusable, making it a very good value. These liners come in different sizes, so be sure to buy the size that fits your cookie sheets.

Wax paper comes in very handy in the cookie kitchen. I use it to shape dough into rolls, to wrap dough before chilling it in the refrigerator, and to line tins and other cookie containers. I also use wax paper to hold sifted dry ingredients and to transfer ingredients from one place to another.

Plastic wrap is another staple to have on hand. I use it to cover ingredients, dough, and, in some cases, cooled cookies. When cookie dough or cookies need to be refrigerated before baking, plastic wrap seals them from exposure to other flavors and from the moist air, which can change their consistency.

Chapter 3

Ingredients for the Cookie Cupboard

Keep your cupboard stocked with basic and often-used ingredients. Then you can bake your favorite cookies whenever the inspiration hits you. Your cookies will be as good as the quality of ingredients you put into them, so make sure that you stock your cupboard with good-quality ingredients. When you go to the store, you may be tempted to buy whatever is on sale. Trying new things is fine, but buying products that you're sure will work is your best bet.

This chapter introduces you to the ingredients used in cookie baking. It discusses how to choose the right ingredients for your cookies, how to store them for maximum freshness, what to have on hand so that you'll always be ready for baking cookies, and what to substitute when you just can't make it to the store for the right ingredient.

Dry Ingredients

Dry ingredients are exactly what their name implies: They're dry with no liquid or fat. This category covers many staple ingredients, including flour, cornmeal, cornstarch, sugar, and cream of tartar. Leavening agents, items that help doughs and batters rise by releasing carbon dioxide gas when combined with liquid, are also included here. Baking powder and baking soda are the leavening agents most often used in cookie baking.

When buying from bulk sources, buy only the amount you'll use within a short period of time. If you buy a large quantity and don't use it, it's not a good value. Also, if you keep some dry ingredients too long, they may attract little critters, such as mealy bugs. You definitely don't want to make them welcome in your pantry!

Baking powder

This is one of the leavening agents used most often in baking. It comes in a round metal can with a tight-fitting plastic lid. Baking powder is made up of two parts of a baking acid, such as cream of tartar, and one part baking soda. There is also a small amount of cornstarch added to stabilize the mixture and absorb acid. Most baking powder is double acting, which means it reacts first when mixed with liquid ingredients and again when heated. Baking powder is perishable, so store it in a cool, dry place. Check the bottom of the can for the expiration date and replace every six months.

If you're unsure whether your baking powder is still effective, combine 1 teaspoon with ½ cup hot water. If it makes lively bubbles, the baking powder is still good.

If you're inspired to bake cookies but find you're out of baking powder, don't despair. You can simulate the rising power of a teaspoon of baking powder by combining ½ teaspoon cream of tartar and ¼ teaspoon baking soda. If you want to have a larger quantity of simulated baking powder on hand, you can combine 1 tablespoon baking soda, 2 tablespoons cream of tartar, and 1½ tablespoons cornstarch. The cornstarch keeps the powder and cream of tartar separated until they are required to work.

Don't be too generous when adding baking powder. Too much will leave a chalky taste and will cause your cookies to deflate rather than rise. A teaspoon of baking powder per cup of flour is the standard amount.

Baking soda

Also called bicarbonate of soda, baking soda is another of the most often used leavening agents in baking. Always mix it with dry ingredients first because it reacts immediately when wet, causing it to produce carbon dioxide bubbles, starting its rising action. As soon as liquid is mixed with baking soda in a batter, the mixture should be put in the oven before this process has time to begin. You want the rising to take place in the oven, not on the kitchen counter. Baking soda reacts well with the natural acidity of other ingredients, such as molasses, buttermilk, and sour cream. This reaction releases more carbon dioxide, creating more bubble in the dough and, as a result, making a more tender mixture.

Only a small amount of baking soda is needed to make batters rise. The standard amount is ¼ teaspoon of baking soda per each cup of flour.

Cornmeal

Cornmeal comes in a variety of colors and textures. Most cookies use fine yellow cornmeal, which can be found in boxes in the supermarket or in bins in specialty food shops. Cornmeal will last for up to a year if stored in a cool, dry place in an airtight container. If the cornmeal is labeled as stone-ground, it is perishable and should be stored in the refrigerator.

Cornstarch

This fine white powder is milled from the inner grain of corn and is used primarily as a thickener for custards and sauces. Cornstarch is often mixed with all-purpose flour to lighten its texture. Cornstarch is sold in cardboard boxes in the baking supplies section in supermarkets. It will last indefinitely if stored in a cool, dry place.

Cream of tartar

Cream of tartar is used mostly to stabilize egg whites while whipping so they can reach maximum volume. It's occasionally used as a leavening agent. Cream of tartar is found in small jars in the spice section of supermarkets and specialty shops. It will last indefinitely if stored in an airtight container in a cool, dry place.

This white crystalline powder is a byproduct of the wine-making industry. It is the crystallized sediment that is found on the bottom and clinging to the sides of wine tanks or casks after the wine has been fermented. This sediment goes through a refining process to make it into the product you buy in the supermarket.

Flour

Flour is the primary ingredient in most cookie recipes. Because it provides structure to cookies, cookies wouldn't hold together without it. Flour is made from many types of grains, but the most commonly used flour is made from wheat. Several types of wheat flour are available, including bread flour and cake flour, but the most common type used in making cookies is all-purpose flour.

Grains from which other types of flour are made include barley, corn, millet, oats, rice, and rye. Many people who have an allergy to wheat are able to successfully use these other types of flour to make cookies. Other cultures also often use these other types of flour for baking.

Flour is best stored in an airtight container in a dark place at room temperature for up to six months. Clean your container before adding new flour and don't place fresh flour on top of old flour.

Flour contains *gluten,* a protein that's activated when dough is mixed. Gluten traps gases that are released when baked. The gases expand with heat, thereby causing the mixture to rise. The result is cookies that rise slightly as they bake, as most drop cookies do. The amount of gluten in the flour determines its strength and leavening power. Flour from hard wheat, such as bread flour, has a high amount of gluten, while cake flour made from soft wheat has much less.

The following is a list of various types of flour used in cookie baking:

- **All-purpose flour:** This is a blend of hard and soft wheats with a medium texture and a gluten content of 12 percent. It's used for most cookies and baked goods. Bleached and unbleached all-purpose flour can be substituted for each other with no problems. The difference between these two flours is that the nutrients are bleached out of bleached flour to make it white. All-purpose flour is available in 2- 5-, 10-, and 25-pound bags in most supermarkets.

- **Whole-wheat flour:** This flour contains the wheat germ and bran that is milled out of white flour. Whole-wheat flour is denser and coarser, with a higher nutritional value and a gluten content of approximately 13 percent. It is often combined with all-purpose flour in cookie doughs and batters and produces a chewy, dense cookie. Whole-wheat flour has a shorter shelf life than white flour. It will last up to a month at room temperature or a year in the freezer. Whole-wheat flour is available at many supermarkets and specialty food stores.

- **Cake flour:** This is made from soft flour with a low gluten content, about 9 percent. It's used when a delicate, slightly crumbly texture is desired in cookies. Cake flour is available in 2-pound boxes in many supermarkets. Be careful not to buy self-rising cake flour.

If you need cake flour for a recipe and don't have any on hand, here's what to do: Use 1 cup all-purpose flour minus 2 tablespoons for every 1 cup of cake flour required. To use cake flour in place of all-purpose flour, for every 1 cup all-purpose flour required, use 1 cup plus 2 tablespoons cake flour. *Note:* Adding the extra 2 tablespoons to each cup brings up the gluten content of cake flour so that it matches that of all-purpose flour. This is an extremely common substitution.

To sift or not to sift?

Sifting is a technique that separates dry ingredients and adds air to them. This makes the ingredients lighter and breaks up any lumps. Sifting is generally accomplished with a sifter or a strainer.

Sifting flour before use isn't really necessary, because it's been sifted many times during processing. Flour packages state that the contents have been presifted. However, sifting aerates flour, giving it more volume. In many recipes, this is a good thing. If a recipe calls for sifted flour, sift it before measuring. If a recipe calls for "flour, sifted," sift after measuring. In delicate cookies, sifting the flour is always a good idea.

Oats

Making oatmeal cookies without oats would be impossible. Oats come in two styles, quick-cooking and old-fashioned rolled oats. Either of these is fine for making cookies, but don't use instant oats. They're processed differently than quick-cooking and old-fashioned oats, so they won't yield the same results in cookie baking. Quick-cooking oats are sold in supermarkets in tall cardboard cylinders. Old-fashioned rolled oats are available in health food stores in large bins. Store them in a tightly sealed container in a dark, dry place, or in the freezer if you use them very little. They'll keep for several months.

Dairy Liquids

Dairy liquids provide moisture to cookie doughs and batters and create steam, helping cookies rise as they bake. Store all fresh and fluid dairy liquids in the refrigerator. Check the pull date of each and don't use the product if it is too far past the date. Canned milk can be kept indefinitely until opened. Then it should be stored in the refrigerator in a tightly sealed container.

If you're unsure whether milk is still good, give it the sniff test. If it has off odors, discard it and buy some fresh milk.

The following list contains various types of milk products:

- ✔ **Fresh milk:** For the recipes in this book, I used cow's milk. You can use whole milk, 2 percent, or 1 percent milk with equal success for any of these recipes.

Skim milk is too thin in consistency and doesn't work well in cookie making.

✔ **Buttermilk:** This was originally the milk liquid left over after churning butter. Today it's made by adding special bacterial cultures to skim milk to produce the tangy flavor and thickened texture.

✔ **Evaporated milk:** This is canned homogenized milk that has half of its water removed through evaporation. It doesn't have added sugar, but it does have a caramelized taste because it has been sterilized and the heat from that process lightly caramelizes the lactose (milk sugar). It comes in cans and is available in whole, lowfat, and fat-free varieties, which can usually be substituted for each other.

Evaporated milk can be substituted for fresh milk by adding an equal amount of water to it. Once opened, transfer it to a clean container and store tightly sealed in the refrigerator for up to five days.

✔ **Sweetened condensed milk:** This is a blend of homogenized milk and sugar that is heated to evaporate more than half of the water, leaving a sweet, sticky mixture. Sweetened condensed milk is available in whole, lowfat, and fat-free varieties. Generally, they can be substituted for each other. Once opened, transfer it to a clean container and store tightly sealed in the refrigerator for up to five days.

✔ **Half-and-half:** As the name implies, this is half milk and half cream. If you don't have any on hand, you can make your own by mixing milk and cream together in equal proportions.

✔ **Cream:** This is the fat part of milk that rises to the top. Several types of cream are available. *Whipping cream,* also called light whipping cream, is between 30 and 36 percent butterfat. *Heavy whipping cream* is between 36 and 40 percent butterfat. *Light cream,* also called table cream or coffee cream, is between 18 and 30 percent butterfat. Whipping cream and heavy cream are the ones used for whipping and mixing into batters. Light cream is used more for sauces; it doesn't have enough body to whip and hold its shape.

Eggs

Eggs are an essential ingredient in most cookies. They add flavor, tenderness, color, and richness and bind ingredients together. They also act as a leavening agent to raise cookies as they bake. Let eggs warm up to room temperature (which will vary, depending on the season) before using them to make cookies so that they can blend easily with other ingredients or whip to their fullest volume.

Following is a list of egg products used in cookie baking and information on how to store and use them:

- **Whole eggs:** Buy the freshest eggs you can. Check the date on the end of the carton to be sure that they're fresh. Inspect each egg to be sure that it's not cracked or dirty. There is absolutely no nutritional difference between brown and white eggs, so you can use either. If you choose, you can use free-range eggs. Just be sure that they're the correct size. Store eggs in their original carton in the refrigerator, with the pointed ends down.

If you're unsure about the age of your eggs, use this test. Place an egg in a bowl of cool water. A fresh egg will sink to the bottom of the bowl, while an old egg will rise near the top. Throw the old eggs away.

Whole eggs don't freeze in their shells, but they can be frozen when lightly beaten with either a pinch of salt or sugar for each egg. Egg yolks can also be frozen by the same method. Egg whites freeze easily and when defrosted are as good as fresh. For more details on freezing egg whites, see Chapter 19.

After frozen eggs have been defrosted, don't freeze them again — it's an invitation to bacteria.

- **Liquid fresh egg whites:** This product is made of 100 percent pure fresh liquid eggs whites that are pasteurized and have no preservatives, colorings, or gums. The only drawback to using this product is that they can't be whipped because the pasteurization process destroys the property that helps them hold their shape. I discuss them in more detail in Chapter 19.

- **Dried egg whites:** If keeping egg whites in the freezer is too much trouble or if there are none in the house, you can use dried egg whites. You can read more about them in Chapter 19.

Egg substitutes are composed of approximately 80 percent egg whites and contain no egg yolks. Because of this, they don't react the same way as whole eggs in baking. They may also contain other ingredients, such as vegetable oils, tofu, and nonfat milk. I don't recommend using egg substitutes in cookie baking. If you use an egg substitute in place of the eggs called for in a recipe, there's no guarantee that the recipe will work as it's supposed to.

Fats

Fats contribute several important qualities to cookies. They add flavor and color, and they tenderize, moisturize, and leaven doughs and batters. The degree of tenderness and the flavor depend on the type of fat used. Always use the type of fat specified in a recipe.

Butter

Butter provides the best flavor and richest mouth-feel to cookies. I prefer unsalted butter because it has a fresher flavor and I can control the amount of salt in a recipe. If you use salted butter, eliminate the salt called for in the recipe. Different brands of butter contain different amounts of water. Find the brand you prefer and stock up when it's on sale.

Butter comes in ¼-pound sticks and in 1-pound solids. Buy whichever you prefer. If you use the solid pound, you need a kitchen scale to measure the correct amount for each recipe.

Don't use whipped butter for baking cookies. It has too much air beaten into it and won't yield the same results.

Butter freezes very well and will last in the freezer for up to a year. I recommend keeping unsalted butter in the freezer until you need it. Defrost overnight in the refrigerator, at room temperature, or in a microwave oven on low power for 10-second intervals.

Take care where you store butter in the refrigerator because it easily picks up other flavors. Keep it tightly wrapped and away from strong-flavored foods. Unsalted butter will stay fresh for up to 10 days in the refrigerator.

Margarine

This solid fat is made from vegetable oils that are hydrogenated, a process of forcing pressurized hydrogen gas through liquids, which changes them to solid. Skim-milk solids, preservatives, salt, and emulsifiers are also added. Margarine can be substituted for butter, but the flavor and texture will be noticeably different. Margarine is softer and more oily than butter. Because it also has a higher melting point than butter, the mouth-feel isn't the same.

If you use margarine for baking cookies, use it in the regular solid form, which is the most similar to butter. Margarine made from any vegetable oil will work for baking cookies. Choose a type whose flavor you enjoy. Margarine is available in 1-pound packages of 4 sticks. Store margarine in the refrigerator for up to a month or in the freezer for up to a year.

Don't use lowfat or nonfat dairy spreads in baking cookies. Many of these contain a high percentage of water, which will dramatically affect cookie dough and batter in a negative way. Using these products won't yield the same results as butter or margarine.

Butter blends

This solid fat is a combination of about 40 percent butter and 60 percent margarine. It can be used as a substitute for butter or margarine. It comes in ¼-pound sticks and should be stored the same way as butter or margarine.

A stick of butter or margarine is 8 tablespoons, the equivalent of ¼ cup. Each stick weighs 4 ounces, or ¼ pound.

Shortening

Solid vegetable shortening adds volume to cookies because it holds air in batters. It can be interchanged with butter. However, shortening lacks butter's delicious taste. It's best to use shortening in recipes where the texture is more important than the flavor. Mixing a small amount of shortening with butter is a good way to adjust the texture of some cookie batters. Shortening stays solid at room temperature and keeps up to a year.

Because shortening doesn't melt as quickly as butter, cookies made with shortening won't spread as rapidly and will be puffier than those made with butter.

Cream cheese

Cream cheese adds tenderness to dough. In some cookie recipes, cream cheese is mixed with butter to make a delicate dough. Most recipes call for full-fat cream cheese. Lowfat cream cheese, usually called Neufchâtel, is often used to replace butter in lowfat cookie recipes. Cream cheese is available in 8-ounce packages in the supermarket dairy case. Store cream cheese tightly covered in the refrigerator and use by the pull date on the carton. Soften at room temperature or in a microwave oven at low power in 10-second intervals.

Oils

Vegetable oils provide moisture and tenderness to cookie doughs. Several vegetable oils, including canola, peanut, safflower, and light olive oil, can be used in cookie baking. Choose one that doesn't have a strong flavor. You can interchange oil for butter if you're concerned about fats, but the results will be different. See Chapter 19 for more information about this.

If you're concerned about lowering the fat content of your cookies, think of butter as an accent flavor rather than a main ingredient. Eliminate most of it from your recipe and use a small amount of canola oil in its place. The result will still be a tasty cookie. Also use parchment paper to line cookie sheets. It has absolutely no fat or calories. Or you can use a nonstick vegetable spray to coat the cookie sheets instead of using parchment paper. Either of these methods will ensure a reduction of the fat in your cookies.

A good general rule when substituting oil for butter is to use 1 tablespoon of oil in place of 4 tablespoons of butter.

Replacing solid fat with oil may make the cookies slightly flatter, but using some cake flour in place of regular flour can prevent this from happening. Also, reduce the sugar in the recipe by two or three tablespoons, and the finished cookie will be close to the original full-fat one.

Store unopened oil at room temperature for several months. Once opened, store oil tightly capped in the refrigerator. If the oil becomes cloudy in the refrigerator, it will become clear when it reaches room temperature.

Flavorings

Extracts, essences, spices, coffee, chocolate, and cocoa are good choices for flavoring cookie doughs and batters. *Extracts* are made from concentrated natural oils, derived from plants, that are mixed with alcohol. *Essences* are concentrated flavorings that are derived from natural sources, such as plants, by distillation or infusion. *Distillation* is accomplished by heating a liquid until it evaporates and then cooling it to produce a concentrated form. *Infusion* involves steeping or soaking an ingredient in hot liquid to extract its essence.

Chocolate and cocoa

Chocolate and cocoa are two of the most-loved ingredients used in cookie baking. Chocolate holds a special place in most people's hearts and mouths. I always use the same type of chocolate for baking cookies that I like to eat. Taste the chocolate before using it, just in case it doesn't appeal to you. However, be aware that, no matter how much you like chocolate, unsweetened chocolate won't taste good because it has no sugar and a pronounced bitter taste. Many brands of chocolate are available, so finding one that you like is easy. Look for chocolate in supermarkets, cookware shops, health food stores, and catalogs and on Web sites. Chocolate is usually melted before adding it to a cookie dough or batter, but often it is chopped into small pieces. Chocolate chips are used occasionally.

Chocolate and cocoa are often considered the same, but there is a difference. Although they both come from the cocoa bean, the difference becomes apparent during the manufacturing process. Cocoa is the dry powder that is hydraulically pressed from the liquid that comes from the cocoa bean. Cocoa is often added to cookie doughs and batters in its dry form, but a more intense chocolate flavor can be obtained by adding boiling water to cocoa. In some cases, both chocolate and cocoa are used together in a recipe to create layers of chocolate flavor. What could be better than that? (See Chapter 16 for recipes that use chocolate and cocoa.)

Chocolate

Several types of chocolate are made from chocolate liquor, depending on the other ingredients added.

Chocolate liquor is not alcoholic, as the name implies. It is the rich, dark liquid that is pressed from roasted cocoa beans during the manufacturing process and is used as the basis of all types of chocolate.

- ✓ **Unsweetened or baking chocolate** contains pure chocolate liquor and no added sugar. It is very bitter and never eaten plain.

- ✓ **Extra bittersweet, bittersweet, semisweet, or sweet chocolate** contains at least 50 percent cocoa butter and varying amounts of sugar. These chocolates also contain cocoa butter, vanilla, and lecithin as an emulsifier.

  Lecithin is a fatty substance found in egg yolks and some vegetables. It is used an emulsifier, a sort of moisturizer, in chocolate. Emulsifiers act to hold fat suspended in a mixture so that it maintains its proper balance. In the case of chocolate, emulsifiers are active agents that suspend cocoa butter within the mixture to promote optimum texture.

- ✓ **Milk chocolate** contains many fewer cocoa components than the previous category. It also has more sugar, milk solids or powder, vanilla, and lecithin.

- ✓ **White chocolate** is made from cocoa butter, sugar, milk solids or powder, vanilla, and lecithin. It contains no cocoa liquor. Some imitations are often passed off as white chocolate. These are known as *summer coating* or *confectionery coating* and are easier to handle than white chocolate because they don't need to be tempered. However, these don't contain cocoa butter but use another vegetable fat. As a result, they don't taste like chocolate. Be sure that the white chocolate you buy has cocoa butter.

- ✓ **Couverture** (koo vehr TYOOR) is chocolate that has a higher-than-usual percentage of cocoa butter. Any of the dark chocolates, milk chocolate, or white chocolate can be couverture. Professionals use it to create thin coatings on candies and truffles and for glazes. It is also used for baking chocolate. Couverture chocolate can be found in bulk in many cookware and specialty food shops.

✔ **Chocolate chips** come in many flavors. Some of these flavors are created with artificial ingredients. Read the label and buy those that contain real substances. Artificial ingredients make artificial-tasting cookies.

Don't substitute one type of chocolate for another. You may not get the outcome you hoped for. Different types of chocolates react in different ways in recipes. If you want to substitute one chocolate for another, you'll have to do some experimenting to get the proportion just right.

Store chocolate in a cool, dry place wrapped in foil or brown paper. Don't refrigerate or freeze chocolate because it will pick up moisture that will cause the chocolate to thicken and seize when it melts. Stored properly, dark chocolate will last for several years. Because of the milk they contain, milk chocolate and white chocolate are more delicate. Under optimum storage conditions, they will last for up to a year.

Cocoa powder

Cocoa powder is different than cocoa for drinking. It doesn't have sugar added to it. Cocoa powder, used for baking and candy making, contains between 15 and 25 percent cocoa butter. Lowfat cocoa powder, used mostly for drinks, contains between 10 and 13 percent cocoa butter.

Store cocoa powder in its tightly sealed container in a cool, dry place. Stored properly, it will last indefinitely.

Extracts

Vanilla is by far the most popular extract. Almond, lemon, and orange are also used often in baking. Buy pure extracts rather than synthetic extracts, except for flavors that aren't available naturally, such as butterscotch. Pure extracts have a fresh, natural flavor, and because extracts are concentrated, only a small amount is needed to impart flavor. Their role is to intensify other flavors and round them out. Store extracts tightly capped in glass bottles in a cool, dry place to prevent evaporation and give them an indefinite shelf life.

Vanilla extract is made by steeping vanilla beans in an alcohol and water solution. Vanilla beans are the pod of a climbing orchid that is native to southern Mexico. Pure vanilla extract is expensive to produce, so be sure you buy the real thing and not a synthetic reproduction.

Essences

Rosewater, orange flower water, strawberry, and apricot essences are often used to flavor cookies. Essences are potent, so you need only a small amount.

They'll last indefinitely if stored tightly capped in glass bottles in a cool, dark, dry place.

Spices

Spices are fruits, seeds, berries, buds, bark, and the dried roots of various plants usually grown in tropical regions. Each has a particular flavor and aroma it imparts to cookies. Spices are used either whole or ground. After spices are ground, their oils, which give them their flavor, begin to evaporate. Use fresh ground spices or buy them ground in small quantities that will be used quickly.

Store spices in tightly sealed containers (glass is best) in a cool, dry place. Don't store spices in the cabinet closest to the stove. Heat and light will shorten their shelf life. If you buy spices in plastic bags, transfer them to glass jars. Label and date your spices so that you know what's in each jar and how long it has been there. The most popular spices for cookies are allspice, anise seed, cardamom, cinnamon, cloves, ginger, and nutmeg. Sometimes black pepper is used to give cookies a flavorful zing.

You can have freshly ground spices anytime you like. Use a clean coffee grinder to grind whole spices as needed. Wipe out the grinder before and after each use. To remove the aroma from the grinder, grind a little fresh bread in it.

A mortar and pestle is an effective tool for crushing and grinding spices. The mortar, a shallow, slope-sided, small bowl, holds the spices, and the pestle, a round, solid, tapered tube, grinds the spices against the side of the bowl. Mortars and pestles are available in marble, ceramic, porcelain, clay, and wood.

You may use a nutmeg grater or grinder, two tools designed for making nutmeg powder and shavings, respectively. Chapter 2 discusses nutmeg graters and grinders.

Instant espresso powder

Instant espresso powder is a good way to imbue cookies with a full-bodied coffee flavor and color while not adding much extra liquid. I dissolve 1 teaspoon instant espresso powder in 1 teaspoon of warm water and add to the other ingredients.

Fruit: Dried and Crystallized

Fruit adds flavor, texture, and color to cookies. Keep a variety of dried, candied, and crystallized fruit in your cupboard so that you're always prepared to bake cookies. Although many types of dried fruits are available, here are some of the most common:

- **Raisins:** Several varieties of raisins are on the market. They add a sweet touch to many cookie recipes. My favorites are Monukka and Thompson seedless raisins because they're plump and juicy. These are available in many stores that sell raisins in bulk. Golden raisins, also called Sultanas, are made by treating grapes with sulfur dioxide before they're dried, a process that maintains their light color. Raisins are available in cardboard boxes or in bulk. Store them in an airtight container in the pantry so that they won't dry out. For prolonged storage, keep raisins in the freezer.

- **Currants:** These are made by drying very small Zante raisins. Currants are generally much smaller and drier than raisins. They are very sweet and can be substituted for raisins. Don't confuse dried currants with fresh red currants. Even though they have the same name, they're completely different fruits and not related. Store currants the same way as raisins.

If the raisins are too dry, you can plump them up by placing them in a small bowl and covering with warm water or liquor, such as bourbon or whiskey, if called for in the recipe. Let the raisins soak for at least 30 minutes and then drain off the liquid.

- **Cranberries:** Dried cranberries add a sweet/tart flavor and texture to cookies. They're available in cartons or in bulk. Store in an airtight container at room temperature.

- **Coconut:** Coconut has a sweet, nutty taste and is a favorite ingredient for cookies. Coconut comes in different forms, including shredded and flaked. It's also available sweetened or unsweetened. Be sure to use the type called for in the recipe. Store coconut in a tightly sealed container in the refrigerator or freezer.

- **Ginger:** Crystallized ginger adds a hot, sweet flavor and a chewy texture to cookies. Chop it finely just before adding to cookie doughs and batters. Store it in an airtight container in the pantry so that it doesn't dry out.

Liquid Sweeteners

Liquid sweeteners add sweetness, texture, moisture, color, and flavor to cookies.

✔ **Honey:** This sweet liquid is made by honeybees. Its flavor varies depending on the area where it's produced and the type of flowers the bees have fed upon. Honey can be light or dark. The color usually corresponds to the flavor: The darker the color, the deeper the flavor. Honey adds flavor, sweetness, moisture, and texture to cookies. Store honey tightly covered in a cool, dry place.

Honey crystallizes with age. To liquefy it, heat the open jar or bottle in a microwave oven or in a pan of warm water over medium heat.

✔ **Corn syrup:** This sweet liquid is made from cornstarch and is available in both light and dark styles. Light corn syrup has been clarified to remove the color. Dark corn syrup contains either refiner's syrup or caramel color and added flavor. Corn syrup adds moisture and texture to cookies. It's available in glass jars in supermarkets. Corn syrup will last indefinitely if stored tightly capped in the refrigerator.

✔ **Maple syrup:** This is produced by boiling the sap of the sugar maple tree until most of the water evaporates. Maple syrup is graded according to color: The lighter the color, the higher the grade. The flavor also corresponds to the color: The lighter the color, the more delicate the flavor. Maple syrup will last indefinitely if stored tightly capped in the refrigerator. If it crystallizes, you can liquefy it by heating the open bottle in a microwave oven or in a pan of warm water over medium heat.

Nuts and Nut Pastes

Nuts add flavor and texture to many cookies and are also used as decoration. A wide variety of nuts used in cookie baking is readily available. Most nuts are available in the form in which they're to be used — either whole, sliced, or slivered.

Buy unsalted nuts for baking. Most whole nuts have a thin, bitter outer skin, which can be removed by toasting or blanching the nuts. Toasting enhances the flavor of most nuts.

Nuts have a high natural oil content, which can easily become rancid. For this reason, store nuts in the freezer in airtight containers or plastic bags, where they'll keep for up to a year. Buy nuts from a source with high turnover so that you can be sure they're fresh.

Nut pastes are made by grinding nuts in a food processor until they release their oil and become a paste. Nut pastes are used in many cookie doughs to provide texture and flavor.

Keep a roll of masking tape and a marker in a kitchen drawer. Use them to write the name and date on each package of nuts or other ingredients you place in your freezer. This way, you know exactly what's in each package and how long it has been there so can use up the older nuts first.

Preserves and Jams

Preserves and jams are used mostly for fillings in sandwich cookies. Buy the best quality you can afford. Until opened, store the jars in the cupboard. Once opened, keep the jars tightly sealed and store in the refrigerator. I like to keep a variety of preserves and jam on hand so that I have a lot of choices.

Salt

This natural crystalline compound is invaluable in the cookie cupboard. Its main role is to enhance the flavor of other ingredients. In baking cookies, use the amount called for in the recipes. Too much salt will disrupt the flavor, and too little may cause a recipe to fail.

Table salt is the most common form of salt. It is fine-grained and flows freely due to additives that prevent it from clumping. Kosher salt has large crystals and is actually less salty than table salt. Sea salt comes in crystals varying in size from coarse to very fine. It's very flavorful and not as salty as table salt. Sea salt is often ground in a salt grinder. Any of these three salts can be interchanged for each other in baking cookies.

Salt will last indefinitely if stored in a cool, dry place. Most types of salt are readily available in supermarkets, health food stores, and specialty food shops.

 To keep salt from clumping in humid weather, add a few grains of rice to the shaker.

Special Ingredients

A couple of ingredients have specific uses in cookie baking. These ingredients include the following:

   ✔ **Fruit purées:** When replacing the fat in cookies, you still need to maintain moisture and texture. A few fruit-based products have been specifically designed to accomplish this. Applesauce is also a good ingredient for replacing fat. Once opened, these ingredients should be stored tightly covered in the refrigerator. They're perishable, so use them within a month.

✔ **Food coloring:** Food coloring is essential for coloring icing and sugar to decorate cookies. The two varieties used are powder and paste. For more information on food coloring, turn to Chapter 21.

Sugar

Sugar adds tenderness, sweetness, texture, stability, and extended life to cookies and also helps in browning. Keep your pantry stocked with the following types of sugar. They're all easy to find in most supermarkets. Store sugar indefinitely in an airtight container at room temperature in a cool, dry place.

Don't store dry ingredients such as flour, sugar, and cornstarch in their original containers after you open them. Doing so is an invitation to critters such as ants and mealy bugs. Transfer them to canisters or other airtight containers. I like to use clear plastic canisters so that I can see what's inside.

✔ **Granulated sugar:** Also called table sugar, this sugar is highly refined into tiny white grains. It's made from either sugar cane or sugar beets, and it's impossible to tell the difference in taste or texture between the sources. Granulated sugar is the most common form and is readily available. It's packed in boxes and bags and comes in cubes as well as grains.

✔ **Superfine sugar:** This sugar is more finely granulated than table sugar. It dissolves very easily and leaves no trace of grittiness. Superfine sugar and granulated sugar can be interchanged for each other. In the United Kingdom, superfine sugar is called castor or caster sugar.

✔ **Powdered sugar:** Also called *confectioners' sugar* or *icing sugar,* this is granulated sugar that has been ground to a powder. It usually has a small amount of cornstarch mixed with it to prevent caking due to moisture absorption. It always needs to be sifted before use. Powdered sugar dissolves easily. It is used in icings and frostings and to dust and decorate the tops of cookies. The amount of Xs on the package indicates the fineness of the mesh screen through which the sugar has been sifted. The more Xs, the finer the sugar.

✔ **Brown sugar:** This is white sugar that has been processed with molasses, which gives it a soft, moist texture and distinctive flavor. Brown sugar comes in both light and dark styles. The difference in the color is the amount of molasses the sugar contains. Light brown sugar is more commonly used than dark, but they can be interchanged for each other. Brown sugar hardens easily if exposed to air. It needs to be tightly packed when measured to expel the air trapped between its crystals.

If your brown sugar becomes too hard, soften it in the microwave oven on low power in 15-second intervals.

If you don't have light brown sugar for a recipe, you can make a good substitute. For 1 cup of light brown sugar, mix ½ cup dark brown sugar and ½ cup sugar. Or mix 1 cup sugar with 3 tablespoons of molasses.

✔ **Pearl sugar:** This is white sugar that has been processed into small round grains, resembling pearls. These grains are four to six times larger than those of granulated sugar. Pearl sugar is used to decorate the tops of cookies and provide texture.

Don't even try to use a sugar substitute (also known as an artificial sweetener) when baking cookies unless you want to court disaster. Sugar substitutes are many times sweeter than sugar. They react negatively when heated and don't provide the same texture as sugar.

Substitutions

Just in case you run out of an ingredient when you're in the middle of baking, Table 3-1 contains a list of substitutions that work well enough to let you continue baking. Remember to make a note to replace the missing ingredient next time you go shopping.

Table 3-1	Common Substitutions
In Place Of	*Use*
1 cup light brown sugar	1 cup sugar plus 3 tablespoons molasses, or ½ cup sugar plus ½ cup dark brown sugar
1 cup dark brown sugar	1 cup sugar plus ¼ cup molasses
1 cup sugar	1 cup superfine sugar, or 2 cups powdered sugar, or 1 cup firmly packed light brown sugar
1 cup cake flour	1 cup minus 2 tablespoons all-purpose flour
1 teaspoon baking powder	½ teaspoon cream of tartar plus ¼ teaspoon baking soda
1 ounce unsweetened baking chocolate	3 tablespoons cocoa powder plus 1 tablespoon butter
1 ounce semisweet chocolate	½ ounce unsweetened chocolate plus 1 tablespoon sugar
1 cup light corn syrup	1¼ cups granulated sugar and ⅓ cup water boiled together until the sugar dissolves
1 cup milk	½ cup evaporated milk plus ½ cup water

Chapter 4

Foolproof Techniques for Outstanding Cookies

* * *

In This Chapter

▶ Getting the oven and pans ready

▶ Brushing up on measuring and sifting

▶ Working with eggs and nuts

▶ Discovering the secrets of dough mixing

▶ Mastering correct baking techniques

* * *

Knowing and understanding the correct techniques for preparing, mixing, handling, baking, and finishing cookies will make your baking experience a breeze. You probably already know some of these techniques, while many others will be new to you. Take your time to read through this chapter and flip back to it as often as you need to while baking. Soon you'll know it all and will be baking cookies like a master. The saying "practice makes perfect" definitely applies here.

Preparing Ovens and Pans

Always bake cookies in a preheated oven. Preheating most ovens takes about 8 to 10 minutes. If cookies go into a cool oven, they'll melt and become flat instead of holding their shape.

Use heavy baking pans that won't warp when exposed to the heat of the oven. Pans with low or no rims are best because they allow the oven heat to circulate evenly and bake the cookies evenly. Several types of cookie sheets are available. I prefer to use shiny aluminum cookie sheets because dark pans conduct the heat much quicker. If you use dark pans, reduce the oven temperature by 25 degrees to prevent the bottoms of the cookies from burning.

Prepare the pans and cookie sheets before baking to keep cookies from sticking. Here are a couple of methods:

- ✔ To save on cleanup time, I prefer to line cookie sheets with nonstick parchment paper. If nothing drips on the cookie sheets, they don't have to be washed.

- ✔ A reusable pan liner works the same way as parchment paper and can be used hundreds of times. These liners are available in a variety of sizes to fit different cookies sheets and baking pans. Cookware shops, catalogs, and Web sites sell them.

- ✔ Butter and flour also work very well to keep cookie doughs and batters from sticking to the cookie sheets. When baking chocolate cookies, try dusting the pan with cocoa powder instead of flour.

Don't overgrease cookie sheets. Doing so causes cookies to spread too much, making them too thin. It will also overbrown the bottoms.

Always use a cold cookie sheet for baking each batch. If cookies are placed on a hot cookie sheet, they'll begin to spread before reaching the oven. If you don't have enough cookie sheets, let the cookie sheets cool before placing another batch of cookies on them. Slide the parchment paper sheet off the cookie sheet directly onto the cooling rack. Have the next batch of cookies ready on a piece of parchment paper that can be slipped onto the cool cookie sheet and placed immediately in the oven.

If you're preparing cookie molds, follow these directions. Spray madeleine and ladyfinger pans with a nonstick coating or use a pastry brush to lightly coat them with oil or butter and then dust with flour and shake out the excess. Lightly dust shortbread, speculaas, and springerle molds with flour before pressing the dough into them. For information about preparing a pizzelle iron, please see Chapter 14.

Measuring and Sifting

In regular cooking, you can get away with adding a pinch of this and some of that. But in cookie baking, it's really important to pay attention to the quantities of ingredients that each recipe calls for. If you add extra amounts or not enough of an ingredient, you're not going to end up with what you expect. Most likely, you'll have a failure on your hands. Who needs that? Dry and liquid ingredients are measured with different types of measuring cups because of their particular characteristics. By following correct measuring techniques for each type of ingredient, you'll guarantee success for each cookie recipe you tackle.

Sift the flour if the recipe calls for it. When flour is sifted, air is added to it, lightening it, getting rid of any lumps, and increasing the volume. Some recipes call for flour to be measured first and then sifted. This is different from sifting the flour before it's measured. The order of these steps makes a difference in the final amount of flour and in the finished cookies. Each recipe is written in a particular way because that's how it works. The best policy is to follow the recipes step by step, and you're sure to come out with great cookies every time!

Checking and double-checking is a good idea when measuring ingredients.

Measuring dry ingredients

There are two main methods of measuring dry ingredients (see Figure 4-1):

✔ The scoop-and-sweep method involves scooping the measuring cup into the ingredient and then sweeping off the excess at the top with a long, flat implement, such as a spatula or a knife. I prefer this method because it's quick, easy, and accurate.

Use the scoop-and-sweep method to get an accurate measure with measuring spoons. Many boxes of baking soda, cans of baking powder, and some spice containers have a straight side so that you can level off the spoon as you draw the ingredient from the container.

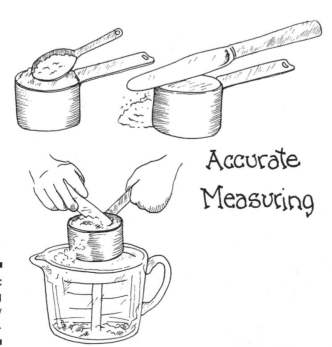

Accurate Measuring

Figure 4-1:
Measuring
dry
ingredients.

> ✔ Lightly spoon the ingredient into the cup and then sweep off the excess at the top with a long, flat implement, such as a spatula or knife. This method aerates the ingredients. It works well but takes more time than the scoop-and-sweep method.

Brown sugar traps a lot of air between its crystals, so pack it down in the cup to get an accurate measurement. The same method is used for measuring shortening. For ingredients such as coconut or chopped nuts, spoon them into the cup and press down lightly.

Sweep off the excess ingredient over the container holding it, not over the mixing bowl, or you'll have more of the ingredient than you need in your recipe.

Measuring liquid ingredients

When measuring liquid ingredients, use a liquid measuring cup, described in Chapter 2. Pour the ingredients carefully into the cup until it reaches the desired amount. For accuracy, place the measuring cup on a flat surface and read the measurement at eye. Reading the liquid level from above looks different than at eye level. Too much liquid will throw off the recipe. If you have more of the specific liquid than the recipe calls for, pour it out by using the liquid measuring cup's pour spout.

Measurement equivalents

Knowing the equivalents of various measurements is helpful in case you have to make some adjustments to a recipe. Table 2-1 gives equivalents for commonly used measurements.

Table 4-1		Common Measurement Equivalents
Dry ingredients		
3 teaspoons	=	1 tablespoon
2 tablespoons	=	⅛ cup
4 tablespoons	=	¼ cup
5 tablespoons plus 1 teaspoon	=	⅓ cup
8 tablespoons	=	½ cup
12 tablespoons	=	¾ cup
16 tablespoons	=	1 cup

Liquid ingredients		
1 pint	=	2 cups
1 quart	=	4 cups
Weights		
½ pound	=	8 ounces
1 pound	=	16 ounces

Sifting

Sifting is a pretty straightforward activity. I like to put my sifter over a large piece of wax paper that lies flat on the countertop. If the flour is to be *measured and then sifted,* I measure the amount of flour called for in the recipe into dry measuring cups. If other dry ingredients (such as baking powder or spices) are to be sifted with the flour, measure those and add them to the sifter. Then work the contents through the mesh screen of the sifter onto the wax paper.

If, on the other hand, the flour is to be *sifted and then measured,* I sift it and then carefully spoon it into a dry measuring cup. When the quantity I need is correctly measured, I return any excess flour to its canister or other receptacle. If other dry ingredients are to be sifted with the flour, I measure them and resift the flour with them.

Sifting ingredients before measuring makes a difference in their volume. Read the recipe to see whether it calls for sifting before or after measuring. I discuss sifters in Chapter 2.

If you don't have a sifter, you can use a fine mesh strainer instead, as shown in Figure 4-2.

How to Sift Flour If You Don't Have a Sifter

Figure 4-2: Use a strainer to sift flour if you don't have a sifter.

1. Pour flour into a strainer

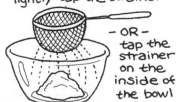

2. Use your hand to lightly tap the strainer

– OR – tap the strainer on the inside of the bowl

Different Strokes for Different Ingredients

All ingredients are not equal, especially when it comes to handling those ingredients. People have a tendency to think that everything can be handled in the same way, for example, putting everything in the refrigerator. That's not always the case. There's a great deal of difference between storing ingredients at room temperature or in the freezer. How ingredients are handled affects the eventual outcome of your cookies. This section talks about eggs, nuts, and spices. It does not include chocolate, which is covered in depth in Chapter 20.

Egg talk

Eggs are one of the main ingredients in cookie making. Eggs are fragile and need to be handled with care. They also need to be handled safely so there's no possibility of contamination from bacteria. Many recipes call for eggs to be separated into their two parts: yolk and white. You can separate them in several different ways (described later in this section). Knowing how to whip eggs so they gain the most volume is important, too. You can find more information on storing eggs in Chapter 3.

All the recipes in this book use large eggs. Using a different size egg will change the proportions of the ingredients and cause a different outcome.

Adding eggs to batter

Because eggs are an important ingredient, don't forget to add them to the mixture when they're called for. Add eggs while the mixer is on so they'll blend thoroughly with the other ingredients.

Here are some tips for successfully adding eggs to batter:

- ✔ Crack an egg into a separate bowl before adding it to the bowl containing the batter. Repeat this procedure with each egg. Don't crack eggs directly into the mixing bowl because the shell may splinter and scatter into the batter. Using this method will not only keep shell fragments out of the batter but will also prevent a spoiled egg from ruining it.

- ✔ When eggs are added to creamed butter and sugar, they have a tendency to sit on top of the mixture. Use a rubber spatula to scrape down the sides of the bowl so that the eggs will blend with the mixture.

- ✔ The addition of the eggs to a butter and sugar mixture makes it look curdled. Don't worry. After you add the dry ingredients, the mixture will smooth out.

Salmonella precautions

The presence of salmonella bacteria in eggs is a big concern today. Salmonella is a type of bacteria that causes an intestinal tract infection. Its symptoms are stomach pain, headache, nausea, vomiting, fever, chills, and diarrhea. Though definitely unpleasant and sometimes serious, salmonella rarely causes death and can be treated with antibiotics. By following some basic precautions, you won't be troubled.

✔ Buy fresh eggs in small quantities that will be used within two weeks.

✔ Salmonella grows in the temperature range of 40 to 160 degrees. Keep eggs refrigerated in the coldest part of the refrigerator, which is lower than 40 degrees.

✔ Wash your hands with warm, soapy water before and after handling raw eggs. Wash any bowls or utensils that come in contact with raw eggs after use.

✔ Don't use eggs with cracked shells.

✔ Don't leave eggs at room temperature longer than two hours.

Separating eggs

Many recipes call for eggs to be separated into their two parts — yolks and whites. The yolks are put in one bowl and the whites into another. Eggs are separated so that the whites can be whipped separately, a technique that is employed often in baking. A recipe occasionally calls for more egg yolks than whites. If that's the case, the whites can be frozen for use at another time (see Chapter 19).

Any touch of egg yolk (fat) in egg whites will keep them from whipping. Keeping the whites completely free of yolks is very important when separating eggs. Separate each egg over a small bowl before adding to a larger bowl of whites. If the white separates cleanly, add it to the bigger bowl. Nothing is more frustrating than ruining a big bowl of perfect egg whites with a blotch of egg yolk, especially if it's the last egg in the batch.

Separate egg whites into a different bowl than the one you will use to whip them, and transfer each egg white into the larger bowl before separating the next. This way, if a stray bit of yolk gets into the egg whites, it won't ruin the entire bowl. Egg whites whip to their fullest volume at room temperature but are easier to separate when cold. Separate the eggs when cold and then cover the bowl of whites tightly with plastic wrap and let stand at room temperature for 20 to 30 minutes before whipping. Here are a few methods of separating eggs.

✔ **Hand method:** Gently crack the egg shell against a hard surface, as close to its center as possible. Break it apart and place the egg's contents in your cupped hand. Slightly separate your fingers and — while retaining the yolk in your hand — let the egg white drip through your fingers into a bowl. Save or discard the egg yolk, depending on the recipe you're making.

Wash your hands after separating each egg so that nothing will get contaminated.

✔ **Egg separator method:** A tool called an egg separator does essentially the same thing as using your hand. It has a small center bowl to hold the egg yolk. Place the separator over a bowl, crack the egg into the center of the separator, and let the egg white drop into the bowl. This tool is available in plastic, aluminum, or ceramic.

✔ **Shell-to-shell method:** Crack the egg shell as close to its center as possible. Carefully pass the egg yolk back and forth between both sides of the shell, letting the egg white drip into a bowl directly under your hands (see Figure 4-3).

How to Separate an Egg

Figure 4-3:
Separating eggs using the shell-to-shell method.

1. Hold the egg in one hand over two small bowls

2. Crack the shell on the side of one bowl

3. Let the white fall into one of the bowls

4. Pass the yolk back & forth, each time releasing more white

5. When all the white is in the bowl, drop yolk in the other bowl.

Whipping egg whites

When egg whites are whipped, air is incorporated into them so that they'll cause cookies (and other baked goods) to rise. Using an electric mixer, either a stand model or the hand-held kind, is the easiest way to whip egg whites. Using a whisk or rotary beater is very tiring, though it can be done. In order to know when to stop beating egg whites, you have to know what your recipe calls for and whether you need to look for soft peaks or stiff peaks. When beating egg whites, stop occasionally and notice how they look before proceeding:

✔ **Soft peaks:** This means that the egg whites should be beaten until they are fluffy and slightly hold their shape. They fall over gently when the beater is removed. Reaching this stage takes 3 to 4 minutes with a stand mixer.

✔ **Stiff peaks:** Egg whites beaten to this stage stand up at attention. They hold their shape easily and are glossy. Reaching this stage takes 5 to 6 minutes with a stand mixer. The challenge here is not to overbeat the egg whites until they're dry or, worse, until they fall apart.

For the best success when whipping egg whites, follow these tips:

✔ Egg whites that are more than a week old whip easier than very fresh whites.

✔ Have egg whites at room temperature.

✔ Use a grease-free bowl and beaters. Any fat that mixes with the egg whites will keep them from whipping to full volume.

✔ Plastic bowls are porous and hold onto other ingredients, such as fat. Don't use them for whipping egg whites because the tiniest amount of fat will keep the egg whites from whipping. Use metal or glass bowls that are at room temperature.

✔ Adding about ¼ teaspoon cream of tartar to egg whites before whipping helps them whip to full volume.

✔ Overbeaten egg whites form a lumpy foam that breaks down and becomes watery.

An ode to nuts

Nuts usually need to be toasted, ground, or chopped before they're added to cookie batters. Read through the recipe and find out what preparation is needed before starting to mix the batter or dough. No matter which type of nuts are used, the methods for toasting, grinding, and chopping are the same. All nuts have a high oil content, which tends to make them turn rancid quickly at room temperature. For long-term storage, keep nuts in different stages of preparation in clearly marked airtight containers or zipper-type freezer bags in the freezer. This way, you'll be ready when the cookie-making mood strikes. Airtight storage helps lock out freezer smells. Date the containers and bags so that you'll know how long they've been in storage. Most nuts can be frozen for up to a year. Let nuts come to room temperature before grinding them. Frozen nuts don't chop up as finely as nuts at room temperature.

Some people are allergic to nuts, especially peanuts. To prevent problems when serving your cookies at a public gathering, place a label on them stating that they contain peanuts.

Found a peanut . . .

While nuts grow on trees, peanuts grow under the ground. That's because a peanut isn't a nut at all, but a legume. The seeds are encased in a dry, thin shell that is easily broken open. Inside the shell, the seeds are covered with a brown papery skin.

Peanuts are native to South America, but came to the United States by a circuitous route.

Portuguese explorers took them to Africa, and the nuts came to the United States with African slaves. Their buttery flavor is enhanced by roasting. Peanuts are very popular and easy to find in supermarkets and many other food shops.

Shelling nuts

You'll probably get your nuts already shelled and in bags in the baking aisle of your local grocery or supermarket. Many health and natural food stores sell nuts in bulk bins, too. If you do buy or have nuts in the shell that you want to use for baking, you'll need to shell them first.

Peanuts are the easiest nuts to shell. Their shells are soft and crack easily in the hand. Pop the shells between your thumbs and forefingers, separate the sides of the shell, and let the nuts drop out into a bowl. Almonds, pecans, walnuts, and hazelnuts have hard shells. You need to crack their shells with a nutcracker. This takes a bit of physical strength, but you don't have to be Hercules. Crack the shells and separate them. You may need to use a sharp knife or a pick, a tool with a sharp point and very thin blade, to remove the nut meat from the shell. Macadamia nuts are the hardest nuts of all. I've never tried to crack one myself, but I hear it's a tough job. Don't worry, though. Macadamia nuts are nearly always available already shelled.

Skinning nuts

Almonds and hazelnuts often need to be skinned when used in cookie recipes. You'll know that they need to be skinned if a recipe calls for blanched almonds or skinned hazelnuts. The skins are removed because they tend to be a little bitter. If you buy Spanish peanuts, you'll have to pop the skins off by hand, which can be tedious. Try to buy Valencia peanuts because they come skinless.

To skin almonds, blanch them first by dropping them into a pan of boiling water for 1 minute (see Figure 4-4). Use a slotted spoon or skimmer to remove them and immediately place them in a bowl of cold water. Drain the almonds, dry them, and gently squeeze them between your fingers. They'll pop out of their skins.

To skin hazelnuts, first toast them in a jelly roll pan or cake pan in a 350-degree oven for about 18 minutes, until the skins split and the nuts turn light golden. Remove the pan from the oven and immediately transfer the nuts to a kitchen towel. Fold the towel around the nuts so that they're completely enclosed and rub them to remove the skins.

HOW TO SKIN NUTS

TO SKIN ALMONDS, BLANCH FIRST. DROP THEM INTO A PAN OF BOILING WATER FOR 1 MINUTE.

USE A SLOTTED SPOON OR SKIMMER TO REMOVE THEM. IMMEDIATELY PLACE THEM IN A BOWL OF COLD WATER.

DRAIN THEM, DRY THEM AND GENTLY SQUEEZE BETWEEN YOUR FINGERS. THEY WILL 'POP' OUT OF THEIR SKINS!

Figure 4-4: Skinning almonds.

Chopping and grinding nuts

Nuts can be chopped with a chef's knife on a cutting board. Be sure to use a sharp knife. Don't try to chop too large a quantity at one time, or you may have nuts flying all over the kitchen. About 1 cup is good to start with. Place the nuts in the center of the cutting board and use a large chef's knife with an 8- to 10-inch blade. Hold the knife by the handle with one hand and place your other hand carefully over the top part of the blade to help center it. Rock the knife back and forth, lifting it occasionally to gather in more nuts, while applying downward pressure. As the nuts get chopped, gather them back into the center and keep chopping until the nuts are the size that you want.

The best way to grind nuts is in a food processor, using the steel blade (see Figure 4-5). Most nuts have a high oil content that gets released when they're ground. To keep them from turning to paste, add 1 tablespoon of sugar for each cup of nuts before processing them. For oily nuts, such as hazelnuts, macadamia nuts, and Brazil nuts, add 2 tablespoons of sugar for each cup of nuts before grinding. If you're grinding nuts for a particular recipe, take the sugar from the amount in the ingredients list. If you're grinding nuts to keep in the freezer, the extra tablespoon or two of sugar won't make a difference in whatever recipe they're used for.

Some recipes call for a rough grind, while others call for a fine grind. Use the on/off or pulse key and pulse the nuts for 30 seconds to a minute for rough grind and up to 2 minutes for a fine grind. Check occasionally to see whether the nuts are being chopped as finely as you want.

Be sure that your food processor is clean and dry before chopping nuts in it, especially if the last thing you chopped in it was onions!

HOW TO GRIND NUTS

Figure 4-5:
Grinding nuts in a food processor.

THE BEST WAY TO GRIND NUTS IS IN A FOOD PROCESSOR USING THE STEEL BLADE

TO KEEP THEM FROM TURNING INTO PASTE, ADD A TABLESPOON OF SUGAR FOR EACH CUP OF NUTS BEFORE PROCESSING.

FOR THE OILIEST NUTS, (HAZELNUTS, MACADAMIAS, AND BRAZIL) ADD 2 TABLESPOONS OF SUGAR FOR EACH CUP OF NUTS!

Toasting nuts

Toasting enhances the flavor of nuts. Spread the nuts in an even layer on a jelly roll pan or in the bottom of a cake pan (see Figure 4-6). Toast them in a preheated 350-degree oven. The type of nuts determines the toasting time. Almonds, walnuts, pecans, and pine nuts toast quickly. Set a timer for 5 minutes. Shake or stir the nuts and toast for another 3 to 5 minutes, until light golden. Check the nuts often while they toast because it doesn't take too long for them to burn. A good indication that they're ready is that their skins split so you can see the color of the nut and you can smell their aroma. Remove all the nuts from the oven and transfer them to a cool pan so that they won't continue to brown on the hot baking pan. Place the cool baking pan on a cooling rack.

Hazelnuts need to toast for about 15 minutes because they're thicker than most other nuts.

Put a little spice in your life

Spices are great flavor enhancers and add zest to cookies. Keep a stock of fresh spices in your cupboard. Fresh ground spices have the most flavor, so I highly recommend grinding them as needed. You'll be amazed at the difference in flavor. (See Chapter 3 for more information on spices.)

Use a nutmeg grater or grinder to grate or grind nutmeg right before using. See Chapter 2 for descriptions of these tools. Other spices, such as cloves, allspice, and any other spices in berry form, can be ground in your coffee grinder. To keep your spices from tasting like coffee, wipe out your coffee grinder thoroughly with a paper towel or keep a separate coffee grinder for grinding spices. I grind a small amount that I know I'll use quickly so the flavor remains strong.

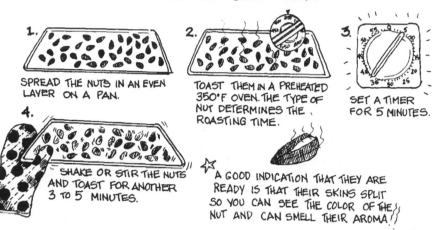

Figure 4-6:
Toasting
nuts.

Dough Mixing 101

Most cookie doughs are pretty forgiving and can be mixed in a few different ways without hurting or changing their texture. Check each recipe for the mixing method. The method chosen in the recipes describes the best way to mix the ingredients, which are listed in order of use. The main methods for mixing are in a food processor, with an electric stand mixer, with a hand-held mixer, or, in a few cases, by hand. Even if the doughs or batters are over-mixed or overhandled, they'll usually turn out just fine. But try to avoid overmixing because it can make cookie dough tough.

These important tips help make cookie mixing go smoothly:

- Have all ingredients at room temperature, unless the recipe states otherwise. Butter can be softened quickly in a microwave oven. Use low power in 15-second intervals and check after each interval. It could melt before you know it.

- Beat butter or fat until fluffy first before adding the sugar. Otherwise, the mixture will be too grainy.

- Add ingredients to the batter in stages. This gives the mixture time to incorporate each new addition so it blends better, making a more homogenous dough.

The type of cookies determines how the dough or batter is handled after mixing. For more information on dough handling, please see the chapter that contains the recipe you're making.

Baking Considerations

Some other recipe steps are worth your attention. The arrangement of cookies on the cookie sheet can have a direct impact on the way they turn out. If you're baking at higher altitudes, some adjustments need to be made in both oven temperature and baking time. How do you know when the cookies are done? There are ways to tell. And cooling cookies after baking is more important than you might think.

Arranging cookies on the cookie sheet

Space cookies evenly on the cookie sheet. If they're too close together, they'll spread into each other as they bake. If you're baking only a few cookies, spread them out so that they're spread out evenly on the cookie sheet. Bake cookies of the same size and shape on each baking sheet so that they bake in the same amount of time.

To keep cookies from spreading as they bake, chill them on the cookie sheet for at least 30 minutes before baking.

Baking more than one sheet of cookies at a time

If you're baking two sheets of cookies at the same time, always switch the cookie sheets to different oven racks halfway through baking. Doing so ensures that they'll bake evenly. Leave at least 2 inches of space around the cookie sheets so that air can circulate around them evenly.

High-altitude baking

If you're baking at 3,000 feet or below, you don't need to make any adjustments to your recipes. Above 3,000 feet, liquids boil quicker, causing moisture to evaporate and resulting in drier and flatter cookies. In this case, the best results are obtained by lowering the oven temperature by 25 degrees and reducing the sugar in recipes by 2 tablespoons for each cup. Above 5,000 feet, do the same as recommended for above 3,000 feet and also reduce the baking powder by half.

Testing for doneness

All cookie recipes in this book give the oven temperature and baking time. Every oven is different, so set the timer for the least amount of time given and begin to check the cookies for doneness at that stage. Adding a few minutes of baking time is a lot easier than trying to salvage overbaked or burned cookies.

When testing for doneness, open and close the oven door as quickly as possible to prevent heat loss.

Most cookies are done when they're light-colored and firm. But sometimes it's hard to tell whether they're ready to come out of the oven. If you're not sure, touch the top of the cookie. It should hold up to the touch and not collapse. If it collapses, it needs to bake a little longer.

Cooling

Completely cool cookies before storing them, or they'll become soft and mushy. Place cookie sheets with the cookies on cooling racks. Doing so allows air to circulate all the way around the cookies, keeping the bottoms from getting soggy. Many cookies need to cool directly on racks. If this is the case, let them cool on the cookie sheet for a couple minutes and then use a flat metal spatula to transfer them to the rack.

Part II
Popular Types of Cookies

"Folks around here really go for giant drop cookie exchanges. Just fill 'em with dough and heave ho."

In this part . . .

This section tells you all you need to know to make drop, rolled, and refrigerator cookies. These are the types of cookies that are probably the most familiar to you. In fact, as a kid you may have even had some experience making them. I like to think of these cookies as the ones you're likely to have around the house for everyday munching. Also, they're great for school lunches and for road trips. Though a lot of tips and techniques are provided in this part, don't let that put you off — drop, rolled, and refrigerator cookies are easy to make and easy to eat!

Chapter 5

Drop Cookies

Drop cookies are the easiest types of cookies to make and probably the one most of us are familiar with. When you made your first cookies as a child, they were probably drop cookies such as chocolate chip cookies or oatmeal cookies (see Chapter 18 for more kid-oriented recipes and tips on ways to involve children in cookie baking). Maybe we like them so much because we only have to drop the dough onto cookie sheets in order to make wonderful cookies. During baking, these cookies flatten out, usually taking on a circular shape, which is easy for kids to hold.

The making of drop cookies lends itself to crowd participation. Hand out spoons to family and friends and let them all take a turn at dropping the dough onto the cookie sheets. If you let others help, they'll expect to be paid — in cookies!

I know you'll be excited about the prospect of eating the cookies after they come out of the oven. But wait until the cookies cool a little before eating them. Be especially careful with chocolate cookies or cookies that have chocolate chips because chocolate keeps its heat longer than other ingredients and it will still be hot even if the cookies are cool. Burning your fingertips or the roof of your mouth with hot cookies will spoil some of the pleasure of eating freshly baked cookies. But when they're warm, they're oh, so good.

Don't Be a Drop Cookie Dropout

Making drop cookies is fun because it's easy to get right down into the dough and work with it. You can get your hands into it because the dough needs a little push to move it off the spoon so it drops onto the cookie sheet. It's comforting to see all those mounds of cookie dough that will soon be transformed into delicious round cookies. And talk about simple — it doesn't get any simpler than making drop cookies. I can guarantee you won't be a dropout when it comes to making drop cookies. The hard part of making these cookies is not eating them all at once.

Drop cookies are made just as their name implies. The dough is dropped from a spoon or scoop onto a cookie sheet. In order to be dropped, the dough must be fairly stiff. There are different textures of drop cookies: chewy, crunchy or crispy, and cakelike. The difference lies in the ingredients and how they're combined, and in how the cookies are baked. Most drop cookies are made by creaming the butter or other fat and sugar together and then adding the other ingredients. The recipes in this chapter fall into the three different texture categories.

- ✓ **Chewy:** Chocolate Chip-Walnut, White Chocolate Chunk-Macadamia Nut, Oatmeal-Raisin, and Peanut Butter.

- ✓ **Crunchy or crispy:** Molasses Spice Drops and Maple Pecan Crisps

- ✓ **Cakelike:** Chocolate Macaroons

A few recipes in this book call for the dough to be chilled before baking. This step is important because chilling keeps the dough from spreading too much when it bakes. Chilling also allows the moisture to be evenly distributed throughout the dough.

Use a small ice cream scoop rather than a spoon to gather up the dough and drop it onto the cookie sheet (see Figure 5-1). Doing so keeps your hands cleaner and gets the cookies in the oven quicker. You can easily vary the size of drop cookies by adjusting the amount of dough on the spoon or in the scoop. If you want to make miniature cookies, use a melon baller to scoop out the dough. You'll have to use your fingers, though, to help the dough drop from this tool, as it doesn't have its own release mechanism.

Try to keep cookies of the same size together on cookie sheets so that they'll bake evenly.

Leave plenty of room between the drop cookies on the baking sheet. They spread as they bake. If they're too close together, you'll end up with one giant cookie the size of the baking sheet. If you make your cookies bigger, you may need to extend the baking time by a few minutes to make sure that they're done.

USE AN ICE CREAM SCOOP
TO SHAPE DOUGH!

Figure 5-1:
Scooping and dropping the dough by using an ice cream scoop.

If you're not sure how to tell whether the cookies are done, there are a couple ways to figure this out. For most cookies, except dark and chocolate cookies, you can tell whether they're done by looking at them. They should look firm and set. Another way to tell whether cookies are done is to lightly touch the top of a cookie with your fingertips. If the cookie is done, the top will feel firm and will spring back instead of holding the imprint of your fingertips.

Drop cookies are versatile. They can be simple, everyday cookies or elaborate, sophisticated cookies fancy enough to serve at an elegant soiree. Some of them can be made into sandwich cookies (see Chapter 9 for tips on making sandwich cookies). You can also decorate drop cookies with chocolate painting or piping and with confectioners' sugar or a dusting of cocoa powder to dress them up (see Chapters 20 and 21 for decorating ideas). Presenting your cookies on attractive plates and in unusual ways can make them even more appealing.

Chunky Drop Cookies

Chunky drop cookies are some of the most loved in the United States. Most of us were introduced to them as children and have very fond memories of making and eating them. In fact, for many of us, these cookies were the very first cookies we ate, and we instantly fell in love with them. I like to think of them as comfort food. A typical characteristic of these cookies is that they include nuts or chips, so they fall into the chewy texture category. Chocolate chip cookies have always held a special place in my heart and mouth! All cookies in this section make excellent big cookies (see Chapter 17 for more information on big cookies). You can even decorate them for a birthday or other special occasion (see Chapter 21 for decorating tips).

Chocolate Chip-Walnut Cookies

These chewy all-American favorite cookies may be the kind you made on your first foray into the kitchen. They typically are made with semisweet chocolate chips, but it's okay to use milk chocolate chips if you prefer. You also can substitute mini-chips or leave out the nuts if you prefer.

Preparation time: *1½ hours; includes chilling*

Baking time: *10 minutes*

Yield: *5 dozen*

2½ cups all-purpose flour	*¾ cup sugar*
1 teaspoon baking soda	*2 teaspoons vanilla extract*
½ teaspoon salt	*2 eggs*
1 cup (2 sticks) unsalted butter, softened	*2 cups chocolate chips*
1 cup light brown sugar	*1 cup roughly chopped walnuts or other nuts*

1 Combine the flour, baking soda, and salt in a mixing bowl.

2 Using a mixer, beat the butter in a large mixing bowl until fluffy, about 2 minutes. Add the brown sugar, sugar, and vanilla and mix together until smooth.

3 Add the eggs one at a time, stopping to scrape down the sides of the bowl with a rubber spatula after each addition.

4 Blend in the flour mixture from Step 1 in three stages and stir in the chips and nuts.

5 Cover the bowl tightly with plastic wrap and chill for 30 minutes.

6 Line a cookie sheet with parchment paper. Scoop out walnut-sized mounds of the cookie dough and place on the cookie sheet, leaving 2 inches between the mounds. Chill the cookies for 30 minutes.

7 While the cookies are chilling, preheat the oven to 375°.

8 Bake for 10 to 12 minutes, until golden. Remove the cookie sheet from the oven and transfer the cookies from the parchment to cooling racks. Store in an airtight container at room temperature for up to a week. Freeze for longer storage.

Vary It! *To make a crispy variation of these cookies, reduce the sugar to ½ cup and add ¼ cup light corn syrup and 3 tablespoons milk to the batter/sugar mixture in Step 2.*

Per serving: *Calories 114 (From Fat 56); Fat 6g (Saturated 3g); Cholesterol 15mg; Sodium 44mg; Carbohydrate 14g (Dietary Fiber 0g); Protein 1g.*

White Chocolate Chunk-Macadamia Nut Cookies

Macadamia nuts and white chocolate give this cookie an extra-sweet bonus. Mix the nuts and white chocolate chunks thoroughly so that they're evenly distributed.

Preparation time: *10 minutes*

Baking time: *8 minutes*

Yield: *3 dozen*

2 cups all-purpose flour

¾ teaspoon baking soda

½ teaspoon baking powder

½ teaspoon salt

1 cup (2 sticks) unsalted butter, softened

1 cup light brown sugar

1 egg

2 teaspoons vanilla extract

8 ounces (1½ cups) white chocolate (white baking squares), cut into small chunks, or white baking chips

¾ cup roughly chopped, unsalted, toasted macadamia nuts (see Chapter 4 for information on toasting nuts)

1 Preheat the oven to 375°. Line a cookie sheet with parchment paper.

2 Combine the flour, baking soda, baking powder, and salt in a mixing bowl.

3 Using a mixer, beat the butter in a large mixing bowl until fluffy, about 2 minutes. Add the brown sugar and mix together until smooth.

4 Add the egg and vanilla. Stop to scrape down the sides of the bowl with a rubber spatula. Blend in the flour mixture from Step 2 in three stages and stir in the white chocolate and the nuts.

5 Scoop out walnut-sized mounds of the cookie dough and place on the cookie sheet, leaving 2 inches between the mounds. Bake for 8 to 10 minutes, until the cookies are golden. Remove the cookie sheet from the oven and transfer the cookies from the parchment to cooling racks. Store in an airtight container at room temperature for up to a week. Freeze for longer storage.

Per serving: Calories 152 (From Fat 87); Fat 10g (Saturated 5g); Cholesterol 21mg; Sodium 76mg; Carbohydrate 15g (Dietary Fiber 0g); Protein 2g.

Oatmeal-Raisin Cookies

These cookies are perfect with a cold glass of milk or a hot cup of coffee or tea. They're great to pack for a picnic, but first and foremost, they're wonderful when still warm from the oven. For extra zip, try using dried cherries or cranberries in place of the raisins.

Preparation time: *20 minutes*

Baking time: *11 minutes*

Yield: *3 dozen*

¾ cup all-purpose flour	*¾ cup light brown sugar*
1½ cups old-fashioned rolled oats	*1 egg, lightly beaten*
1 teaspoon baking powder	*1½ teaspoons vanilla extract*
1 teaspoon ground cinnamon	*½ cup raisins*
¼ teaspoon salt	*½ cup chopped walnuts*
½ cup (1 stick) unsalted butter, softened	

1 Preheat the oven to 350°. Line a cookie sheet with parchment paper.

2 In a large mixing bowl, combine the flour, oats, baking powder, cinnamon, and salt and set aside.

3 Using a mixer, beat the butter in a large mixing bowl until fluffy, about 2 minutes. Add the brown sugar and mix together until smooth. Combine the egg and vanilla and add to the mixture, blending thoroughly.

4 Stir in the dry ingredients from Step 2 in three batches, blending well after each addition. Stir in the raisins and nuts.

5 Drop the batter by rounded tablespoonfuls onto the cookie sheet, leaving 2 inches between the mounds. Bake for 11 to 12 minutes, until set. Remove the cookie sheet from the oven and transfer the cookies from the parchment to cooling racks. Store in an airtight container at room temperature for up to a week. Freeze for longer storage.

Per serving: *Calories 82 (From Fat 36); Fat 4g (Saturated 2g); Cholesterol 13mg; Sodium 31mg; Carbohydrate 11g (Dietary Fiber 1g); Protein 1g.*

Peanut Butter Cookies

Don't expect these cookies to last long — they taste too good! For the best flavor, use a natural style or freshly ground peanut butter in these cookies. I don't recommend using lowfat peanut butter to make these cookies because it doesn't have near the flavor of regular peanut butter.

Preparation time: *15 minutes*

Baking time: *11 minutes*

Yield: *4½ dozen*

2 cups all-purpose flour	*½ cup sugar*
1 teaspoon baking soda	*1¼ cups light brown sugar*
¼ teaspoon salt	*2 eggs, lightly beaten*
¾ cup (1½ sticks) unsalted butter, softened	*1 teaspoon vanilla extract*
1 cup smooth or chunky peanut butter at room temperature	*¾ cup chopped salted peanuts*

1 Preheat the oven to 350°. Line a cookie sheet with parchment paper.

2 Sift together the flour, baking soda, and salt and set aside.

3 Using a mixer, beat the butter in a large mixing bowl until fluffy, about 2 minutes. Add the peanut butter and blend together well. Add the sugar and brown sugar and mix together until smooth. Combine the eggs and vanilla and add to the mixture, blending thoroughly.

4 Stir in the dry ingredients from Step 2 in three batches, blending well after each addition. Stir in the peanuts.

5 Shape the dough into tablespoon-size balls and place on the cookie sheet, with 2 inches between the balls. With a damp fork, press the dough to flatten slightly and make a crosshatch pattern on top (see Figure 5-2).

6 Bake for 11 to 12 minutes, until the cookies are golden and set. Remove the cookie sheet from the oven and transfer the cookies from the parchment to cooling racks. Store in an airtight container at room temperature for up to a week. Freeze for longer storage.

Per serving: *Calories 109 (From Fat 56); Fat 6g (Saturated 2g); Cholesterol 15mg; Sodium 76mg; Carbohydrate 12g (Dietary Fiber 1g); Protein 2g.*

Trivia: Chocolate chip cookie pedigree

The original chocolate chip cookies were called Toll House cookies. They were named after the Toll House restaurant in Whitman, Massachusetts, which was a toll house on the road to Boston, built in the early 18th century. Ruth Wakefield purchased the building and the inn it housed in the 1930s. Ms. Wakefield cut a chocolate bar into small pieces and blended it into cookie dough. A classic was created — the chocolate chip cookie. These are the most popular cookies in the United States.

When you *sift*, you pass dry ingredients (such as flour, cocoa powder, and powdered sugar) through a fine mesh screen, such as a sifter or strainer. Sifting lightens the ingredients by adding air and breaks up any lumps. Sifting is also used to combine dry ingredients.

MAKING CROSSHATCH PATTERNS ON PEANUT BUTTER COOKIES

Figure 5-2:
Making the traditional crosshatch pattern on peanut butter cookies.

2"

SHAPE THE DOUGH INTO TABLESPOON-SIZE BALLS. PLACE ON COOKIE SHEET WITH 2" BETWEEN BALLS. WITH A DAMP FORK, PRESS THE DOUGH TO FLATTEN SLIGHTLY. AND MAKE A CROSSHATCH PATTERN ON TOP.

Not So Chunky Drop Cookies

The cookies in this section fall into the crunchy or crispy and cakelike types. These are less chewy and more delicate because they have a smoother texture than chunky cookies. For that reason, they go pretty fast, so you'll want to make a lot. I like to serve these cookies with afternoon tea because they're a little less filling than their chunky cousins.

Chocolate Macaroons

The word macaroon has its origins in the Greek word *makaria*, which means pleasure or contentment. A childhood favorite for many, Chocolate Macaroons are a treat you can sink your teeth into. Macaroons are unusual because they're one of the few types of cookies that don't contain flour.

Preparation time: *10 minutes*

Baking time: *12 minutes*

Yield: *2½ dozen*

1 cup slivered almonds

⅔ cup sugar

Pinch of salt

¼ cup unsweetened Dutch-processed cocoa powder

2 ounces (⅓ cup) bittersweet or semisweet chocolate, finely chopped

1 cup shredded sweet coconut

2 egg whites at room temperature

1 Preheat the oven to 350°. Line a cookie sheet with foil.

2 Place the almonds, sugar, salt, cocoa powder, and chocolate in the work bowl of a food processor fitted with the steel blade. Process by using on/off until the almonds are finely ground, about 2 minutes. Stir in the coconut. (To make these cookies using a mixing bowl and mixer, start with finely ground almonds. Combine the almonds, coconut, sugar, salt, cocoa powder, and chcolate in the bowl and blend briefly.)

3 Lightly beat the egg whites and pour them through the feed tube while the food processor is running. Process until the mixture is well blended, about 30 seconds. (If you're using a mixing bowl and mixer, add the egg whites and blend on medium speed until the mixture is well blended, 30 seconds to 1 minute.)

4 Spoon out 1-inch mounds on the cookie sheets, leaving 1 inch between them. Bake for 12 to 14 minutes, until set. Remove the cookie sheet from the oven and transfer the cookies from the foil to cooling racks. Store in an airtight container at room temperature for up to a week. Freeze for longer storage.

Per serving: *Calories 67 (From Fat 33); Fat 4g (Saturated 2g); Cholesterol 0mg; Sodium 17mg; Carbohydrate 8g (Dietary Fiber 1g); Protein 1g.*

A *pinch* of something refers to a tiny amount of a dry ingredient (approximately ¹⁄₁₆ teaspoon), such as salt or spices, that can be grasped between the thumb and finger.

Molasses Spice Drops

These cookies remind me of gingersnaps, but their texture is chewier. They're delicious with a glass of milk or a hot cup of tea.

Preparation time: *10 minutes*

Baking time: *10 minutes*

Yield: *3½ to 4 dozen*

⅔ cup canola oil	1 teaspoon baking soda
1 cup sugar	Pinch of salt
¼ cup dark molasses	½ teaspoon ground cloves
1 egg	½ teaspoon ground ginger
2 cups all-purpose flour	1 teaspoon ground cinnamon

1 Preheat the oven to 350°. Line a cookie sheet with parchment paper.

2 Using a mixer, combine the canola oil, sugar, molasses, and egg in a large mixing bowl and mix until smooth.

3 In another large mixing bowl, combine the flour, baking soda, salt, cloves, ginger, and cinnamon. Toss to blend well. Add the dry ingredients to the molasses mixture in three batches, blending well after each addition.

4 Scoop or spoon out rounded tablespoons of the batter onto the cookie sheets, leaving 2 inches between the balls. Run the scoop or spoon under cold water, shake off the excess, and lightly press down the balls.

5 Bake for 10 to 11 minutes, until set. Remove the cookie sheet from the oven and transfer the cookies from the parchment to cooling racks. Store in an airtight container at room temperature for up to a week. Freeze for longer storage.

Per serving: Calories 68 (From Fat 29); Fat 3g (Saturated 0g); Cholesterol 4mg; Sodium 31mg; Carbohydrate 9g (Dietary Fiber 0g); Protein 1g.

Maple Pecan Crisps

Maple and pecan are a perfect flavor match. They come together deliciously in this crisp cookie. Don't try to substitute maple syrup for maple extract. It takes too much syrup to duplicate the same flavor, which changes the texture of these cookies. Maple extract can be found in the baking section of most supermarkets.

Preparation time: *10 minutes*

Baking time: *10 minutes*

Yield: *2½ dozen*

½ cup (1 stick) unsalted butter, softened	¼ teaspoon maple extract
¾ cup golden brown sugar	Pinch of salt
1 egg	1 cup all-purpose flour
1 teaspoon vanilla extract	3 tablespoons pecans, finely chopped

1 Preheat the oven to 350°. Line a cookie sheet with parchment paper.

2 Using a mixer, beat the butter in a large mixing bowl until fluffy, about 2 minutes. Add the brown sugar and mix together until smooth. Separate the egg, saving the white to use later in the recipe. Blend the vanilla and maple extracts into the egg yolk. Add to the butter mixture and blend well.

3 Stir the salt into the flour and add to the butter mixture in three stages, blending well after each addition.

4 Drop the batter by teaspoons onto the cookie sheet, leaving 2 inches between the cookies. Beat the egg white until frothy and brush lightly on top of the cookies, pressing them down into rounds. Sprinkle the top of each cookie with the pecans, pressing them slightly to stick.

5 Bake for 10 to 11 minutes, until light brown and set. Remove the cookie sheet from the oven and set for 5 minutes on cooling racks so the cookies have time to set further. If they're removed from the cookie sheet while they're hot, they'll crumble and fall apart. Use a wide spatula to transfer the cookies from the parchment to cooling racks. Store in an airtight container at room temperature for up to a week. Freeze for longer storage.

Per serving: Calories 71 (From Fat 34); Fat 4g (Saturated 2g); Cholesterol 15mg; Sodium 9mg; Carbohydrate 9g (Dietary Fiber 0g); Protein 1g.

Chapter 6

Rolled Cookies

In This Chapter

▶ Understanding the steps involved in making rolled cookies

▶ Mastering rolling and cutting techniques

▶ Decorating rolled cookies

Rolled cookies get their name from how they're made — from the act of rolling out a firm dough and then cutting it into various shapes before baking. Rolled cookies have a long history, stretching back to the early 14th century in Europe, where the first records of rolled gingerbread have been found in German monasteries. One aspect of making rolled cookies that many people find gratifying is using a rolling pin, a wonderful tool. After rolling the dough, you can then cut the dough with your cookie cutters just the way you want it. The first rolling pins were probably fashioned from logs of wood.

In modern times, rolled cookies have been popular for at least a century, if not longer. Many recipes are heirlooms and have been passed from one generation to the next. Some families may also have cookie cutters that they pass from one generation to another. However, even if you haven't inherited any cookie cutters, you can still make many different shapes and sizes of rolled cookies. You can choose from a huge variety of cookie cutters and other utensils to cut out cookies. They're part of the reason that rolled cookies are lots of fun to make!

Handling the Dough

Making rolled cookies is a multistep process. The nice part about this is that if you're pressed for time, you can stretch out the cookie-making process by taking time in between the steps. First, you mix the dough and then chill it. Next, you roll the dough and cut it out into various shapes, depending on the cookie cutters you use. Finally, you bake the cookies and can choose to decorate them when they're cool. Each step requires that you pay attention, so it's nice to know that you can take a break between the steps and still make great rolled cookies. These cookies lend themselves very well to being made as a group or family project. While one person rolls the dough, another can cut it with the cookie cutters. Someone else can place the cookies on the baking sheet, and yet another person can be in charge of baking the cookies. And of course, everyone can get in on the act by eating the cookies.

Set aside time when rolling out the dough for these cookies. If you rush, your cookies will most likely be rolled unevenly and will bake that way.

Making the dough

A firm, buttery dough is generally used for rolled cookies. To make this type of dough, butter is beaten until fluffy, sugar is added, and then the mixture is creamed together. Eggs and other ingredients, such as flour, flavorings, and, in some cases, nuts, are added. The dough is easy to make and can be mixed by using a mixer and bowl or a food processor.

Chill out!

Most rolled cookie dough needs to be chilled in the refrigerator or freezer for a period of time before it's rolled out. The dough for rolled cookies always needs to be chilled after mixing. Chilling changes the dough's texture and makes it firmer and easier to handle. If the dough is too cold, though, it will crack and break into pieces. Let the dough stand at room temperature for a short time — 20 to 30 minutes — to bring it to the right consistency. If the dough happens to become too soft while sitting on the kitchen counter, all you have to do is chill it again. Getting the consistency just right takes a little practice, but once you master that, it becomes second nature.

Divide the dough into halves or quarters and wrap each portion separately in plastic wrap. Rolling one portion of dough at a time is a lot easier than rolling all the dough at once. Just leave the other portions in the refrigerator or freezer until you're ready for them.

Some cookie doughs can be prepared in advance and kept in the refrigerator for a few days before baking. Chilling lets the moisture of all the ingredients distribute evenly throughout the dough. Be sure that the dough portions are tightly wrapped in plastic so that they don't pick up unwanted flavors from other foods in the refrigerator. Most cookie doughs can be frozen for a few months.

Roll, roll, roll your dough . . .

The dough for rolled cookies is rolled out with a rolling pin before it's cut. Rolling the dough flattens it into a thin, smooth layer that can be easily cut into the desired shapes. There are two ways of rolling the dough: the traditional way and a more modern way. Here is the traditional way. Start with the dough in a rectangle about ½ inch thick. Dust a smooth surface and the top of the dough lightly with flour and roll from the center of the dough out to the edges. When you reach an edge, lift the pin and bring it back to the center and repeat in the same direction as necessary. Do not roll the pin back and forth — doing so toughens the dough. Give the dough a quarter turn to make sure that it's not sticking. You can also use a large offset spatula to run underneath the dough to prevent sticking. Dust the dough with flour as needed to prevent it from sticking.

Rub the rolling pin with flour before rolling out the dough so that it doesn't get too sticky.

If the dough is soft or sticky, you may wish to employ the more modern way of rolling the dough — between sheets of lightly floured wax paper. Occasionally lift both sheets of wax paper off the dough to be sure that the dough isn't sticking to them. You may need to lightly flour the dough again. Do this a few times while working with the dough to be sure that it's evenly rolled out and doesn't stick (see Figure 6-1). I like this method the best and use it for rolling all the doughs for the recipes in this chapter. It makes cleanup a breeze.

Roll the dough to an even thickness. The easiest way to do this is by rolling the dough from the center, pushing the rolling pin away from yourself. Give the dough a quarter turn and continue rolling in the same manner. Turning the dough also helps to make sure that the dough isn't sticking to the work surface, if you're not rolling it between layers of wax paper.

You can buy rings that fit on the ends of a rolling pin that can measure the thickness of your dough. They come in standard sizes of ⅛, ¼, and ⅜ inch. These are helpful for achieving an even thickness as you roll the dough. These rings are available in some cookware catalogs and on Web sites. I also find that using a ruler for an occasional check as I'm rolling out dough works very well. Once you get used to rolling out dough, you can tell by feeling and by sight whether it's the thickness you want.

Use a 2-inch-wide pastry brush to brush excess flour off cookie dough after it has been rolled out. If the extra flour stays on the dough, it will bake into a tough crust.

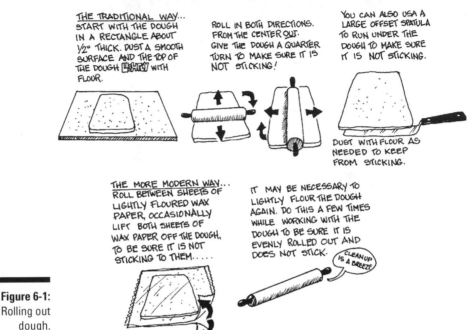

Figure 6-1:
Rolling out
dough.

Work with a small amount of dough at a time and keep the rest chilled until needed. After cutting out the dough (see the following section), gather the scraps, reroll, and recut. Scraps aren't as tender as the first batch (because they absorb more flour), so try to avoid cutting from scrap dough more than two times. Cut as many cookies as possible the first time.

If the dough was rolled out on a work surface and it's stuck, gather it back into a ball, shape into a rectangle, cover with plastic wrap, and chill again in the freezer until it's firm enough to roll.

Rolling pins are available in various materials, including wood, glass, marble, ceramic, plastic, stainless steel, and copper. A hardwood rolling pin is the most popular choice. The most effective rolling pin is a heavy one that has an equal thickness along its length. Whether to buy one with handles or not is a matter of personal preference. The weight of the rolling pin does most of the work of rolling out the dough.

After using the rolling pin, clean it with a damp sponge and then dry it with a kitchen towel. Don't immerse a wooden rolling pin in water or it could warp. Never put it in the dishwasher.

The cutting edge

Cutting out the cookies is the most enjoyable part of making rolled cookies for some people because they get to use their cookie cutters (see Chapter 2 for more information on cookie cutters). Cookie cutters come in myriad shapes and sizes. Made from either metal or plastic, they're available separately or in sets of graduated sizes of the same shape. Many cookie cutters are based on certain themes, such as holidays. If you're just starting out, I recommend buying a star-shaped cutter, a round shape, and a heart-shaped cutter. These are my favorite shapes.

If you find that the cookie cutter is sticking to the dough as it's cutting, dip the cookie cutter into flour and shake off the excess. Do this after every three or four cuts. Press down firmly on the cookie cutter so that it cuts all the way through the dough. Use different sizes and shapes of cookie cutters to cut the most out of the dough, leaving fewer scraps. After cutting out the cookies, gather the scraps together, press into a ball, chill again briefly, reroll, and cut again (see Figure 6-2). Or form the scraps into a roll, wrap in wax paper, chill, and then slice into coins before baking.

CUTTING OUT COOKIES WITH CUTTERS

1. DIP THE COOKIE CUTTER INTO FLOUR AND SHAKE OFF THE EXCESS TO PREVENT IT FROM STICKING DO THIS EVERY 3 OR 4 CUTS!

2. BE SURE TO PRESS DOWN FIRMLY ON THE COOKIE CUTTER SO IT CUTS ALL THE WAY THROUGH!

3. USE DIFFERENT SIZES AND SHAPES OF COOKIE CUTTERS TO CUT THROUGH MOST OF THE DOUGH, LEAVING FEWER SCRAPS.

4. AFTER CUTTING OUT THE COOKIES, GATHER THE SCRAPS AND PRESS INTO A BALL. CHILL BRIEFLY. RE-ROLL AND CUT AGAIN. OR... FORM THE SCRAPS INTO A ROLL. WRAP IN WAX PAPER AND CHILL. THEN SLICE INTO COINS BEFORE BAKING.

5. ONCE THE COOKIES ARE CUT, USE A SMALL, OFFSET SPATULA TO TRANSFER TO COOKIE SHEETS. TO KEEP COOKIES FROM LOSING THEIR SHAPE, DIP THE SPATULA IN FLOUR AND SHAKE OFF EXCESS.

6. CLEAN THE COOKIE CUTTERS WITH A DAMP CLOTH. IF THEY HAVE DOUGH STUCK TO THEM, USE HOT, SOAPY WATER TO WASH THEM.

Figure 6-2: Cutting out cookies with cookie cutters.

Tips for making great rolled cookies

Rolled cookies are a snap to make if you follow these tips. This gets you to the eating part sooner.

✔ If the dough for rolled cookies is a bit soft, you may be tempted to work lots of extra flour into the dough to keep it from sticking to the work surface. The extra flour makes the dough tough, resulting in cookies that aren't the correct consistency. They wind up tasting not nearly as good as they could. To prevent the need for too much flour, roll out the dough between sheets of lightly floured wax paper.

✔ Roll out the cookie dough on a smooth surface to help prevent sticking. A large wooden surface, such as a table, countertop, or a cutting board, is the best because it has enough texture to keep the dough from sliding.

✔ To prevent cookies from losing their shape, use a metal spatula to transfer cut cookies to the baking sheet. Metal spatulas are thinner than plastic ones and have sharper edges. You can slip it under the dough easily without disturbing the edges. Plastic spatulas wind up squeezing the dough together, making it contort as you lift it up.

Once the cookies are cut, use a small offset spatula to transfer them to cookie sheets. To keep the cookies from losing their shape, dip the spatula in flour and shake off the excess to prevent it from sticking to the cookies. Clean cookie cutters by wiping them with a damp cloth. If they have dough stuck to them, use hot, soapy water to wash them. Don't put them in the dishwasher because they usually wind up on the bottom of the machine, potentially causing damage to the cookie cutters and to your dishwasher.

An offset spatula has a flexible metal blade with a bend or angle near the wooden handle that is stepped down about an inch, forming a Z shape. Offset spatulas come in a variety of sizes with the length of the blade measuring from 3 to 12 inches. This type of spatula comes in very handy for lifting cutout shapes of cookie dough because it can get under the dough without hitting the sides of cookie sheets.

Think creatively when it comes to cookie cutters. Use different shaped glasses or tiny bowls with thin rims as cutters. To keep the rims from sticking to the dough, dip them in flour and shake off the excess before cutting. You can also make your own cookie cutters. Trace your design on stiff cardboard to make a pattern. Place the pattern on top of the dough and use a sharp knife to cut out the shape.

Don't press too hard when using glasses or glass bowls as cookie cutters. Too much pressure could break the glass. If that should happen, throw away the dough!

Baking Your Rolled, Cutout Cookies

Space cookies evenly on the cookie sheet. If they're too close together, they'll spread into each other as they bake. If you're baking only a few cookies, spread them out so that they cover the cookie sheet evenly. Make all the cookies on a cookie sheet the same size and shape so that they'll bake in the same amount of time.

Decorating Your Cookies

Rolled cookies are some of the best types to decorate, and the decorating ideas are endless. They can be drizzled or painted with chocolate or dusted with confectioners' sugar or cocoa powder. Dipping in chocolate is also a great way to dress up rolled cookies. Rolled cookies are especially popular during the holiday season, when adults and children alike enjoy decking them out in various frostings and sprinkles. They're beautiful when decorated with Royal Icing (see the recipe in Chapter 21), especially if they're cut into seasonal shapes such as hearts or bunnies and the icing is colored to match the season. A sprinkling of colored crystal sugar is also an attractive way to decorate cookies (see Chapters 20 and 21 for more decorating ideas).

Ready to Rock and Roll

Rolled cookies vary in texture from crisp and crunchy to soft and chewy. As mentioned earlier, they lend themselves to decorating. And after you get started decorating, you may not want to stop! But don't feel obligated to decorate your cookies (see Chapters 20 and 21 for decorating ideas). The main enjoyment, after all, comes in eating them.

Mocha Hazelnut Snaps

Mocha Hazelnut Snaps have a crispy and crunchy texture, similar to gingersnaps. Although these aren't difficult to make, they involve a little more work because you need to toast the hazelnuts before mixing the ingredients together. Your extra efforts will be rewarded when you take the first bite of these yummy cookies. Try dipping them into coffee or milk.

Specialty tools: *Rolling pin, cookie cutters*

Preparation time: *40 minutes*

Baking time: *10 minutes*

Yield: *5 dozen*

⅔ cup whole raw hazelnuts

4½ ounces semisweet or bittersweet chocolate, finely chopped

¼ teaspoon instant espresso powder

¾ cup confectioners' sugar

1¼ cups all-purpose flour

½ cup (1 stick) unsalted butter, cold

2 teaspoons vanilla extract

1 Preheat the oven to 350°. Place the hazelnuts in a single layer in a baking pan and toast for 15 to 18 minutes, until the skins split and the nuts are golden. Remove and transfer the nuts to a kitchen towel. Fold the ends of the towel to cover the nuts so they'll stay warm. Line a cookie sheet with parchment paper.

2 Melt the chocolate in the top of a double boiler set over warm water. Stir frequently with a rubber spatula to ensure even melting. Rub the hazelnuts in the towel to remove most of the skins.

3 Place the hazelnuts, espresso powder, and confectioners' sugar in the work bowl of a food processor fitted with a steel blade. Pulse using the on/off switch until the hazelnuts are finely chopped, about 2 minutes. Add the flour and process to blend. Cut the butter into small pieces and add to the flour mixture. Pulse until the butter is cut into tiny pieces, about 1 minute. Add the melted chocolate and vanilla extract and process until the mixture is well blended, about 1 minute.

(If not using a food processor, follow these steps. Grind the nuts in a clean coffee grinder or use the fine side of a grater. Toss the nuts with the espresso powder. Soften the butter briefly in a microwave oven or let it stand at room temperature. Using a mixer and mixing bowl, beat the butter until fluffy. Add the confectioners' sugar and cream together well. Add the flour in three stages, blending well and stopping to scrape down the sides of the bowl after each addition. Add the melted chocolate and vanilla extract and blend well. Add the hazelnuts mixed with espresso powder and mix thoroughly.)

4 Divide the dough in half and place each half on a large sheet of wax paper. Cover each with another sheet of wax paper. With a rolling pin, roll each portion of dough into a large rectangle about ⅛ inch thick. Peel off the wax paper and use the cookie cutter to cut out shapes. Transfer the cookies to the lined cookie sheets, leaving 1 inch between them.

5 Bake for 9 to 10 minutes, until firm and set. Remove the cookie sheet from the oven and transfer the cookies from the parchment to cooling racks. Store the cookies in an airtight container at room temperature for up to a week. Freeze for longer storage.

Per serving: Calories 55 (From Fat 37); Fat 4g (Saturated 2g); Cholesterol 6mg; Sodium 0mg; Carbohydrate 4g (Dietary Fiber 0g); Protein 1g.

Almond-Cinnamon Stars

These festive cookies are perfect for the Christmas holiday season. The recipe calls for finely ground almonds, which you can sometimes buy in stores that carry many types of nuts. However, grinding almonds is easy if you use the steel blade of a food processor. Use whole, slivered, sliced, or chopped almonds and, for each cup of nuts, include 1 tablespoon of sugar to absorb the natural oil that's released when they're ground. Pulse using the on/off switch until the almonds are finely ground, about 1 minute.

Specialty tools: Rolling pin, 2½-inch star-shaped cookie cutter

Preparation time: 3¼ hours; includes chilling

Baking time: 12 minutes

Yield: 4 dozen

½ cup plus 2½ tablespoons (1¼ sticks) unsalted butter, softened

½ cup sugar

1 cup finely ground almonds

½ teaspoon ground cinnamon

½ teaspoon vanilla extract

1 egg, lightly beaten

2 cups all-purpose flour

Pinch of salt

Confectioners' sugar for garnish

1 Using a mixer, beat the butter in a large mixing bowl until light and fluffy, about 2 minutes. Add the sugar and blend the mixture until smooth, about 2 more minutes. Scrape down the sides of the bowl with a long-handled rubber spatula. Add the almonds in two stages, blending well after each addition. Beat in the cinnamon and vanilla and then add the egg and blend well.

2 Combine the flour and salt and add to the almond mixture in three stages, stopping to scrape down the sides of the bowl often. Beat the dough until smooth, about 2 minutes. Gather the dough together, wrap in plastic, and chill in the refrigerator for at least 3 hours, or until firm, before using. The dough can be kept in the refrigerator for 3 days, or it can be frozen. If frozen, defrost it overnight before using.

3 Preheat the oven to 350°. Line a baking sheet with parchment paper. Roll out the dough on a lightly floured work surface to a thickness of ¼ inch. Using a 2½-inch star-shaped cookie cutter, cut out stars from the dough.

4 Place the stars on the cookie sheets, leaving 1 inch between the cookies. Bake for 12 to 14 minutes, until the cookies are golden and set. Remove the cookie sheet from the oven and transfer the cookies from the parchment to cooling racks. Lightly dust the tops of the cookies with confectioners' sugar. Store between layers of wax paper in an airtight container at room temperature for up to 5 days.

Per serving: Calories 67 (From Fat 36); Fat 4g (Saturated 2g); Cholesterol 11mg; Sodium 2mg; Carbohydrate 7g (Dietary Fiber 0g); Protein 1g.

Put some confectioners' sugar in a small strainer and shake it over the cookies for a beautiful effect with little effort. You can do the same with a sifter — just give the handle a couple cranks or squeezes, depending on the type of sifter you have.

Walnut-Lemon Stars

These delicate lemon-flavored stars will become one of your favorites. They're adorned with crystal sugar, which adds a crunchy texture. Crystal sugar is oblong grains of sugar that are about six times larger than those in regular granulated sugar. It's mainly used for garnishing cookies and other baked goods and sold in a rainbow of colors. Crystal sugar can be found in the baking section of most grocery stores.

Specialty tools: *Rolling pin, 1½-inch star-shaped cookie cutter*

Preparation time: *4½ hours; includes chilling*

Baking time: *18 minutes*

Yield: *4 dozen*

¾ cup (1½ sticks) unsalted butter, softened	¼ cup finely ground walnuts
½ cup confectioners' sugar, sifted	Pinch of salt
1 teaspoon vanilla extract	Zest of 2 medium lemons, finely minced
1¼ cups all-purpose flour	¼ cup crystal sugar

1 Using a mixer, beat the butter in a large mixing bowl until fluffy, about 2 minutes. Add the confectioners' sugar and blend together until smooth. Blend in the vanilla.

2 Combine the flour, walnuts, salt, and lemon zest in a small bowl. Add to the butter mixture in three stages, stopping to scrape down the sides of the bowl after each addition. Gather the dough into a disk, wrap tightly in plastic wrap, and chill for at least 4 hours. The dough can be frozen for up to 3 months. If frozen, defrost overnight in the refrigerator.

3 Line a cookie sheet with parchment paper. Roll out the dough between sheets of lightly floured wax paper to a thickness of ¼ inch thick. Use a 1½-inch star-shaped cutter to cut out shapes. Transfer the stars to the cookie sheets, leaving 1 inch between the cookies. Sprinkle the stars with the crystal sugar.

4 Chill the cookies for 1 hour. Preheat the oven to 325°. Bake for 18 to 20 minutes, until the cookies are golden. Remove the cookie sheet from the oven and transfer the cookies from the parchment to cooling racks. Store between layers of wax paper in an airtight container at room temperature for up to 5 days. Freeze for longer storage.

Per serving: Calories 46 (From Fat 28); Fat 3g (Saturated 2g); Cholesterol 8mg; Sodium 3mg; Carbohydrate 4g (Dietary Fiber 0g); Protein 0g.

Rolled Sugar Cookies

Crisp sugar cookies are all-time favorites. You can garnish them with *nonpareils,* which are tiny multicolored sugar pellets. You can make ornaments by poking a hole near the top before baking. After they're cool, string a decorative ribbon through the hole.

Specialty tools: *Rolling pin, cookie cutters, paper pastry cone (optional)*

Preparation time: *1½ hours; includes chilling*

Baking time: *8 minutes*

Yield: *4 dozen*

2½ cups all-purpose flour

2 teaspoons baking powder

Pinch of salt

1 cup superfine sugar

¼ cup confectioners' sugar

½ cup plus 2 tablespoons (1¼ sticks) unsalted butter, softened

1 egg

1½ teaspoons vanilla extract

Colored crystal sugar or nonpareils (optional)

Royal Icing (optional) (see Chapter 21)

1 Combine flour, baking powder, salt, superfine sugar, and confectioners' sugar in the work bowl of a food processor fitted with the steel blade. Pulse briefly to blend. Cut the butter into small pieces and add. Pulse until the butter is cut into very tiny pieces. In a small bowl, lightly beat the egg with the vanilla and add to the butter mixture. Pulse until the dough forms a ball, about 30 seconds. Wrap tightly in plastic and chill, at least 2 hours.

(To mix the dough using a mixer and bowl, beat the butter until fluffy, about 2 minutes. Sift the confectioners' sugar and add to the butter with the superfine sugar. Cream together well. Lightly beat the egg with the vanilla extract and add. Blend well. Combine the flour, baking powder, and salt and add to the mixture in three stages, blending well after each addition. Proceed to wrap and chill the dough.)

2 Preheat the oven to 375°. Line a cookie sheet with parchment paper.

3 Divide the dough in two and roll each section between sheets of lightly floured wax paper to a thickness of ¼ inch. Gently peel off the wax paper and use a variety of cookie cutters to shape the dough. Transfer the cookies to the cookie sheet, leaving 2 inches between the cookies. If desired, sprinkle crystal sugar or nonpareils over the cookies.

4 Bake for 8 to 10 minutes, until the cookies are firm. Remove the cookie sheet from the oven and transfer the cookies from the parchment to cooling racks.

5 If using the Royal Icing to decorate the cookies, wait until the cookies are completely cool before icing them. Place the icing in a parchment paper pastry cone and snip off a small opening at the pointed end. Pipe decorations onto the cookies and set until firm.

Per serving: *Calories 64 (From Fat 23); Fat 3g (Saturated 2g); Cholesterol 11mg; Sodium 21mg; Carbohydrate 10g (Dietary Fiber 0g); Protein 1g.*

Almond Butter Cookies

Although delicious on their own, Almond Butter Cookies are great for making sandwich cookies (see Chapter 9 for information on how). Use raspberry or apricot jam or a rich chocolate buttercream for a filling.

Specialty tools: *Rolling pin, 3-inch round fluted-edge cookie cutter*

Preparation time: *3½ hours; includes chilling*

Baking time: *12 minutes*

Yield: *3 dozen*

½ cup plus 2 tablespoons (1¼ sticks) unsalted butter, softened

½ cup sugar

1 cup finely ground blanched, toasted almonds (see Chapter 4 for information on toasting nuts)

¼ teaspoon ground cinnamon

1 egg

½ teaspoon almond extract

2 cups all-purpose flour

Pinch of salt

Confectioners' sugar for garnish

1 Using a mixer, beat the butter in a large mixing bowl until light and fluffy, about 1 minute. Add the sugar and blend together, about 1 more minute. Add the almonds and cinnamon and beat to blend well.

2 Beat the egg lightly with the almond extract and add to the butter mixture. Blend well and then add the flour with the salt in three stages. Stop and scrape down the sides of the bowl after each addition. Mix to a smooth dough, about 2 minutes. Wrap the dough in plastic and chill for at least 3 hours, until firm enough to roll out. The dough can be held in the refrigerator for 3 days or can be frozen for 2 months. If frozen, defrost in the refrigerator overnight.

3 Preheat the oven to 350°. Line a cookie sheet with parchment paper. Roll out the dough on a lightly floured surface to a thickness of ¼ inch. Use a 3-inch round fluted-edge cutter to cut out shapes. Transfer the circles to the cookie sheet, leaving 1 inch between them. Bake for 12 to 15 minutes, until the cookies are golden and set. Remove the cookie sheet from the oven and transfer the cookies from the parchment to cooling racks.

4 Dust the cookies heavily with the confectioners' sugar. Store in an airtight container at room temperature for up to a week. Freeze for longer storage.

Per serving: *Calories 87 (From Fat 47); Fat 5g (Saturated 2g); Cholesterol 15mg; Sodium 6mg; Carbohydrate 9g (Dietary Fiber 1g); Protein 2g.*

Sablés

Pronounced SAH blay, the name of these classic French cookies translates as "sand," which refers to their crumbly texture. They're originally from Normandy but now are found throughout France.

Specialty tools: *Rolling pin, cookie cutters*

Preparation time: *1 hour; includes chilling*

Baking time: *9 minutes*

Yield: *4 dozen*

2¾ cups all-purpose flour	¾ cup (1½ sticks) unsalted butter, cold
⅛ teaspoon salt	2 eggs
¾ cup sugar	1 teaspoon vanilla extract

1 Preheat the oven to 350°. Line a cookie sheet with parchment paper.

2 Combine the flour, salt, and sugar in the work bowl of a food processor fitted with the steel blade. Pulse briefly to blend. Cut the butter into small pieces and add. Pulse until the butter is cut into very tiny pieces. In a small bowl, lightly beat the eggs with the vanilla and add to the butter mixture. Pulse until the dough forms a ball, about 30 seconds.

(To mix the dough using a mixer and bowl, beat the butter until fluffy, about 2 minutes. Add the sugar and cream together well. Lightly beat the eggs with the vanilla extract and add. Blend well, stopping occasionally to scrape down the sides of the bowl. Combine the flour and salt and add to the mixture in three stages, blending well after each addition.)

3 Divide the dough in two and roll each section between sheets of lightly floured wax paper to a thickness of ¼ inch. If the dough is soft, chill on a cookie sheet in the freezer for 10 to 15 minutes. Gently peel off the wax paper and use a variety of cookie cutters to shape the dough. Transfer the cookies to the lined cookie sheet, leaving 2 inches between the cookies.

4 Bake for 9 to 13 minutes, until the cookies are golden and set. Remove the cookie sheets and transfer the cookies from the parchment to cooling racks. Store in an airtight container at room temperature for up to a week. Freeze for longer storage.

Per serving: *Calories 65 (From Fat 28); Fat 3g (Saturated 2g); Cholesterol 17mg; Sodium 9mg; Carbohydrate 8g (Dietary Fiber 0g); Protein 1g.*

Chapter 7

Refrigerator Cookies

I like to think of refrigerator cookies as "made in advance" cookies. I don't mean that you make the cookies and put them in the refrigerator. Instead, you make the dough and keep it in the refrigerator until you're ready to bake it. Refrigerator cookies are convenient because you can make your cookies in two separate stages. If you want something to nibble on after work, or if guests drop in unexpectedly, you can bake a batch of fresh cookies in minutes.

You can buy ready-made refrigerator cookie dough at any grocery store, of course, but those cookies fall far short of the delicious cookies that come from your oven with your own homemade refrigerator cookie dough. With the store-bought variety, all you do is slice and bake. But making cookie dough from scratch takes less time than driving to the store, parking, searching for the exact dough you want, paying for it, and driving home. By the time you've done all of that, you could be enjoying the aroma of your homemade cookies baking in the oven. It really is that easy! Once you start making your own refrigerator cookies, you'll discover how convenient and fun it is to make several recipes in advance to have on hand. In fact, you'll notice that friends will find excuses to drop by so they can enjoy some of your freshly baked cookies.

Chilling in the Fridge

The dough for refrigerator cookies is usually soft after mixing and needs to be chilled before it can be baked. Otherwise, it will be too difficult to slice and will spread too much in the oven. The chilling helps the cookie maintain its shape. After mixing, transfer the dough to wax paper or plastic wrap to roll into cylinders (as described in the next section) and then chill the dough for at least 1 hour before slicing. If the dough isn't firm enough, slicing the dough evenly will be too difficult.

Test the dough after it has chilled for an hour to see how it slices. If it slices cleanly and easily, then it's ready to go. The dough cylinders will keep for up to a week in the refrigerator or can be frozen for longer storage. If the dough is frozen, you can also slice it, but if it's too firm, let the dough stand at room temperature briefly to warm up so it won't splinter when cut. Or you can cut off the amount you want from the roll and defrost it in the refrigerator before slicing and baking.

Roll Your Own and Then Slice 'Em Off

Refrigerator cookies from the grocery store are always in cylinders or rolls, which is what makes them so easy to use. All you have to do is slice the cylinders into individual pieces and they're ready to bake. Making your own refrigerator cookies is equally as easy. Simply shape cookie dough into cylinders by following these steps:

1. **Place the cookie dough on one half of a large rectangle of wax paper and cover the dough with the other half of the wax paper.**

   Try to handle the dough as little as possible when placing it in the wrapping.

2. **Place your fingertips in the center of the dough, on top of the wax paper. Gently roll your fingertips over the dough in a back and forth motion (away from you and then toward you).**

   The dough will begin to form a roll.

3. **Keep rolling the dough, moving your fingertips out toward each end, until the cylinder is the desired thickness and length.**

4. **Wrap the cylinder in the wax paper and twist the ends tightly to seal, as shown in Figure 7-1.**

5. **Wrap each roll in another layer of wax paper to prevent it from picking up other flavors in the refrigerator.**

   Seal the ends of the rolls tightly, either by twisting them or turning them to the inside. If your refrigerator shelves have lines or ridges, place the cylinders of cookie dough in a loaf pan or on a flexible cutting board and then place them in the refrigerator. The cylinders won't roll around on the shelves and wind up with lines indented on them.

You can also use a square or rectangle pan to shape the dough. Line the inside of the pan with a piece of wax paper, extending it over the sides. Press the dough evenly in the pan and put it in the refrigerator to chill. Use the wax paper to lift the dough out of the pan and then peel it off the firm dough. Cut the dough into strips after chilling and then cut the strips into individual pieces. This method makes square or rectangular rather than round cookies.

FORMING DOUGH INTO A CYLINDER

1. PLACE CYLINDER ON ONE HALF OF A LARGE RECTANGLE OF WAX PAPER AND COVER WITH THE OTHER HALF.

TRY TO HANDLE THE DOUGH AS LITTLE A POSSIBLE WHEN PLACING IT IN WRAPPING!

2. PLACE YOUR FINGERTIPS IN THE CENTER OF THE DOUGH, ON TOP OF THE WAX PAPER.

3. GENTLY ROLL YOUR FINGERTIPS OVER THE DOUGH IN A BACK + FORTH MOTION IT WILL BEGIN TO FORM A ROLL. KEEP ROLLING, MOVING FINGERTIPS OUT→ TOWARD EACH END UNTIL IT IS THE DESIRED LENGTH + THICKNESS.

4. WRAP THE CYLINDER IN WAX PAPER AND TWIST ENDS TIGHTLY TO SEAL!

AFTER SHAPING THE DOUGH, WRAP EACH ROLL AGAIN TO PROTECT IT FROM PICKING UP THE OTHER FLAVORS IN THE REFRIGERATOR!

Figure 7-1:
Forming cookie dough into a cylinder.

After the cylinders have chilled until they're firm, getting them ready for baking is a snap. Take them out of the refrigerator and unwrap them from the wax paper. Place the cylinder on a cutting board and use a sharp knife to slice it into uniform pieces, usually about ¼ inch thick (see Figure 7-2). Transfer the slices to baking sheets covered with parchment paper, leaving at least 1 inch between them, and bake them in a preheated oven, following the instructions in each recipe.

TIP

To keep the roll of refrigerator cookies round when slicing, rotate it a quarter turn after eight slices. If the slices lose their form, simply use your fingers to push them back into shape.

SLICING THE DOUGH CYLINDER

TAKE THE CHILLED CYLINDERS OUT OF THE REFRIGERATOR AND UNWRAP FROM THE WAXED PAPER. PLACE ON A CUTTING BOARD AND USE A SHARP KNIFE TO CUT INTO UNIFORM PIECES. USUALLY ¼" THICK.

TRANSFER SLICES TO BAKING SHEETS COVERED WITH PARCHMENT PAPER. LEAVE AT LEAST 1" OF SPACE BETWEEN THEM. BAKE IN A PREHEATED OVEN, FOLLOW THE INSTRUCTIONS IN EACH RECIPE.

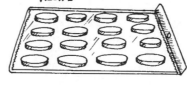

Figure 7-2:
Slicing a cookie dough cylinder.

Almond Coins

This recipe makes a big batch, so you can have freshly baked cookies on hand at all times. Keep a roll in the refrigerator to bake quickly when the kids come home from school.

Preparation time: *2½ hours; includes chilling*

Baking time: *8 minutes*

Yield: *7 dozen*

1¼ cups (2½ sticks) unsalted butter, softened	*¼ teaspoon salt*
2 teaspoons almond extract	*2½ cups all-purpose flour*
1¼ cups confectioners' sugar, sifted	*1 cup finely ground almonds*

1 Using a mixer, beat the butter in a large mixing bowl until fluffy, about 1 minute. Add the almond extract and mix well. Add the confectioners' sugar in two batches. Stop and scrape down the sides of the bowl with a rubber spatula after each addition. In a separate bowl, blend the salt with the flour and add in three stages to the butter mixture. Add the almonds and blend well.

2 Divide the dough into four equal pieces. Place each piece on a large rectangle of wax paper and roll each into a cylinder about 10 inches long and 1 inch thick. Wrap the cylinders in the wax paper and chill for at least 2 hours. The cylinders can be frozen at this point. If frozen, defrost overnight in the refrigerator before using.

3 Preheat the oven to 375°. Line a cookie sheet with parchment paper. Cut each cylinder into ¼-inch-thick slices. Place the slices on the cookie sheet, with 2 inches between the slices.

4 Bake for 8 to 9 minutes, until firm. Remove the cookie sheet from the oven and transfer the cookies from the parchment paper to cooling racks. Store in an airtight container at room temperature for up to a week. Freeze for longer storage.

Per serving: *Calories 53 (From Fat 32); Fat 4g (Saturated 2g); Cholesterol 7mg; Sodium 7mg; Carbohydrate 5g (Dietary Fiber 0g); Protein 1g.*

To *soften* an ingredient, such as butter or cream cheese, is to bring it to a pliable texture. This is done by letting it stand at room temperature or warming it slightly in a microwave oven or a double boiler.

Diamond Circles

These cookies take their name from the outer layer of sugar that sparkles like diamonds. For Cocoa Diamond Circles, replace the 1¾ cups flour with 1¼ cups flour and ½ cup Dutch-processed cocoa powder.

Preparation time: *2 hours and 20 minutes; includes chilling*

Baking time: *10 minutes*

Yield: *5 dozen*

¾ cup (1½ sticks) unsalted butter, softened	⅛ teaspoon salt
1 cup sugar	1¾ cups all-purpose flour
1 teaspoon vanilla extract	1 egg yolk

1 Using a mixer, beat the butter in a large mixing bowl until fluffy, about 1 minute. Add ½ cup of the sugar and mix together until smooth. Add the vanilla and mix well. In a separate bowl, blend the salt with the flour and add in three stages to the butter mixture, stopping occasionally to scrape down the sides of the bowl with a rubber spatula.

2 Divide the dough into four equal pieces. Place each piece on a large rectangle of wax paper and roll each into a cylinder about 7 inches long and 1¼ inches thick. Wrap the cylinders in the wax paper and chill for at least 2 hours. The cylinders can be frozen at this point. If frozen, defrost overnight in the refrigerator before using.

3 Preheat the oven to 400°. Line a cookie sheet with parchment paper.

4 In a small bowl, beat the egg yolk lightly. Place the remaining ½ cup sugar on a large piece of wax paper. Brush the outside of each cylinder with the beaten egg yolk and then roll it in the sugar to coat it completely. Cut each cylinder into ½-inch-thick slices. Place the dough on the cookie sheet, with 1 inch of space between the cookies.

5 Bake for 10 to 11 minutes, until golden. Remove the cookie sheet from the oven and transfer the cookies from the parchment paper to cooling racks. Store in an airtight container at room temperature for up to a week. Freeze for longer storage.

Per serving: *Calories 48 (From Fat 22); Fat 2g (Saturated 1g); Cholesterol 10mg; Sodium 5mg; Carbohydrate 6g (Dietary Fiber 0g); Protein 0g.*

Butterscotch Coins

These yummy cookies are hard to resist. Brown sugar creates the deep flavor of butterscotch. If you want to give these cookies extra excitement, dip them in chocolate after they're cool (see Chapter 20 for decorating with chocolate).

Preparation time: *2¼ hours; includes chilling*

Baking time: *8 minutes*

Yield: *3 dozen*

¾ cup (1½ sticks) unsalted butter, softened

½ cup light brown sugar

½ cup sugar

1 egg and 1 egg yolk

1 teaspoon vanilla extract

2¼ cups all-purpose flour

1 teaspoon baking powder

½ teaspoon baking soda

¾ teaspoon ground cinnamon

⅛ teaspoon salt

1 Using a mixer, beat the butter in a large mixing bowl until fluffy, about 1 minute. Add the brown sugar and sugar and blend together until smooth. In a separate bowl, stir together the egg, egg yolk, and vanilla. Add to the butter mixture and mix well.

2 In a separate mixing bowl, blend together the flour, baking powder, baking soda, cinnamon, and salt. Add to the butter mixture in four stages, blending well after each addition.

3 Divide the dough in half. Place each piece on a large rectangle of wax paper and roll each into a cylinder about 12 inches long and 1½ inches thick. Wrap the cylinders in the wax paper and chill for at least 1 hour. The cylinders can be frozen at this point. If frozen, defrost overnight in the refrigerator before using.

4 Preheat the oven to 350°. Line a cookie sheet with parchment paper. Cut each cylinder into ½-inch-thick slices. Place on the cookie sheet, with 1 inch of space between the cookies. Bake for 8 to 10 minutes, until golden. Remove the cookie sheet from the oven and transfer the cookies from the parchment paper to cooling racks. Store in an airtight container at room temperature for up to a week. Freeze for longer storage.

Per serving: Calories 89 (From Fat 38); Fat 4g (Saturated 2g); Cholesterol 22mg; Sodium 40mg; Carbohydrate 12g (Dietary Fiber 0g); Protein 1g.

Benne Wafers

These cookies take their name from the sesame seeds that were called *benne seeds* by African slaves who brought them to the American South. These rich, chewy wafers are classics.

Preparation time: *2¼ hours; includes chilling*

Baking time: *12 minutes*

Yield: *4 dozen*

2 cups hulled sesame seeds	*1 teaspoon vanilla extract*
½ cup pecans	*½ cup all-purpose flour*
6 tablespoons (¾ stick) unsalted butter, softened	*¼ teaspoon baking powder*
¾ cup light brown sugar	*⅛ teaspoon salt*
1 egg, lightly beaten	*2 tablespoons unsalted butter, melted*

1 Center a rack in the oven and preheat the oven to 350°. Place the sesame seeds in a single layer on a jelly roll pan (12 x 17 x 1 inch) or another shallow pan with a rim. Toast for about 15 minutes, shaking the pan every 5 minutes, until the seeds are lightly browned. Remove from the oven and transfer the sesame seeds to a cool plate. Place the pecans in a shallow baking pan and toast for 8 minutes. Cool the nuts and chop them finely.

2 Using a mixer, beat the 6 tablespoons butter in a large mixing bowl until light and fluffy, about 1 minute. Add the brown sugar and blend together well. Add the egg and vanilla and occasionally scrape down the sides of the bowl with a long-handled rubber spatula. Beat the mixture for 2 minutes.

3 In a medium bowl, sift together flour, baking powder, and salt. Add 1 cup of the toasted sesame seeds to the flour mixture and add to the butter mixture in three stages, blending well after each addition. Stir in the pecans and beat until well mixed, about 30 seconds.

4 Sprinkle ½ cup of the remaining sesame seeds on a large rectangle of wax paper. Place half of the dough on the wax paper and form into a roll about 2 inches in diameter. Dredge the outside of the roll to coat it in the sesame seeds. Roll up the dough tightly in the wax paper and chill in the refrigerator until firm, about 2 hours. Repeat with the remaining half of the dough. The rolls can be kept in the refrigerator for 1 week, if well wrapped.

5 If the oven is not turned on, preheat it to 350°. Line a baking sheet with aluminum foil and brush with the melted butter. Slice off ¼-inch-thick rounds of the dough rolls and place the slices on the foil, with 2 inches between them. Bake for 10 to 12 minutes, until lightly browned. Remove the cookie sheets from the oven and transfer the cookies on the aluminum foil to cooling racks. Gently peel the foil from the cookies when cooled. Store in an airtight container at room temperature for up to a week. Freeze for longer storage.

Per serving: *Calories 74 (From Fat 49); Fat 5g (Saturated 2g); Cholesterol 10mg; Sodium 13mg; Carbohydrate 6g (Dietary Fiber 1g); Protein 1g.*

To *dredge* something is to coat the outside of it with another ingredient, such as finely chopped nuts, sugar, cocoa, or flour. A cylinder of cookie dough can be dredged with sugar by rolling it in the sugar.

Hazelnut Slices

A combination of spices adds extra-special flavor to these delicate cookies. They're sensational when half-dipped in chocolate.

Specialty tools: *7-x-11-x-2-inch baking pan, ruler*

Preparation time: *1½ hours; includes chilling*

Baking time: *20 minutes*

Yield: *5 dozen*

1 cup (2 sticks) unsalted butter, softened

1 cup plus 2 tablespoons confectioners' sugar, sifted

¼ teaspoon ground cinnamon

¼ teaspoon ground nutmeg, preferably freshly grated

¼ teaspoon ground cloves

½ teaspoon vanilla extract

Pinch of salt

2 cups plus 2 tablespoons all-purpose flour, sifted

1 egg white

1 cup roughly chopped, toasted hazelnuts (for information on toasting, see the Tip at the end of the recipe and Chapter 4)

2 tablespoons sugar

8 ounces bittersweet chocolate, finely chopped (optional)

1 Preheat the oven to 350°. Line a baking sheet with parchment paper. Using a mixer, beat the butter in a large mixing bowl until fluffy, about 1 minute. Add the confectioners' sugar and mix together until smooth.

2 Add the cinnamon, nutmeg, cloves, vanilla, and salt to the butter mixture and beat until well mixed. Add one-half of the flour in two stages to the butter mixture and then add the egg white. Add the remaining flour in two stages, beating well after each addition. Blend in the hazelnuts.

3 Lightly sprinkle a 7-x-11-x-2-inch baking pan with the 2 tablespoons sugar. Transfer the mixture to the pan and spread it evenly, making sure that the top is smooth and flat and the sides are square. Chill until firm, about 1 hour.

4 Using a ruler as a guide, cut the chilled dough into strips 1½ inches wide and the length of the baking pan. Cut each strip into ¼-inch-wide slices. Place these on the parchment-paper-lined baking sheet, sugar side up, with at least 1 inch between the slices. Bake until golden, about 20 minutes. Remove the cookie sheet from the oven and transfer the cookies from the parchment paper to cooling racks.

5 If garnishing with the chocolate, melt two-thirds of the chocolate in the top of a double boiler over hot water, stirring occasionally. Remove the top pan of the double boiler and dry the bottom and sides of the pan. Keeping the top pan off the heat, stir in the remaining one-third of the chocolate in three batches, making sure that each batch is melted before adding the next. When all the chocolate is added, test to make sure that it's not too hot by dipping your finger into it. It should be a little less than body temperature and should feel comfortable. You can also test the temperature with an instant-read thermometer. It should be between 89° and 91°.

6 Dip the cookies on the diagonal halfway into the chocolate. Place on parchment-paper-lined baking sheets. When all the cookies are dipped, place the sheets in the refrigerator for 15 minutes to set the chocolate. Store between sheets of wax paper in an airtight, covered container at room temperature for up to a week, or in the refrigerator if it's warm. Freeze for longer storage.

Tip: To toast hazelnuts, place them in a single layer in a shallow pan with a lip, such as a jelly roll pan. Toast them in a preheated 350° oven for 15 to 18 minutes. You'll be able to tell they're ready because you'll smell their appetizing aroma, the skins will split open, and the nuts will be light golden brown. Remove the baking pan from the oven and transfer the warm hazelnuts to a kitchen towel. Wrap the towel around the nuts and let them steam for about 10 minutes. Then rub the nuts in the towel to help remove the skins.

Per serving: Calories 65 (From Fat 39); Fat 4g (Saturated 2g); Cholesterol 8mg; Sodium 4mg; Carbohydrate 6g (Dietary Fiber 0g); Protein 1g.

A *garnish* is an edible decoration added to food to make it more attractive and appealing. The garnish should be harmonious with the dish. Cookies are often garnished with confectioners' or pearl sugar, also called coarse or decorating sugar.

Pearl sugar is white sugar that has been processed into small round grains, resembling pearls. These are about four to six times larger than grains of granulated sugar.

Part III
Stylish Cookies

The 5th Wave   By Rich Tennant

"I couldn't find any rose petals, but I figured brownies make more sense in a milk bath anyway."

In this part . . .

*I*t's okay to get a little fancy with cookies. Doing so gives them the respect that they deserve and also makes them look even yummier. But what's neat about bar, sandwich, and filled cookies is that they're fairly simple to make. They may require an extra step or two, but when you see and taste the results, you'll know that they were worth it. I clearly explain every step so that you need to invest only minimal effort and time to make these cookies. Don't think that these cookies are only for adults, because kids love them, too!

Chapter 8

Bar Cookies

*B*ar cookies are some of the quickest and easiest cookies to make. All you have to do is mix up the batter, spread it in a pan, and bake it. After they cool, you simply cut them into bars or squares. What could be easier than that? Bar cookies include brownies, an all-American favorite.

One feature I like most about bar cookies is that they lend themselves to endless variations. You can add some chocolate chips or nuts to the batter before spreading it in the pan. Or you can sprinkle chopped nuts or coconut on top of the batter after spreading it in the pan Those are just a couple ways to vary bar cookie recipes.

Another attractive quality of bar cookies is they're easy to transport in their pan, making them great to make for a picnic or a potluck gathering. You can even bake bar cookies and keep them in their pan until ready to serve them, thus saving both time and space.

Bar cookies are some of my very favorite cookies because they're great for many occasions. They run the gamut from basic to elegant.

The Best, Bar None

Bar cookies are easy to make, but you can ensure that your cookies will be the best they can be by following these tips and techniques:

- Always use the pan size called for in the bar cookie recipe. If you use a larger or smaller pan, the cookies won't bake correctly and will be too thin and brittle or too thick and soggy.

- Bake most bar cookies in a square aluminum pan. If you use a pan made of a different material, you have to adjust the baking time.

  Glass pans conduct heat very quickly. If you use a glass pan, lower the oven temperature by 25 degrees so they won't burn. And check the cookies about 5 minutes early to see whether they're done.

- To make bar cookies easy to remove from the pan, there are a few different ways to prepare the pans. Grease the pan well with up to 1 tablespoon softened unsalted butter, depending on the size of the pan. In most cases, you can substitute nonstick cooking spray for butter, if you desire. For cakelike bar cookies, such as gingerbread, dust the inside of the pan with flour after greasing with butter to ensure that the bars won't stick in the pan. If the recipe calls for dusting with flour after greasing, don't use nonstick cooking spray because the flour won't stick to the spray.

  Another way to easily remove bar cookies from the pan is to line the pan with aluminum foil. Grease the foil with butter or spray generously with nonstick cooking spray. To remove the cookies, simply lift the foil from the pan.

- After mixing the batter or dough, pour it into the center of the pan. If the batter is thin, use a rubber spatula to push it out to the sides and into the corners of the pan. Spread the batter or dough evenly so that the corners aren't too thin. If they are, they bake quicker and are too dry.

  To spread a thicker bar cookie dough in the pan, the best tool is your fingertips. Using your fingers enables you to manipulate the dough and place it exactly where you want it. Dust your fingertips with flour to keep the dough from sticking to them.

- Cut bar cookies while they're in the pan. Use a ruler to measure for even cuts and cut with a sharp knife. Cut all the way through to the bottom of the pan so that you can easily remove the cookies. The first one removed from the pan often breaks or crumbles, but you don't really need to lose any at all. Try using a small serving spatula to remove bar cookies from the pan.

Bar cookies can be cut into diamond or square shapes or other shapes by using a cookie cutter. Dress them up for company by dusting them with powdered sugar or cocoa powder before serving (see Chapter 21 for more decoration ideas).

To keep bar cookies at their freshest, cut only as many as you need at a time. Because they have a tendency to dry quickly, keep the pan of remaining cookies covered tightly with aluminum foil. Most bar cookies last from 5 days to a week. Some of them can be frozen for longer storage. To make bar cookies really last a long time, wrap them individually in plastic wrap before freezing. Each recipe in this chapter has information about how long the cookies keep.

All-Time Favorites

I picked the recipes here because they're classic bar cookies. They're quick and easy to prepare, although a few of them are more advanced because they involve making a bottom crust and a topping. These cookies disappear quickly when I serve them. I'm often asked to bring along a batch of one of these recipes when I'm invited to a gathering.

There's a good variety of flavors in these recipes. Shortbread, one of my personal all-time favorites, is in a section of its own because it's so special. The Oatmeal Shortbread Bars are similar to classic shortbread, but the addition of oatmeal gives them a different texture and makes them a very casual cookie. They're also quicker to make than the Classic Shortbread recipe because you don't have to chill them before baking.

Oatmeal Shortbread Bars

These bars will disappear so fast it will make your head spin. It's a good thing they are made with only a few ingredients and are a snap to prepare!

Preparation time: *10 minutes*

Baking time: *25 minutes*

Yield: *20 bars*

½ cup (1 stick) unsalted butter, softened	⅓ cup old-fashioned rolled oats
⅓ cup sugar	Pinch of salt
¾ cup all-purpose flour	½ teaspoon ground cinnamon

1 Preheat the oven to 325°. Heavily butter an 8-inch square baking pan.

2 Using a mixer, beat the butter in a large mixing bowl until soft and fluffy, about 2 minutes. Add the sugar and mix together until smooth. In a separate bowl, combine the flour, oats, salt, and cinnamon and add to the butter mixture in two stages, blending well.

3 Dust your fingertips with flour and press the dough evenly into the pan. Bake for 25 minutes, until golden. Remove the pan and cool on a rack for 10 minutes. Cut into bars and transfer them to racks to cool completely. Store in an airtight container at room temperature for up to a week. Freeze for longer storage.

Per serving: Calories 76 (From Fat 43); Fat 5g (Saturated 3g); Cholesterol 12mg; Sodium 8mg; Carbohydrate 8g (Dietary Fiber 0g); Protein 1g.

Coconut-Pecan Squares

If you like coconut, you'll love these chewy bars. Because these squares call for a crust and a topping, you can spread the baking out over two days when making them. You can prepare the crust one day, cover it tightly with aluminum foil after it's cooled, and store it at room temperature. The next day you can prepare the topping and bake the squares. This recipe is great for a busy lifestyle.

Preparation time: *25 minutes*

Baking time: *25 minutes*

Yield: *16 squares*

Crust

½ cup (1 stick) unsalted butter, softened

2 tablespoons confectioners' sugar

1 cup all-purpose flour

Topping

2 eggs

1¼ cups light brown sugar

2 teaspoons vanilla extract

2 tablespoons all-purpose flour

Pinch of salt

1 teaspoon baking powder

1 cup pecans, roughly chopped

1½ cups shredded coconut

1 Preheat the oven to 350°. Spray an 8-inch square baking pan with nonstick cooking spray.

2 For the crust, use a mixer to beat the butter in a large mixing bowl until fluffy, about 2 minutes. Add the confectioners' sugar and mix together until smooth. Blend in the flour. Dust your fingertips with flour and press the crust evenly into the pan.

3 Bake for 15 minutes, until the edges are golden. Remove the pan and cool on a rack.

4 For the topping, use a mixer to beat the eggs in a large mixing bowl until fluffy, about 2 minutes. Gradually add the brown sugar and continue beating on medium-high speed until the mixture is thick and holds a slowly dissolving ribbon as the beater is lifted, about 5 minutes. Blend in the vanilla. In a separate bowl, combine the flour, salt, and baking powder. Add to the butter mixture, mixing thoroughly. Stir in the pecans and coconut and blend well.

5 Spread the topping evenly over the crust. Bake for 25 minutes, until golden and set. Remove the pan from the oven, cool on a rack, and cut into squares. Store in an airtight container at room temperature for up to a week. Freeze for longer storage.

Per serving: *Calories 257 (From Fat 133); Fat 15g (Saturated 7g); Cholesterol 42mg; Sodium 74mg; Carbohydrate 30g (Dietary Fiber 2g); Protein 2g.*

Lemon Squares

These yummy squares are what I crave when I want the taste of lemon. A soft lemon topping sits on a crunchy cookie base. Although these cookies aren't complicated to prepare, I consider them to be advanced because you have to prepare a crust and a topping. But they're well worth any extra effort because they're always a hit when I bring them to any gathering.

Preparation time: *30 minutes*

Baking time: *45 minutes*

Yield: *24 2-inch squares*

Crust

2 cups all-purpose flour

½ cup confectioners' sugar

Pinch of salt

1 cup (2 sticks) unsalted butter, cold, cut into small pieces

Finely minced zest of 1 large lemon

1 teaspoon vanilla extract

Lemon topping

4 eggs

1½ cups sugar

¼ cup all-purpose flour

½ teaspoon baking powder

½ cup freshly squeezed lemon juice

Finely minced zest of 1 large lemon

3 to 4 tablespoons confectioners' sugar to sift over top

1 Preheat the oven to 350°. Spray a 9-x-13-inch baking pan with nonstick cooking spray.

2 For the crust, combine all the crust ingredients in the work bowl of a food processor fitted with the steel blade. Process until the mixture forms a ball, about 1 minute. Dust your fingertips with flour and press the crust evenly into the pan. (To make the crust using a mixer and mixing bowl, soften the butter to room temperature and then beat until fluffy, about 2 minutes. Add the confectioners' sugar and cream together well. Stop occasionally and scrape down the sides of the mixing bowl with a rubber spatula. Add the salt, lemon zest, and vanilla and blend well. Add the flour in three stages, blending well after each addition. Proceed as with the same instructions given for the food processor.)

3 Bake for 20 minutes, until the edges are golden. Remove the baking pan from the oven and cool on a rack.

4 For the topping, use a mixer to beat the eggs in a large mixing bowl on medium-high speed until fluffy, about 2 minutes. Gradually add the sugar and continue beating on medium-high speed until the mixture is thick and holds a slowly dissolving ribbon as the beater is lifted, about 5 minutes. Combine the flour and baking powder and add with the lemon juice and zest. Blend thoroughly.

5 Pour the topping into the pan. Bake for about 25 minutes, until the topping is set. Remove the pan and cool on a rack. Dust the top heavily with confectioners' sugar and cut into squares. Store in a single layer in an airtight container at room temperature for up to 5 days.

Per serving: *Calories 184 (From Fat 78); Fat 9g (Saturated 5g); Cholesterol 56mg; Sodium 26mg; Carbohydrate 25g (Dietary Fiber 0g); Protein 2g.*

Belafonte Bars

This recipe comes from friend and colleague Diane Phillips, who has an abundant lime tree in her backyard. She created this version of lemon squares made with lime, coconut, and macadamia nuts and named them in honor of the great old Harry Belafonte song about the witch doctor who put the lime in the coconut. Like the preceding recipe for Lemon Squares, this recipe has a crust and a topping and is a bit more work than most cookies, but well worth it.

Preparation time: 30 minutes

Baking time: 45 minutes

Yield: 24 2-inch squares

Crust

2 cups all-purpose flour

½ cup confectioners' sugar

Pinch of salt

1 cup (2 sticks) unsalted butter, cold, cut into small pieces

1 cup shredded coconut

½ cup roughly chopped raw macadamia nuts

Topping

4 eggs

1½ cups sugar

¼ cup all-purpose flour

1 teaspoon baking powder

½ cup freshly squeezed lime juice

Finely minced zest of 2 limes

3 to 4 tablespoons confectioners' sugar to sift over top

1 Preheat the oven to 350°. Spray a 9-x-13-inch baking pan with nonstick cooking spray.

2 For the crust, combine all the crust ingredients in the work bowl of a food processor fitted with the steel blade. Process until the mixture forms a ball, about 1 minute. Dust your fingertips with flour and press the crust evenly into the pan.

(To make the crust using a mixer and mixing bowl, soften the butter to room temperature and then beat until fluffy, about 2 minutes. Add the confectioners' sugar, and cream together well. Stop occasionally and scrape down the sides of the mixing bowl with a rubber spatula. Mix the flour and salt with the coconut and macadamia nuts and add to the butter mixture in three stages, blending well after each addition. Proceed with the same instructions given for the food processor.)

3 Bake for 20 minutes, until the edges are golden. Remove the baking pan from the oven and cool on a rack.

4 For the topping, use a mixer to beat the eggs in a large mixing bowl until fluffy, about 2 minutes. Gradually add the sugar and continue beating on medium-high speed until the mixture is thick and holds a slowly dissolving ribbon as the beater is lifted, about 5 minutes. Combine the flour and baking powder and add with the lime juice and zest. Blend thoroughly.

5 Pour the topping into the pan. Bake for about 25 minutes, until the topping is set. Remove and cool on a rack. Dust the top heavily with confectioners' sugar and cut into squares. Store in a single layer in an airtight container at room temperature for up to 5 days.

Per serving: Calories 176 (From Fat 109); Fat 12g (Saturated 7g); Cholesterol 56mg; Sodium 45mg; Carbohydrate 15g (Dietary Fiber 1g); Protein 3g.

Date-Nut Bars

I've been making these chewy bars for many years, and they're always a hit. Try using other dried fruits or nuts to create delicious variations. Although I prefer to use freshly squeezed orange juice, the frozen variety is fine.

Preparation time: *20 minutes*

Baking time: *30 minutes*

Yield: *16 bars*

¾ cup finely chopped pitted dates	*2 eggs*
¼ cup finely chopped dried apricots	*¼ cup light brown sugar*
2 tablespoons orange juice	*⅓ cup sugar*
¼ cup all-purpose flour	*1 cup roughly chopped walnuts*
½ teaspoon baking powder	

1 Preheat the oven to 350°. Spray an 8-inch square baking pan with nonstick cooking spray.

2 Mix the dates and apricots with the orange juice in a small bowl. In a separate bowl, sift together the flour and baking powder.

3 Using a mixer, whip the eggs in a large mixing bowl until frothy, about 1 minute. Add the brown sugar and sugar and continue to whip until the mixture is thick and pale colored and holds a ribbon when the beater is lifted, about 5 minutes. Stir in the flour mixture and blend in the dried fruit and the walnuts.

4 Turn the mixture into the pan, spreading it evenly into the corners. Bake until golden and a crust forms on top, about 30 minutes. Remove the pan from the oven and cool on a rack. Cut into 16 bars. Store in an airtight container at room temperature for up to a week. Freeze for longer storage.

Per serving: *Calories 123 (From Fat 50); Fat 6g (Saturated 1g); Cholesterol 27mg; Sodium 22mg; Carbohydrate 18g (Dietary Fiber 1g); Protein 2g.*

You can change the flavor of a cookie by simply changing the type of nuts used in preparation. Try experimenting with different nuts to find the flavors you like best.

The Art of Shortbread

Historically, shortbread cookies can be traced back to ancient Scotland when they were called bannock, a type of sweetened bread. Shortbread is still very much considered a Scottish specialty. In every tiny village in Scotland, you can find shortbread for sale in the local bakery and the corner store.

Shortbread is relatively simple to make and has only a few ingredients. Use only top-quality ingredients because the recipe contains nothing to mask the flavor of the cookies. Butter gives shortbread cookies their traditional, tender, crumbly texture, which is drier than other bar cookies. But they're definitely richer. Shortbread cookies seem to melt in the mouth. I like to make shortbread cookies with superfine sugar to give them their delicate texture. When it's blended with softened butter, the result is a silky-smooth mixture. Superfine sugar is available in the baking aisle in grocery stores.

Don't substitute margarine for butter in shortbread. You'll be disappointed with the taste, and the texture will be different.

Superfine sugar is more finely granulated than regular sugar. It dissolves very quickly and leaves no gritty texture. If you can't find it, you can replicate it by pulsing regular granulated sugar in a food processor for 30 seconds to a minute.

Shortbread keeps very well, as long as a month in an airtight container between layers of wax paper at room temperature. But I've never had the problem of keeping it too long. It disappears too quickly.

Making shortbread dough

The method for making shortbread differs from the bar cookie recipes discussed earlier. The main difference is that shortbread needs to be chilled before baking. Chilling is necessary because the dough for shortbread is very rich due to the high proportion of butter. The dough must be chilled so the butter can firm back up, which will keep it from flattening out, causing the cookies to spread too much when baked.

Shortbread is called "short" because of the vast quantity of "shortening" (butter) involved in its making.

In shortbread, the salt and flour are blended, meaning the two ingredients are combined so they're smooth and uniform in appearance, texture, and flavor. Blending can be done by hand with a rubber spatula, whisk, or spoon or by using a machine, such as a food processor, electric mixer, or blender.

Before mixing the shortbread dough, have all the ingredients at room temperature. Doing so helps everything to blend easily and creates a light dough.

Scoring and piercing

Shortbread needs to be marked into pieces before it is chilled and cut. This is done by *scoring,* which means marking the dough lightly so the lines are visible and can be easily cut through later. Scoring the dough makes it easy to separate the pieces before baking (see Figure 8-1).

Shortbread dough also needs to be pierced. To *pierce* the dough, puncture it most of the way through with a fork. Doing so allows steam to escape while the cookies bake and helps them bake evenly. Pierce the dough on a diagonal in two or three places. This traditional marking is always seen on shortbread (see Figure 8-1).

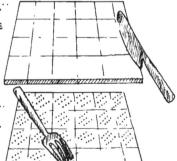

Figure 8-1:
Scoring and piercing shortbread dough.

SCORING AND PIERCING SHORTBREAD DOUGH

⤴ SHORTBREAD NEEDS TO BE MARKED INTO PIECES BEFORE IT IS CHILLED AND CUT!

TO SCORE THE DOUGH....
USE A KNIFE TO LIGHTLY MARK IT SO THE LINES ARE VISIBLE AND CAN BE EASILY CUT LATER. SCORING MAKES IT EASY TO CUT AND SEPARATE PIECES BEFORE BAKING.

TO PIERCE THE DOUGH..... PUNCTURE IT MOST OF THE WAY THROUGH. USE A FORK TO PIERCE THE DOUGH ON A DIAGONAL IN 3 PLACES.

Shortbread shapes

Shortbread cookies are traditionally made in several different shapes (see Figure 8-2):

✔ **Fingers:** These are the classic rectangular shape. Use a ruler to measure out the size of shortbread fingers after patting the dough evenly into the pan. Along the long side of the pan, mark 2½-inch pieces with a sharp knife. Using the ruler as a guide to make even lines, draw the knife across the dough to score it. Across the top (short) side of the pan, mark 1-inch-wide pieces. Use the ruler as a guide to mark these lines in the dough.

✔ **Petticoat tails:** These pie-shaped wedges are cut from a large round after baking. They were given their name because their shape is said to resemble the petticoats worn by 12th-century women during the time of the Norman Conquest of Britain. I'm not exactly sure how this shape got its name, because the Normans invaded Britain, not Scotland. All I can think is that the Scots had a laugh on the British who had tried, without success, to conquer them.

To shape petticoat tails, score the pieces just as if you were cutting slices of pie. These are larger than finger shapes, but you can make them skinnier by scoring thinner wedges. Be sure to pierce these with a fork, too, after scoring.

✔ **Rounds:** Shaped like coins, these round cookies are also called Highlanders. They can be made in different size rounds, from mini (1 inch) to 3-bite size (2½-inches in diameter). Use a round cookie cutter to make uniform sizes.

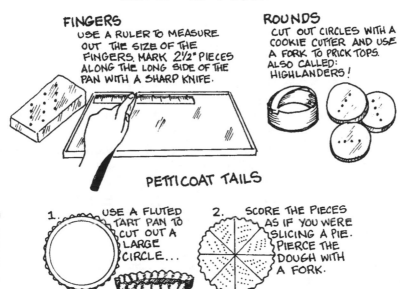

Figure 8-2:
Traditional shortbread shapes.

Classic Scottish Shortbread

Years ago I traveled through Scotland on a mission to find the very best shortbread. Eating all those delicious cookies was a daunting task, but I managed — quite well, in fact. This recipe is a classic that comes from my quest. Shortbread is always served as part of afternoon tea, but it is also found in lunch boxes and on the dessert table for most events in Scotland.

Preparation time: *1¼ hours; includes chilling*

Baking time: *40 minutes*

Yield: *60 bars, 1 x 2 inches each*

2 cups (4 sticks) unsalted butter, softened

1 cup superfine sugar

½ teaspoon salt

4 cups all-purpose flour

1 Using a mixer, beat the butter in a large mixing bowl until fluffy, about 2 minutes. Add the sugar and mix together until smooth.

2 Blend the salt into the flour and add the flour in four stages to the butter. Stop and scrape down the sides of the bowl with a rubber spatula after each addition. After all the flour is added, continue to mix for another 2 to 3 minutes, until the dough is smooth and soft.

3 Lightly flour a 9-x-13-inch baking pan. Dust your fingertips with flour and press the dough evenly into the baking pan. Use a ruler to score the dough into bars that are 1 inch wide and 2 inches long. Use a fork to pierce each bar on the diagonal two times. Cover the pan tightly with plastic wrap and chill for at least 1 hour.

4 Preheat the oven to 275°. Line a cookie sheet with parchment paper. Cut through the scored lines on the chilled dough and place the bars on the cookie sheet, leaving 2 inches between them.

5 Bake for 40 minutes, until set. Remove the cookie sheet from the oven and transfer the cookies to racks to cool. Store in an airtight container at room temperature for up to a week. Freeze for longer storage.

Per serving: Calories 97 (From Fat 56); Fat 6g (Saturated 4g); Cholesterol 17mg; Sodium 20mg; Carbohydrate 10g (Dietary Fiber 0g); Protein 1g.

Shortbread variations

Here's how you can turn basic shortbread into many delectable variations. It's easy to do by simply adding a few other ingredients to the Classic Scottish Shortbread recipe.

- **Cocoa Shortbread:** Replace ½ cup of the flour with ½ cup unsweetened Dutch-processed cocoa powder.

- **Double Ginger Shortbread:** Add 2 teaspoons ground ginger and ½ cup finely diced crystallized ginger to the flour before it is mixed with the butter.

- **Spicy Shortbread:** Blend together 2 teaspoons ground cinnamon, 1 teaspoon ground ginger, ½ teaspoon freshly grated nutmeg, and ¼ teaspoon ground cloves and add to the batter.

- **Cardamom Shortbread:** Add 1 tablespoon ground cardamom to the batter.

- **Nut Shortbread:** Add 1 teaspoon pure vanilla extract and 1 cup toasted, finely chopped nuts to the batter.

- **Lemon Shortbread:** Add 2 teaspoons lemon extract and the finely minced zest of 3 large lemons to the batter.

- **Orange Shortbread:** Add 2 teaspoons orange extract and 1 cup finely chopped candied orange peel to the batter.

- **Royal Scottish Shortbread:** You can make your Classic Scottish Shortbread royal by dipping it halfway in chocolate. Use 8 ounces of semisweet or bittersweet chocolate for best results. Pay close attention to the chocolate as it's melting because it burns very easily with too much heat.

Chop the chocolate into matchstick-size pieces and set aside one-third of them. Melt the remaining two-thirds in the top of a double boiler over hot water, stirring frequently with a rubber spatula to ensure even melting. Make sure the top pan or bowl of the double boiler fits snugly over the bottom pan, especially if you make your own double boiler. Keep the water level in the bottom pan very low — about 1 inch. You don't want any water or steam to mix with the chocolate. If this happens, the chocolate will *seize*, a condition that makes the chocolate like mud. Remove the double boiler from the heat. Remove the top pan of the double boiler and dry the bottom of the pan. Stir in the remaining chocolate in three batches, making sure that each batch is completely melted before adding the next. When all the chocolate has been added, the chocolate will be ready for dipping. To test that it's not too hot, place a dab below your lower lip. It should feel comfortable — not too hot or too cool. If you use a thermometer, the final temperature of the chocolate should be between 89° and 91°. If it's too hot, add a little more finely chopped chocolate until it feels comfortable. To hold the chocolate at the same temperature, place it over a shallow pan with water that is about 2 degrees warmer than the chocolate.

To dip the shortbread cookies, line two cookie sheets with parchment or wax paper. Hold a cookie between your fingers and dip into the chocolate about halfway up the bar. Remove the cookie from the chocolate and let the excess drip off. To help remove the excess chocolate, tap the cookie very lightly against the side of the pan. Place the cookie on the cookie sheet. When the cookie sheet is full, place it in the refrigerator for 10 minutes to set the chocolate.

Cakelike Bars

Cakelike bars are just as their name implies — they're more like cake than cookies. Their texture is softer than most cookies. These can easily pass as a complete dessert on their own. Try serving them with whipped cream or ice cream. You can cut cakelike bars into just about any size you want, from tiny one- or two-bite sizes to pieces closer to the size of a piece of cake. Cut cakelike cookies into squares, bars, triangles, or large rectangles.

Very Rich Cakelike Brownies

These cakelike brownies are tantalizing, mouthwatering, and soul satisfying. They are definitely richer than many cakes, so you may want to cut them into small squares. If you really want to make these memorable, try topping them with ice cream or whipped cream. They can also be dusted with powdered sugar or a mixture of unsweetened cocoa powder and powdered sugar. Or you can frost them with your favorite icing (see Chapters 20 and 21 for decorating ideas and recipes). If you like chewier brownies instead, see the recipe for Chocolate Fudge Brownies in Chapter 16.

Preparation time: *20 minutes*

Baking time: *30 minutes*

Yield: *25 pieces*

7 ounces bittersweet or semisweet chocolate, finely chopped

¾ cup (1½ sticks) unsalted butter, cut into small pieces

4 eggs

1 cup sugar

1 teaspoon vanilla extract

½ teaspoon lemon extract

Zest of 1 large lemon, finely minced

⅓ cup all-purpose flour

Pinch of salt

1 cup walnuts, finely chopped

1 Cut a square of parchment paper to fit the bottom of an 8-inch square baking pan. Using 1 tablespoon butter, generously grease the baking pan and one side of the parchment paper. Dust the pan with 2 teaspoons flour and shake out the excess. Line the bottom of the pan with the buttered square of parchment paper and set aside briefly. Preheat the oven to 350°.

2 Place the chocolate and butter in the top of a double boiler over hot, not simmering, water. Stir frequently with a rubber spatula so they melt evenly.

3 In a large mixing bowl, using a mixer, beat the eggs and sugar together until they are very thick and pale colored and hold a ribbon when the beaters are lifted, about 5 minutes. Blend in the vanilla and lemon extracts and the lemon zest.

4 Combine the flour with the salt and add slowly to the egg mixture with the mixer at low speed. Stop and scrape down the sides of the bowl with a rubber spatula and mix again.

5 Remove the double boiler from the heat, remove the top pan from the water, and dry the bottom of the pan. Pour the melted chocolate and butter into the mixture and blend thoroughly. Add the nuts and mix briefly to blend.

6 Pour the batter into the prepared pan. Bake for 30 to 35 minutes, until a toothpick inserted 2 inches from the edge still has moist crumbs clinging to it. The center will be very moist. Remove the pan from the oven and cool completely on a rack.

7 Cut the brownies into five rows of 1½-inch squares, using a knife dipped in hot water and dried. Store in an airtight container at room temperature for up to 3 days, or in the refrigerator for up to a week. If refrigerated, they'll firm up slightly but still remain very fudgy.

Per serving: Calories 173 (From Fat 107); Fat 12g (Saturated 6g); Cholesterol 49mg; Sodium 17mg; Carbohydrate 15g (Dietary Fiber 1g); Protein 3g.

Gingerbread

This gingerbread is delicious served warm with whipped cream. Gingerbread is especially popular in the fall and during the holiday season. I love the mix of spices that are used in gingerbread. They warm me up just thinking about them. Warm cider, tea, and coffee are great beverages to serve with gingerbread.

Preparation time: *20 minutes*

Baking time: *45 minutes*

Yield: *16 squares*

2½ cups all-purpose flour

2 teaspoons baking soda

1 tablespoon ground ginger

1 teaspoon ground cinnamon

½ teaspoon ground cloves

¼ teaspoon ground nutmeg, preferably freshly grated

¼ teaspoon salt

½ cup (1 stick) unsalted butter, at room temperature

¼ cup light brown sugar

¼ cup sugar

2 eggs, lightly beaten

1 cup dark molasses

1 cup boiling water

½ cup heavy cream for garnish

1 Preheat the oven to 350°. Prepare an 8-x-8-x-2-inch baking pan by generously buttering with 1 tablespoon of butter. Dust the pan with 1 tablespoon of flour and shake out the excess.

2 Sift the flour, baking soda, ginger, cinnamon, cloves, and nutmeg together on a large piece of wax paper and then blend in the salt. Set this mixture aside briefly.

3 Using a mixer, beat the butter in a large mixing bowl until it's soft and fluffy, about 2 minutes. Add the brown sugar and sugar and continue to beat until the mixture is well blended, about 2 more minutes. Stop and scrape down the sides of the bowl with a rubber spatula two times.

4 Blend in the eggs and the molasses, beating well, and then add the boiling water. Scrape down the bottom and sides of the bowl. With the mixer on low speed, add the dry ingredients from Step 2 in several small batches, beating to blend well after each addition.

5 Spread the mixture in the prepared pan and bake for 45 minutes, until the top springs back when lightly touched and a cake tester inserted in the center comes out clean.

6 Remove the pan from the oven and cool on a rack. Using a mixer set on medium speed, whip the cream in a small mixing bowl until it forms soft peaks. Cut the gingerbread into squares and serve with a dollop of whipped cream. Store tightly wrapped in foil at room temperature for up to 4 days. Freeze for longer storage.

Per serving: Calories 213 (From Fat 60); Fat 7g (Saturated 4g); Cholesterol 42mg; Sodium 212mg; Carbohydrate 36g (Dietary Fiber 1g); Protein 3g.

Chapter 9

Sandwich Cookies

In This Chapter

▷ Explaining the popularity of sandwich cookies

▷ Shaping cookies with pastry bags

▷ Getting fancy with your cookies

The Earl of Sandwich gave his name to one of the most popular food inventions of the last 200 years. How, you ask, would we all get by without a sandwich? One of the beauties of sandwiches is their portability. You couldn't have a picnic, go hiking, or eat on the run without sandwiches. Once sandwiches were invented, sandwich cookies weren't far behind. I'm not sure who the clever person was who noticed the popularity of sandwiches and invented sandwich cookies, but I'm sure glad it happened!

Like sandwiches, sandwich cookies are easy to transport. You get double the pleasure with sandwich cookies — two cookies and filling, to boot. What could be better than that? Kids, especially, love sandwich cookies. They can keep busy for a long time eating them. Lots of people love to indulge in certain store-bought brands of sandwich cookies, but making your own yields much tastier results. And you can be creative in the process by combining sandwich cookies with a variety of fillings.

People have their own special ways of eating sandwich cookies. There are no rules when it comes to eating them. Some people like to nibble around the cookie parts first and then either lick out or eat the remaining filling. Others take the cookies apart and eat the filling first and then the cookies. Still others don't bother to dissect them but devour the whole cookie in just a few bites. However you choose to eat your sandwich cookies is strictly up to you. Be as creative as you want. The point is to have a great time and a delicious eating experience!

Sticking Together

Although you can use many different kinds of cookies to make sandwich cookies, be sure to use thin cookies. Once you put them together with a filling, there's more than you might think. Use cookies with textures that are soft and chewy or crisp. You don't want the cookie to break into a million pieces when you bite into it. And you don't want to have to work hard to bite into the cookie, either.

Sandwich cookies look like you've spent a lot of time constructing them, but in reality, that's far from the truth. All you do is put a filling on the bottom of one cookie and cover it up with another cookie. When the cookies are cooled after baking, match up pairs by size. That way, you'll have cookies that fit together perfectly and don't leave room for the filling to leak out.

Be careful about the amount of filling you spread on. If you use too much filling, it will ooze out the sides, and the cookie will be messy to eat and store. Sandwich cookies need just enough filling to hold together.

Wait until no more than 2 days in advance of eating the cookies to put them together with their filling or they'll become soggy. To be certain that the cookies remain fresh, fill them the same day you plan to serve them.

You can make sandwich cookies in lots of shapes, depending on the shape of the cookie cutter you use to cut out the dough. Try hearts, ovals, squares, and rectangles. I love to make sandwich cookies that have the center cut from the top cookie, letting the filling peek through. I think of these as elegant sandwich cookies, perfect for an afternoon tea.

Make ice cream sandwiches with classic cookies such as chocolate chip, oatmeal raisin, or peanut butter.

Mastering Pastry Bag Techniques and Piping

Piping or pressing? It's easy to get piped and pressed cookies confused. Here's the difference: Piped cookies are made by using a pastry bag. The dough is piped (pushed) out through the tip by applying pressure to the pastry bag. When you use a cookie press to make cookies, they're referred to as pressed cookies (see Chapter 11).

Pastry bags are used to shape piped cookies, to fill sandwich and thumbprint cookies, and to decorate cookies. This section introduces you to pastry bags, how to prepare and fill them, and how to handle them effectively.

Pastry bags are made of nylon, polyester, canvas, plastic-lined cloth, or disposable plastic. Nylon and polyester are the most popular materials because they're light and very flexible, even when new, and are easy to care for. Pastry bags come in a wide range of sizes, from 8 to 24 inches. The most useful sizes and easiest to handle are 12 and 14 inches because they can hold a decent amount of a mixture without overfilling. The advantage of these sizes is that they don't have to be refilled as often as smaller pastry bags. Pastry bags and tips are available in cookware and craft shops, in the cookware sections of department stores, in some supermarkets, and through catalogs and Web sites.

Here's how to get a new pastry bag ready to use:

1. **Cut off about ½ inch at the pointed end for the pastry tube to fit through.**

2. **Drop the tube into the bag, thin end down.**

3. **Mark the line to be cut with a pencil, remove the tube from the bag, and use sharp scissors to cut the pastry bag.**

   Cut just enough to hold your smallest tip (see Figure 9-1).

   Don't cut off any more than necessary on a new pastry bag. If the opening is too big, the pastry tip will fall through when you apply pressure on the bag to push out the filling.

Preparing a Pastry Bag

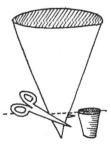

Figure 9-1:
Preparing a pastry bag.

Cut the end of the pastry bag, just enough to hold your smallest tip, without falling through.

You may want to use a coupler. A *coupler* is a two-piece plastic device that's used to attach a pastry tip to a pastry bag. A cylindrical piece with threads in the center fits into the pastry bag. Its wide top keeps it from falling out of the bag while the bottom protrudes from the bag. The pastry tip is placed onto the bottom of the coupler, and a plastic ring with inside threads fitted over the tip is secured by twisting it so that it holds onto the other half of the coupler.

Here are the steps for filling a pastry bag:

1. **Fold the top edge of the pastry bag out and down a few inches to form a cuff.**

2. **Hold the pastry bag underneath the cuff or place the pastry bag upright in a jar or measuring cup.**

3. **Use a rubber spatula to fill the bag no more than halfway for ease of handling.**

4. **Unfold the cuff over the filling.**

5. **Holding the pastry bag by the top end, push the filling down toward the tip.**

6. **Twist the pastry bag tightly at the point where the filling ends, and hold the pastry bag between your thumb and forefinger to secure the filling.**

7. **Squeeze a small amount of the filling back into the bowl to release any air caught in the bag.**

8. **To refill the bag, fold the cuff down and repeat the process.**

A pastry bag that is too full is hard to handle and easily becomes messy. Fill the pastry bag no more than halfway. You can always refill it when the filling is low.

To pipe cookies, hold the pastry bag about an inch above the surface at an angle and apply even pressure (see Figure 9-2). The pressure applied with the palm and fingers of the hand holding the bag is what makes the filling come out of the bag. Use the fingers of the other hand to help guide the bag. They should rest gently above the line of the pastry tube or tip. Move the pastry bag toward you to form a straight line or finger shape.

To stop the filling from coming out of the pastry bag, stop applying pressure with your hand. To pipe a mound, hold the pastry bag above the surface and keep it steady while applying pressure. Release the pressure to stop the flow and pull the pastry bag away from the mound.

Before doing actual cookie work, practice using the pastry bag at least once to make sure your grip on the bag is comfortable and to determine how much pressure you'll need to get the effect you want.

Fill cookies by using a pastry bag in the same way that you pipe out cookies (as shown in Figure 9-2). Hold the pastry bag straight up and down, about 1 inch above the surface of the cookie. Hold the pastry bag steady and apply even pressure with your hand to push the filling out of the pastry bag onto the cookie. Release the pressure of your hand to stop the flow of filling from the bag.

PIPING AND FILLING SANDWICH COOKIES WITH A PASTRY BAG

1. TO PIPE COOKIES HOLD THE PASTRY BAG ABOUT AN INCH ABOVE THE SURFACE AT AN ANGLE AND APPLY EVEN PRESSURE.

HOLD BAG AT A 45° ANGLE.

2. MOVE THE PASTRY BAG TOWARDS YOU TO FORM A FINGER SHAPE. TO STOP FILLING FROM COMING OUT OF THE BAG, STOP THE PRESSURE FROM YOUR HAND.

3. TO PIPE A MOUND, HOLD THE PASTRY BAG ABOVE THE SURFACE AND KEEP IT STEADY WHILE APPLYING PRESSURE. RELEASE PRESSURE TO STOP FLOW AND PULL BAG AWAY FROM MOUND.

1. TO FILL COOKIES, HOLD BAG STRAIGHT UP AND DOWN. ABOUT AN INCH ABOVE THE SURFACE OF THE COOKIE.

2. HOLD THE BAG STEADY AND APPLY EVEN PRESSURE WITH YOUR HAND TO PUSH OUT THE FILLING ONTO THE COOKIE.

STEADY!

3. RELEASE THE PRESSURE OF YOUR HAND TO STOP THE FILLING FROM FLOWING FROM THE BAG.

Figure 9-2: Piping and filling sandwich cookies with a pastry bag.

When you're finished with a pastry bag, squeeze out any remaining filling. Turn the pastry bag inside out and wash it in warm, soapy water. Stand the bag, wide end down, in a drainer or on a countertop to dry. The tips can go in the dishwasher, but be sure to put them in the silverware holder.

Cocoa Sandwiches

You can use a variety of fillings for these cookies. Try peanut butter, for instance, or your favorite variety of jam or preserves.

Specialty tools: *12- or 14-inch pastry bag with a ½-inch plain round pastry tip (#5)*

Preparation time: *15 minutes*

Baking time: *18 minutes*

Yield: *About 15 sandwiches*

¾ cup all-purpose flour

½ teaspoon baking soda

⅓ cup unsweetened natural cocoa powder

¼ teaspoon salt

½ cup (1 stick) unsalted butter, softened

⅔ cup light brown sugar

2 egg whites

1 teaspoon vanilla extract

1 cup peanut butter or 1 cup jam or preserves or 1 cup white chocolate cream filling (see following recipe)

1 Preheat the oven to 325°. Line a cookie sheet with parchment paper.

2 Sift together the flour, baking soda, cocoa powder, and salt. Set aside briefly.

3 Using a mixer, beat the butter in a large mixing bowl until fluffy, about 2 minutes. Add the brown sugar and mix together until smooth. In a separate bowl, blend together the egg whites and vanilla and add to the butter mixture. Stop and scrape down the sides of the bowl with a rubber spatula.

4 Add the dry ingredients from Step 2 in three stages to the butter mixture, stopping to scrape down the sides of the bowl after each addition. Blend thoroughly.

5 Fit a 12- or 14-inch pastry bag with a ½-inch plain round tip (#5). Fill the bag partway with batter. On the cookie sheet, pipe out 1-inch-thick mounds, leaving 2 inches between them. You can also scoop out mounds of dough using a scoop or spoon. Bake for 18 to 20 minutes, until set. Remove the cookie sheet from the oven and transfer the cookies from the parchment paper to cooling racks.

6 For each sandwich cookie, place a heaping teaspoon of filling on the flat side of one wafer. Place a second wafer on top and gently press together until the filling spreads to the sides. Wipe off any filling that drips or spills over the sides. Store at room temperature in a single layer covered with foil for 2 days.

Per serving (based on the White Chocolate Cream Filling): Calories 128 (From Fat 71); Fat 8g (Saturated 5g); Cholesterol 18mg; Sodium 75mg; Carbohydrate 14g (Dietary Fiber 1g); Protein 1g.

White Chocolate Cream Filling

Use this delicious filling with any sandwich cookies. This filling will surprise you when you take a bite because it looks like it's a lot sweeter than it is.

Preparation time: *2 hours, includes chilling*

Yield: *1½ cups*

3 tablespoons heavy whipping cream

¼ pound (4 ounces) white chocolate, finely chopped

3 tablespoons unsalted butter, softened

1 Heat the cream in a small saucepan over medium heat until it comes to a boil. Remove the saucepan from the heat and stir in the chocolate until it is completely melted and smooth.

2 Transfer the mixture to a bowl, cover tightly with plastic wrap, and cool to room temperature. Chill in the refrigerator until the mixture is thick, about 1 hour.

3 Using a mixer and mixing bowl, whip the butter for about 30 seconds. Add the white chocolate mixture and whip on medium speed until soft peaks form, about 2 minutes.

4 Fit a pastry bag with a #5 plain round tip and fill the bag partway with the mixture. Onto the center of one cookie pipe a small mound for the filling, and top with a second cookie to form sandwiches. You can also spoon a small amount (about 2 teaspoons) of the filling onto one cookie for the filling.

Per serving (1 tablespoon): Calories 46 (From Fat 34); Fat 4g (Saturated 2g); Cholesterol 7mg; Sodium 6mg; Carbohydrate 3g (Dietary Fiber 0g); Protein 0g.

Hazelnut-Almond Sticks

Ganache is the creamy chocolate filling in the center of these sophisticated cookies. *Ganache* is a smooth, velvety mixture of melted chocolate and cream that is thickened by chilling before use. It is often used as the center of truffles. The texture of ganache can vary, depending on the proportions of chocolate and cream.

These cookies are actually little meringues that bake at a low temperature. Meringues always seem to stick to parchment paper because some of their sugar seeps out while they're in the oven. To keep them from sticking, line the baking sheets with aluminum foil. When the cookies are cool, the foil peels off very easily.

Specialty tools: *14-inch pastry bag with a large ½-inch plain round pastry tip (#5)*

Preparation time: *25 minutes*

Baking time: *12 minutes*

Yield: *1½ dozen*

Cookies

1¼ cups toasted, skinned, and finely ground hazelnuts (see Chapter 4 for information on toasting nuts)

1½ cups finely ground almonds

3 egg whites

¾ cup sugar

¼ cup all-purpose flour, sifted

Ganache

¼ cup heavy cream

3 ounces bittersweet or semisweet chocolate, finely chopped

1 Preheat the oven to 325°. Line a cookie sheet with aluminum foil. Spray the foil with a nonstick baking spray.

2 Combine the hazelnuts and almonds in a bowl and set aside briefly. In a large mixing bowl with a mixer, whip the egg whites until frothy. Slowly add the sugar and whip until the whites hold firm, but not stiff, peaks. Fold the nuts into the meringue mixture. Sprinkle the flour on the mixture and fold in.

3 Fit a 14-inch pastry bag with a ½-inch plain round pastry tip (#5) and fill partway with the mixture. Pipe out sticks about 3 inches long onto the foil, leaving 1 inch between them.

4 Bake for 12 to 15 minutes, until the cookies are firm. Remove the cookie sheet from the oven and cool slightly before transferring the cookies from the foil to cooling racks. The cookies can be prepared up to 3 days in advance and held at room temperature covered with foil before they're assembled.

5 For the ganache, warm the cream in a saucepan until it begins to simmer. Remove the saucepan from the heat and stir in the chocolate until it is completely melted and the mixture is smooth. Transfer the mixture to a bowl, cover tightly with plastic wrap, and cool to room temperature. Chill the mixture for 1 hour, until thick.

6 Using a mixer, whip the ganache until it thickens, about 1 minute.

7 Fit a 14-inch pastry bag with a large ½-inch round plain pastry tip (#5) and fill the bag partway with the whipped ganache. Pipe a line of ganache on the center of half of the cookies. Top each covered cookie with a plain cookie, forming sandwiches. Press each sandwich together lightly. Store in a single layer in an airtight container at room temperature for up to 3 days.

Note: *Hazelnuts need to toast for about 15 minutes because they're thicker than most other nuts.*

Per serving: *Calories 201 (From Fat 126); Fat 14g (Saturated 3g); Cholesterol 5mg; Sodium 11mg; Carbohydrate 16g (Dietary Fiber 3g); Protein 5g.*

Parchment paper pastry cones and other pastry bag substitutes

One of the great features of pastry bag substitutes such as parchment paper pastry cones (see Chapter 19) and plastic pastry bags and bottles is that they're disposable. This feature makes cleanup go really quickly. Another great feature is that you can have a supply of them handy in advance so you don't have to spend time making them when you're ready to use them.

You can buy precut parchment paper triangles or cut a triangle with equal sides and a larger base from parchment paper (17½" 12½" 12½"). To form a cone from the triangle follow these steps (see the accompanying figure):

1. **Hold the triangle in front of you with the top point facing down.**

2. **Take the right corner and curve it in, bringing the point down to meet the bottom point.**

3. **Hold the two ends together with your hand. With your other hand, wrap the left point of the triangle around the outside and bring**

the point down to meet the other points, forming a cone.

Make sure that the pointed end of the cone is tightly closed.

4. **Use a piece of clear tape to secure the back seam and fold the top edges in twice, about ¼ inch each to make the edge even.**

To fill the cone, hold it near the pointed end and use a rubber spatula to place the filling into the cone, no more than halfway. Fold in each side of the top of the pastry cone to the center and then roll the top down until it meets the filling. Use sharp scissors to cut off a small opening, about ¼ inch, at the tip.

Hold the pastry cone between your thumb and fingers and use the pressure from your fingers to push the filling from the pastry cone. Hold the pastry cone about 1 inch above the surface and squeeze evenly to release the mixture. To stop the flow, release pressure on the pastry cone.

(continued)

(continued)

In a pinch, you can use a plastic sandwich bag to make a pastry bag. Cut a small piece off one of the corners and insert a pastry tube or a coupler to attach a small pastry tip. Fill the bag partway with the mixture and close it tightly. Push the mixture towards the tip, twist, and pipe.

You can also use a plastic squeeze bottle. Place the mixture into a plastic bottle with a thin nozzle that attaches to the top. Snip off a tiny opening at the end of the nozzle. Turn the bottle upside down and squeeze the bottle evenly to release the contents.

Be sure to use food-safe plastic bottles to hold any fillings, batters, or decorating materials. Don't use an old glue bottle or a bottle that's contained gardening chemicals. Keep the plastic bottles that you use in the kitchen separate from those in the laundry room or garage.

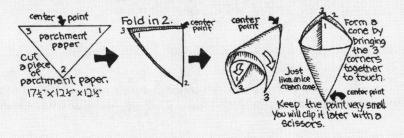

Making a Paper Cone for Decorating

Sandwiches with a Touch of Class

Sandwich cookies can be very elegant and can really dress up your table or event by their presentation. To give them a refined feel, keep the cookies small and choose elegant fillings, such as ganache, buttercream, and preserves. Sandwich cookies show that you've put time and loving care into making them. They're like miniature layer cakes. I like to think of elegant sandwich cookies as edible art. Some people ooh and aah over them and say they're too pretty to eat. But they *are* made for eating. You can always make other batches for another occasion.

By using cookie cutters in particular shapes, such as a heart shape for Valentine's Day or a tree shape for Christmas, you can turn certain cookies into holiday cookies (see Chapter 15). You might try making Ischl Tartlets for Valentine's Day. Cut them into heart shapes and fill them with red raspberry preserves. Let your imagination go, and you'll be delighted by the new cookies you create.

Make the cookies for sandwich cookies uniform so that the completed treat looks as good as it tastes. One way to ensure uniformity in the size of the cookies is to use cookie cutters.

Pofer Cookies

I first ate Pofer Cookies in Switzerland. Variations are found throughout northern Italy, Austria, and Germany. If you don't want to sandwich them together, they're delicious on their own. These cookies are really beautiful, besides being delicious. The scalloped edges made by the round, fluted cookie cutters give them an elegant look, and the preserves glisten like little jewels in the center of the sandwich, making them hard to resist. For special flair, dip them in chocolate or drizzle chocolate over them.

Specialty tools: *1-inch and 3-inch round fluted-edge cutters, rolling pin*

Preparation time: *3¼ hours; includes chilling*

Baking time: *10 minutes*

Yield: *3½ dozen*

¾ cup plus 1 tablespoon (1½ sticks plus 1 tablespoon) unsalted butter, softened

1 cup sugar

2 cups finely ground almonds

¼ teaspoon ground cinnamon

½ teaspoon vanilla extract

2 eggs

4 cups all-purpose flour

Pinch of salt

1¼ cups apricot or raspberry preserves

1 cup confectioners' sugar for garnish

1 Using a mixer, beat the butter in a large mixing bowl, about 2 minutes. Add the sugar and mix together until smooth. Add the almonds, cinnamon, and vanilla and blend well.

2 In a separate bowl, beat the eggs lightly and add to the butter mixture. Blend well and then add the flour with the salt in three stages. Stop and scrape down the sides of the bowl after each addition. Mix to a smooth dough, about 2 minutes. Wrap the dough in plastic and chill for at least 3 hours, until firm enough to roll out. The dough can be held in the refrigerator for 3 days or can be frozen. If frozen, defrost overnight in the refrigerator.

3 Preheat the oven to 350°. Line a cookie sheet with parchment paper. Roll out the dough on a lightly floured work surface to about ¼ inch thick. Cut out circles using a 3-inch round fluted-edge cutter. Take half the circles and cut out their centers using a 1-inch round fluted-edge cutter. Gather together the scraps and center cutouts, reroll, and recut. Place the circles on the cookie sheet, leaving 1 inch between them. Bake for 10 to 15 minutes, until golden and set. Remove the cookie sheet from the oven and transfer the cookies from the parchment paper to the cooling racks.

4 When the cookies are cool, place a teaspoon of preserves on the solid cookies. Heavily dust the cookies with the center holes with confectioners' sugar and place these on top of the cookies with the preserves, forming sandwiches. Store in a single layer in a tightly sealed container at room temperature for up to 2 days.

Per serving: *Calories 349 (From Fat 64); Fat 7g (Saturated 3g); Cholesterol 20mg; Sodium 11mg; Carbohydrate 71g (Dietary Fiber 1g); Protein 3g.*

Ischl Tartlets

These Austrian specialties use the same types of ingredients as Pofer Cookies but are a bit more delicate. My favorite shape for these is a heart, but you can use any cookie cutter shape you choose. These cookies take their name from the spa town of Bad Ischl (pronounced "eesh uhl"), outside of Salzburg.

Specialty tools: *1-inch round cutter, 3-inch-diameter heart cutter, rolling pin*

Preparation time: *1¼ hours; includes chilling*

Baking time: *15 minutes*

Yield: *3½ dozen*

1¾ cup all-purpose flour, sifted

1 scant cup sugar

1½ cups finely ground almonds

½ teaspoon ground cinnamon

1¼ cups (2½ sticks) unsalted butter, softened

1 cup apricot or raspberry preserves

Confectioners' sugar for garnish

1 Place the flour, sugar, almonds, and cinnamon in a food processor fitted with a steel blade. Pulse the mixture for 10 seconds. Cut the butter into pieces and add to the dry ingredients. Pulse the mixture for 30 seconds. Then turn the machine on and leave until the dough forms a ball, another 30 seconds. Wrap the dough in plastic and chill for 1 hour. (To make the dough with a mixer and mixing bowl, beat the butter until fluffy, about 2 minutes. Add the sugar, and cream together. Toss the cinnamon with the flour and almonds. Add this to the butter in four stages, blending well after each addition. Stop occasionally and scrape down the sides of the mixing bowl with a rubber spatula. Proceed with the same instructions given for the food processor.)

2 Preheat the oven to 350°. Line a cookie sheet with parchment paper.

3 Roll out the pastry dough on a lightly floured work surface to ⅛-inch thick. Use a 3-inch-diameter heart cutter to cut out the cookies. In half of the hearts, cut out the center with a 1-inch-diameter round cutter. Gather together the scraps and the cutout centers, reroll, and recut. Place the cookies on the lined cookie sheet, with at least 2 inches between them. Bake for 15 minutes, until golden and set. Remove the cookie sheet from the oven and transfer the cookies from the parchment paper to cooling racks. The cookies can be prepared up to 3 days in advance and held at room temperature covered with foil before they're assembled.

4 When the hearts are cool, place a spoonful of preserves on the solid hearts. Heavily dust the hearts with the hole in the center with confectioners' sugar and place these on top of the preserves. The tartlets will keep for 1 day at room temperature, in a single layer covered with foil.

Per serving: *Calories 131 (From Fat 71); Fat 8g (Saturated 4g); Cholesterol 15mg; Sodium 4mg; Carbohydrate 15g (Dietary Fiber 1g); Protein 2g.*

Chapter 10

Filled Cookies

In This Chapter

▶ Making an impression with thumbprint cookies

▶ Baking flavor-filled little pies

▶ Hiding the filling inside the cookies

Filled cookies include thumbprints and little tartlets, as well as cookies that are rolled up with a filling inside. Most of these cookies are shaped individually, so they take a little time to assemble, but they're well worth the effort.

What all filled cookies have in common is that the dough is rolled around the filling or the filling is placed inside the dough either before or after baking. The fillings vary from a simple dollop of jam or preserves to a mixture with several ingredients. Filled cookies are popular because they please both our eyes and our taste buds.

Thumbs Up to Thumbprints!

Thumbprint cookies take their name from the way they're made. A thumb is pressed into the center of a small ball or mound of dough to form a well for the filling. These are some of the simplest and most delicious cookies to make. It's easy to get overly zealous, however, when pressing your thumb into the center of the ball of dough and flatten it too much. If this happens, the filling will ooze out when the cookies bake, making a big, sticky mess on the cookie sheet. When placing the cookies on the cookie sheets, leave at least an inch of room between them because they spread when they bake. You don't want to wind up with one big cookie! Each thumbprint cookie should be a complete little package to be savored on its own.

To make an indentation in the center of the ball of cookie dough, press gently with your thumb (see Figure 10-1). Doing so pushes the dough from the center to the sides, forming a ridge in which to enclose the filling.

When thumbprint cookies are arranged on a serving plate, they look like a bunch of jewels, twinkling in the light with their different-colored fillings. Feel free to try different jams and preserves for the filling. If you're serving the cookies for a special occasion, use a filling in a color that's appropriate for the event (red for Valentine's Day and Christmas and yellow or orange for the fall, for example). Although thumbprint cookies are easy, they're also elegant and versatile. I love to serve them on a mixed cookie platter for afternoon tea. They're also a perfect after-dessert treat for a dinner party, and they're great as a bedtime snack.

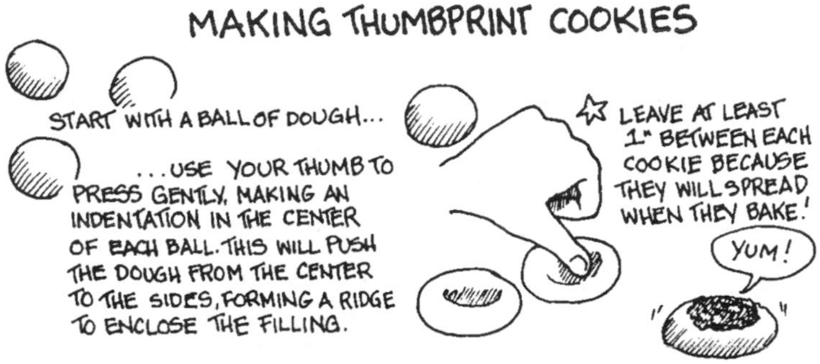

MAKING THUMBPRINT COOKIES

START WITH A BALL OF DOUGH...

...USE YOUR THUMB TO PRESS GENTLY, MAKING AN INDENTATION IN THE CENTER OF EACH BALL. THIS WILL PUSH THE DOUGH FROM THE CENTER TO THE SIDES, FORMING A RIDGE TO ENCLOSE THE FILLING.

LEAVE AT LEAST 1" BETWEEN EACH COOKIE BECAUSE THEY WILL SPREAD WHEN THEY BAKE!

YUM!

Figure 10-1: Making thumbprint cookies.

Raspberry-Hazelnut Thumbprints

These classic cookies are very festive. They combine two of my favorite flavors, raspberry and hazelnut. I like to make these in the fall and winter because their colors go best in these seasons.

Preparation time: *20 minutes*

Baking time: *16 minutes*

Yield: *4 dozen*

2 cups all-purpose flour

½ teaspoon baking powder

1 teaspoon ground cinnamon

1 cup (2 sticks) unsalted butter, softened

⅓ cup sugar

¼ cup light brown sugar

2 eggs

2 teaspoons vanilla extract

1½ cups finely chopped toasted hazelnuts (see the Tip at end of recipe and Chapter 4)

½ cup raspberry jam

1 Preheat the oven to 350°. Line a cookie sheet with parchment paper.

2 Sift together the flour, baking powder, and cinnamon. Set aside. Using a mixer, beat the butter in a large mixing bowl until fluffy, about 1 minute. Add the sugar and brown sugar and mix together until smooth.

3 Separate the eggs and lightly beat the egg yolks with the vanilla. Add to the butter mixture and blend thoroughly. Add the flour mixture in three stages, blending well after each addition. Stop and scrape down the sides of the bowl occasionally. Stir in ½ cup hazelnuts and blend well. Gather the dough into a disk, cover tightly in plastic wrap, and chill for about 30 minutes, until firm but still pliable.

4 Place the egg whites in a small bowl and stir lightly. Place the remaining 1 cup hazelnuts in a small bowl. Break off walnut-size pieces of the dough and roll into balls. Coat the balls with the egg white and then roll in the hazelnuts, coating completely. Place the balls on the cookie sheet with 1 inch of space between them. Use your thumb to press an indentation into the center of each ball. Place about ½ teaspoon jam in each indentation.

5 Bake for 16 to 18 minutes, until the cookies are golden and set. Remove the cookie sheet from the oven and transfer the cookies from the parchment paper to cooling racks. Store in a single layer between sheets of wax paper in an airtight container at room temperature for 3 days.

Tip: *To toast hazelnuts, place them in a single layer in a shallow pan with a lip, such as a jelly roll pan. Toast them in a preheated 350° oven for 15 to 18 minutes. You'll be able to tell they're ready because you'll smell their appetizing aroma, the skins will split open, and the nuts will be light golden brown. Remove the baking pan from the oven and transfer the warm hazelnuts to a kitchen towel. Wrap the towel around the nuts and let them steam for about 10 minutes. Then rub the nuts in the towel to help remove the skins.*

Per serving: *Calories 93 (From Fat 57); Fat 6g (Saturated 3g); Cholesterol 19mg; Sodium 8mg; Carbohydrate 8g (Dietary Fiber 1g); Protein 1g.*

Apricot-Almond Thumbprints

This version is as equally delicious as the classic Raspberry Hazelnut Thumbprints. I have a hard time choosing which I like more.

Preparation time: *20 minutes*

Baking time: *16 minutes*

Yield: *4 dozen*

2 cups all-purpose flour

½ teaspoon baking powder

1 teaspoon ground cinnamon

1 cup (2 sticks) unsalted butter, softened

⅓ cup sugar

¼ cup light brown sugar

2 eggs

1 teaspoon vanilla extract

1 teaspoon almond extract

1½ cups finely chopped toasted almonds (see the Tip at end of recipe and Chapter 4 for more information on toasting nuts)

½ cup apricot preserves

1 Preheat the oven to 350°. Line a cookie sheet with parchment paper.

2 Sift together the flour, baking powder, and cinnamon. Set aside. Using a mixer, beat the butter in a large mixing bowl until fluffy, about 1 minute. Add the sugar and brown sugar and mix together until smooth.

3 Separate the eggs and lightly beat the egg yolks with the vanilla and almond extracts. Add to the butter mixture and blend thoroughly. Add the flour mixture in three stages, blending well after each addition. Stop and scrape down the sides of the bowl occasionally. Stir in ½ cup almonds and blend well. Gather the dough into a disk, cover tightly in plastic wrap, and chill for about 30 minutes, until firm but still pliable.

4 Place the egg whites in a small bowl and stir lightly. Place the remaining 1 cup almonds in another small bowl. Break off walnut-size pieces of the dough and roll into balls. Coat the balls with the egg white and then roll in the almonds, coating completely. Place the balls on the cookie sheet, with 1 inch between them. Use your thumb to press an indentation into the center of each ball. Place about ½ teaspoon of preserves in each indentation.

5 Bake for 16 to 18 minutes, until golden and set. Remove the cookie sheet from the oven and transfer the cookies to racks to cool. Store in a single layer between sheets of wax paper in an airtight container at room temperature for 3 days.

Tip: *To toast the almonds, place them in a shallow pan with a lip. Toast in a 350° oven for 5 minutes. Shake the pan and toast for another 2 to 3 minutes, until the nuts are light golden. Remove the pan from the oven and transfer the nuts to a cool plate to cool completely.*

Per serving: *Calories 94 (From Fat 55); Fat 6g (Saturated 3g); Cholesterol 19mg; Sodium 8mg; Carbohydrate 8g (Dietary Fiber 1g); Protein 2g.*

Hidden Surprises and Mini-Pies

Have you ever walked into a bakery and picked a sweet to eat just because it looked good, even though you didn't know what was inside? That's fun, but it's even more fun to take the first bite and be thrilled by how yummy it tastes. Eye appeal is part of the enticement of cookies. Cookies such as rugelach — a classic Jewish cookie — have hidden fillings inside that you can't see, but the cookies look so good you know that they'll yield delicious surprises. Date Pinwheels are another great example. You can see a little of the filling rolled between the layers of dough, but until you take that first bite, you have no idea what a treat awaits you! Hamantaschen, another classic Jewish cookie, also fits perfectly in this category. *Jewish Cooking For Dummies* by Faye Levy (Hungry Minds, Inc.) contains hamantaschen recipes and illustrations.

Rugelach (pronounced RUGH-uh-luhkh), too, is a classic cookie with hidden surprises. Rugelach look like mini-croissants. The dough starts out rolled into a circle, which is cut into several pie-shaped wedges that are rolled up individually around their filling. Because the filling is hidden inside, it's hard to know what it is. But the anticipation makes the first bite that much sweeter. If you've never tried to make rugelach, I urge you to do it. Definitely make plenty of them — you'll need a lot once everyone discovers how good they are!

Mini-pies are a form of filled cookie. They're tiny — only two-bite size. Because mini-pies have both a crust and a filling, you can make them in stages, so the job is very easy to fit into a busy lifestyle. Simply make the dough, press it into the mini-muffin tins, and keep it in the freezer until you're ready to make the filling and bake the cookies.

Rugelach

These cookies are classics of Jewish cuisine. They take a bit of work, but they're definitely worth it. The delicate dough melts in your mouth. This recipe is one of my mother's specialties.

Preparation time: *2½ hours; includes chilling*

Baking time: *18 minutes*

Yield: *4 dozen*

Dough

2 cups all-purpose flour

1 tablespoon sugar

1 package (8 ounces) cream cheese, at room temperature

1 cup (2 sticks) unsalted butter, softened

Filling

⅔ cup sugar

⅓ cup light brown sugar

1 tablespoon ground cinnamon

¾ cup walnuts

¾ cup raisins

½ cup apricot or raspberry jam or preserves

1 For the dough, combine the flour and sugar in the work bowl of a food processor fitted with a steel blade. Pulse briefly to blend. Cut the cream cheese and butter into pieces and add. Pulse until the dough is cut into tiny pieces and then process until the mixture forms a ball, about 1 minute. Divide the dough into four equal pieces. Wrap each in plastic and chill in the freezer for at least 2 hours. If frozen, let the dough stand at room temperature until pliable, but still firm. (To make the dough using a mixer and mixing bowl, beat the butter and cream cheese together until fluffy, about 2 minutes. Combine the sugar with the flour and add to the butter mixture in three stages, blending well after each addition. Stop occasionally and scrape down the sides of the bowl. Proceed by following the instructions given for the food processor.)

2 For the filling, combine the sugar, brown sugar, cinnamon, walnuts, and raisins in the work bowl of a food processor fitted with a steel blade. Pulse to chop the walnuts into small pieces, about 15 seconds.

3 Preheat the oven to 350°. Line a cookie sheet with parchment paper.

4 To assemble, work with one piece of dough at a time while keeping the others chilled. Roll each piece on a floured surface into a large circle. Spread a very thin layer of jam on the dough toward the center, leaving a ½-inch border. Evenly sprinkle one-fourth of the filling over the dough. Cut each circle into 12 equal pie-shaped pieces. Starting from the wide end, roll each piece toward the point into a tight sausage shape (see Figure 10-2). Place each piece on the cookie sheet, leaving 1 inch between each cookie.

5 Bake for 18 to 20 minutes, until golden. Remove the cookie sheet from the oven and transfer the cookies to racks to cool. Store in an airtight container at room temperature for up to a week. Freeze for longer storage.

Per serving: *Calories 137 (From Fat 59); Fat 7g (Saturated 4g); Cholesterol 16mg; Sodium 21mg; Carbohydrate 20g (Dietary Fiber 1g); Protein 1g.*

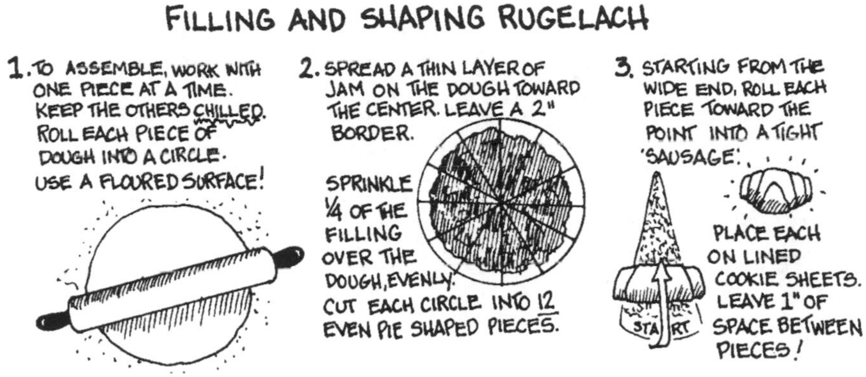

FILLING AND SHAPING RUGELACH

1. TO ASSEMBLE, WORK WITH ONE PIECE AT A TIME. KEEP THE OTHERS CHILLED. ROLL EACH PIECE OF DOUGH INTO A CIRCLE. USE A FLOURED SURFACE!

2. SPREAD A THIN LAYER OF JAM ON THE DOUGH TOWARD THE CENTER. LEAVE A 2" BORDER.

SPRINKLE ¼ OF THE FILLING OVER THE DOUGH, EVENLY. CUT EACH CIRCLE INTO 12 EVEN PIE SHAPED PIECES.

3. STARTING FROM THE WIDE END, ROLL EACH PIECE TOWARD THE POINT INTO A TIGHT 'SAUSAGE'.

PLACE EACH ON LINED COOKIE SHEETS. LEAVE 1" OF SPACE BETWEEN PIECES!

START

Figure 10-2: Filling and shaping rugelach.

Pecan Tassies

These gems are miniature pecan pies. Use either mini-muffin tins or 2-inch individual tartlet pans. The name *tassie* apparently has two different sources. The Scots use the word tassie to mean a small cup, which is what these mini-pies look like. Tassie is also the name that many people in the southern United States use to mean tiny pies. In the South, pecan pie is revered.

Specialty tools: *2-inch mini muffin tins or 2-inch tartlet pans*

Preparation time: *30 minutes*

Baking time: *23 minutes*

Yield: *3 dozen*

Dough

½ cup pecans

1⅓ cups all-purpose flour

⅔ cup sugar

Pinch of salt

¾ cup (1½ sticks) unsalted butter, softened

1 egg

Filling

½ cup light brown sugar

4 tablespoons dark corn syrup

1½ teaspoons vanilla extract

1 egg and 1 egg yolk

¾ cup pecans, finely chopped

1 For the dough, place the pecans and flour in the work bowl of a food processor fitted with the steel blade. Pulse until the pecans are finely ground, about 1 minute. Add the sugar and salt and pulse briefly to blend. Cut the butter into small pieces and add. Pulse until the butter is cut into very tiny pieces, about 1 minute. Add the egg and process until the dough forms a ball. Wrap in plastic and chill for 1 hour. (To make the dough using a mixer and mixing bowl, beat the butter until fluffy, about 2 minutes. Add the sugar, and cream together well. Lightly beat the egg and add to the butter mixture. Blend thoroughly, stopping to scrape down the sides of the bowl. Finely chop the pecans with a chef's knife and toss with the flour and salt. Add the dry ingredients to the mixture in the bowl in three stages, blending well after each addition. Proceed following the instructions given for the food processor.)

2 For the filling, combine all the ingredients in a medium mixing bowl and stir together well. Preheat the oven to 375°. Spray the inside of the muffin tin or tartlet pan with non-stick cooking spray.

3 Pinch off walnut-size pieces of the dough and roll each into a ball. Place each ball in the mini-muffin tin or tartlet pan and press with your thumb to form a deep indentation. Spoon the filling into each indentation just up to the top. Place the muffin tin or tartlet pan on a cookie sheet.

4 Bake for 23 to 25 minutes, until the edges of the dough are golden and the filling is set. Remove the cookie sheet, cool on racks, and turn the tartlets out of the pans. Store in a single layer in an airtight container at room temperature for up to 5 days. Freeze for longer storage.

Vary It! *The dough in this recipe can be baked without a filling. When the crust is cool, it can hold lemon curd, ganache, jam, peanut butter, or a spoonful of ice cream. You can even do a two-tone filling that is half of one type and half of another. Varying the filling is a great way to get more mileage out of a recipe.*

Per serving: *Calories 77 (From Fat 43); Fat 5g (Saturated 2g); Cholesterol 17mg; Sodium 9mg; Carbohydrate 8g (Dietary Fiber 0g); Protein 1g.*

Date Pinwheels

Although these cookies take a bit of work, they're worth it. You can make both the filling and the dough in advance and put them together before baking.

Preparation time: *12½ hours; includes chilling*

Baking time: *12 minutes*

Yield: *3½ dozen*

Filling

⅓ cup sugar

½ cup water

¾ cup roughly chopped, pitted dates

¼ cup walnuts, roughly chopped

1 tablespoon orange juice

Dough

2 cups all-purpose flour

¼ teaspoon baking powder

Pinch of salt

½ cup (1 stick) unsalted butter, softened

1 cup light brown sugar

1 egg

1 teaspoon vanilla extract

1 tablespoon finely minced orange zest

1 For the filling, combine the sugar, water, and dates in a 2-quart heavy-bottomed saucepan. Cook over medium heat until the mixture is thick. Remove and stir in the walnuts and orange juice. Cool and then purée in a food processor fitted with a steel blade. Transfer to a bowl, cover tightly with plastic wrap, and hold at room temperature.

2 For the dough, sift together the flour, baking powder, and salt. Using a mixer, beat the butter in a large mixing bowl until light and fluffy, about 1 minute. Add the brown sugar and mix together until smooth. In a small bowl, beat the egg lightly with the vanilla extract and add the orange zest. Add to the butter mixture and blend well. Add the flour mixture in three stages, blending well after each addition. Form the dough into a disk, wrap tightly in plastic, and chill overnight.

3 On a lightly floured surface, roll out the dough to a large rectangle about 10 by 15 inches and ¼ inch thick. Evenly spread the date mixture over the dough. Roll up from the long side to a tight roll. Wrap in wax paper, cover with plastic wrap, and chill for at least 1 hour.

4 Preheat the oven to 375°. Line a cookie sheet with parchment paper. Slice the roll into ¼-inch-thick slices. Transfer the cookies to the cookie sheet, leaving 1 inch between them. Bake for 12 to 15 minutes, until golden and set. Remove the cookie sheet from the oven and transfer the cookies to racks to cool. Store in an airtight container at room temperature for up to a week. Freeze for longer storage.

Per serving: Calories 82 (From Fat 25); Fat 1g (Saturated 1g); Cholesterol 11mg; Sodium 10mg; Carbohydrate 14g (Dietary Fiber 0g); Protein 1g.

Part IV
Shaping Up Your Cookies

The 5th Wave   By Rich Tennant

"We're making hand-formed cookies, why?"

In this part . . .

You can dig in and be as creative as you like with shaped cookies — pressed, hand-formed, and molded cookies — because they're totally handmade. If you liked playing with modeling clay as a child, you'll have a great time here! There's a lot of variety to choose from.

Chapter 11

Pressed Cookies

*1*f you like fancy cookies, pressed cookies are the way to go. Pressed cookies take on a professionally tailored or finished look because of their uniformity. Using a pastry bag or cookie press enables you to make sure that your cookies have a uniform shape and size. Because of their tailored quality, these cookies are perfect for parties or fancy occasions.

Pressed cookies can be made in variety of shapes and sizes depending on the template or disk you use with your cookie press or the tip you use with your pastry bag. Many cookie presses have disks that are appropriate for various seasons and holidays. For example, you can make hearts for Valentine's Day, Christmas trees for the Christmas season, and pumpkins for Halloween.

Pressed cookies lend themselves very well to a variety of decorations. They look good with a little drizzled or piped chocolate on top, or they can be dipped in chocolate, halfway or all the way (see Chapter 20 for tips on chocolate embellishments). If you're feeling creative, try piping dots of icing around the top of a cookie and pressing edible candied flowers or candy coffee beans on top of the icing, depending on the flavor of the cookie (see Chapter 21 for more decorating tips). Arranging cookies on interesting platters or in unusual containers is another way to show them off (see www.dummies.com/bonus/cookies for more presentation ideas).

Let the Presses Roll!

One of the main tools for making pressed cookies is a cookie press, shown in Figure 11-1. Also sometimes called a gun, a cookie press (see Chapter 2) consists of a cylindrical container that holds the cookie dough. The bottom end holds the disk or template that shapes the cookie dough into the design.

Disks and templates are easy to change, making it very simple to create cookies in many different shapes. Pressed cookies are also made with a pastry bag and tips. The design that the pastry tip makes determines the shape of the cookies.

STANDARD COOKIE PRESS WITH TEMPLATES

Figure 11-1:
A standard cookie press with templates.

When assembling a cookie press, follow the manufacturer's instructions. Here are some general instructions on assembly:

1. **Place the dough inside the cylindrical container.**

2. **Choose the disk or template in the shape that you want and attach it to the bottom of the cylinder with the ring that screws onto the cylinder.**

3. **Attach the plunger mechanism.**

When you're ready to bake the cookies, all that's left to do is press the top lever to release the cookie dough. Each press of the lever releases a specific amount of cookie dough, so each cookie is the same size.

The most suitable dough for pressed cookies is a buttery mixture with a medium stiffness. If the dough is too thin, it will run out of the cookie press on its own and will be hard to control. If the dough is too stiff, you'll need the strength of Hercules to push it out of the press. Cookie dough made with nuts or chopped fruit can get stuck in the pastry tip or cookie press, so it's best to use a smooth dough for this type of cookie. If you do use a dough with nuts, grind or grate them very finely to prevent this problem.

The dough for pressed cookies often needs to be chilled to firm it up a bit before pressing. However, if it's too cold, it needs to stand at room temperature to warm up to the right consistency. In some cases, chilling the pressed cookies for 15 to 30 minutes before baking them is a good idea. Doing so helps them to maintain their shape, which they would lose if the dough bakes while soft.

At first, using a cookie press can be a little tricky. Think of the first couple cookies out of the press as a trial run. These always seem to break off partway through, leaving the dough hanging halfway in the press. After pressing the first couple cookies, the rest should be easy to press out. To ensure smooth cookie pressing, hold the cookie press perpendicular to the cookie sheet. Don't push the bottom edge of the press into the cookie sheet. Instead, hover it just above the sheet, about ¼ inch. This position gives the dough room to come out of the press.

For good results when making pressed cookies, have the cookie sheets at room temperature. If they're too warm, the cookies will start to melt before they go into the oven.

Using a Pastry Bag to Press Cookies

Pressing cookies out of a pastry bag is no different than piping icing with a pastry bag (see Chapter 9 for pastry bag techniques). You use the same technique for cookies, but use large pastry tubes to create the shapes. These tubes are about 2 inches tall and are sold in cookware shops and craft stores and through catalogs and Web sites. They're very easy to find. Generally I like to use a large star tip, such as #4 or #5. This size makes rosettes and also gives definition to other shapes by creating ridges. If I want to create a smooth surface, I use a large open tube, such as #5.

Delicious Pressed Cookies

The following pages contain some of my favorite pressed cookie recipes. I've included cookies of various textures that range from chewy to crispy. They also include a wide variety of flavors. I hope you'll enjoy them as much as I do!

Chocolate Butter O's

Here's a way to get some good experience with your cookie press or pastry bag and be rewarded at the same time. These delicate butter cookies are perfect for afternoon tea or coffee. To make butter cookies without the chocolate, leave out the cocoa powder and finely chopped chocolate, increase the flour to 2 cups, and use 2 egg yolks.

Preparation time: *25 minutes, include chilling time*

Baking time: *9 minutes*

Yield: *4½ dozen*

1 cup (2 sticks) unsalted butter, softened	*1 egg yolk*
¾ cup confectioners' sugar	*1¾ cups all-purpose flour*
2 tablespoons unsweetened Dutch-processed cocoa powder	*2 ounces bittersweet or semisweet chocolate, very finely chopped or shaved*

1 Line a cookie sheet with parchment paper.

2 Using a mixer, beat the butter in a large mixing bowl until fluffy, about 2 minutes. Sift together the confectioners' sugar and cocoa powder and add to the butter mixture in two batches. Stop and scrape down the sides of the bowl with a rubber spatula after each addition. Add the egg yolk and beat until very well blended.

3 Add the flour to the butter mixture in three stages and stir in the chocolate and blend thoroughly.

4 If you're using a cookie press, chill the dough for 30 minutes. Preheat the oven to 350°. Assemble the cookie press and insert the dough in the cylinder. Choose the disk or template and attach it to the press. Fit a 14-inch pastry bag with a large pastry tube that has a ½-inch plain round tip (#5). Fold a cuff back on the top of the pastry bag and stand the bag in a tall jar or measuring cup. Use the rubber spatula to scoop some of the cookie dough into the pastry bag, filling it no more than halfway. Fold the cuff up and push the mixture down towards the pastry tip. Tightly twist the bag at the point where the cookie dough ends.

5 Hold the cookie press perpendicular to the cookie sheet, about ¼ inch above it. Press down on the handle to release the dough. Repeat to release all the dough. Refill the cookie press as needed with the remaining dough. If using a pastry bag, hold it 1 inch above the cookie sheets and pipe out round circles of dough about 1 inch in diameter.

6 Bake for 9 to 10 minutes, until the cookies are golden. Remove the cookie sheet from the oven and transfer the cookies from the parchment to cooling racks. Store in an airtight container at room temperature for up to a week. Freeze for longer storage.

Per serving: *Calories 58 (From Fat 35); Fat 4g (Saturated 2g); Cholesterol 13mg; Sodium 1mg; Carbohydrate 5g (Dietary Fiber 0g); Protein 1g.*

Almond Macaroons

These typical macaroons are chewy and delicious. Many countries have a tradition of macaroons, and most of them are similar to these (see Chapter 5 for another macaroon recipe). For example, French-style macaroons have a smooth surface and are often made into sandwich cookies with a filling of jam, buttercream, or ganache (see Chapter 9 for sandwich cookie fillings).

This recipe calls for almond paste, a confection made of ground almonds that is used in pastry and dessert making. Almond paste, which has a sweet almond flavor and a slightly grainy texture, can be found in the baking section of many supermarkets or in cookware shops. I prefer to use the kind that comes in a roll.

Preparation time: *15 minutes*

Baking time: *15 minutes*

Yield: *3½ dozen*

1 roll (7 ounces) almond paste	*½ teaspoon almond extract*
¾ cup granulated sugar	*1 tablespoon all-purpose flour*
2 egg whites, lightly beaten	

1 Preheat the oven to 325°. Line a cookie sheet with aluminum foil. Coat the foil with butter. Dust with flour and shake off the excess.

2 Using a mixer, combine the almond paste and sugar in a large mixing bowl. Blend together on low speed until the mixture is crumbly. Beat on medium speed until the mixture is well combined. Add the egg whites and almond extract and blend until smooth. Add the flour and mix together well.

3 If you're using a cookie press, chill the dough for 15 minutes. Assemble the cookie press and insert the dough in the cylinder. Choose the disk or template and attach it to the press. Hold the cookie press perpendicular to the cookie sheet, about ¼ inch above it. Press down on the handle to release the dough. Repeat to release all the dough. Refill the cookie press as needed with remaining dough. If using a pastry bag, hold it 1 inch above the cookie sheets and pipe out round circles of dough about 1 inch in diameter. To use a pastry bag, fit a 12- or 14-inch pastry bag with a pastry tube that has a ½-inch plain round opening (#5). Fill the pastry bag halfway with the macaroon mixture. Pipe out 1-inch-diameter mounds on the prepared cookie sheet, leaving 2 inches between the mounds.

4 Bake for 15 minutes, until the cookies are golden. Remove the cookie sheet from the oven and place on a cooling rack. When the sheet is completely cool, lift the macaroons off the aluminum foil. The macaroons are best eaten within 2 days. Store in an airtight container at room temperature.

Per serving: Calories 37 (From Fat 12); Fat 1g (Saturated 0g); Cholesterol 0mg; Sodium 3mg; Carbohydrate 6g (Dietary Fiber 0g); Protein 1g.

Some cookies, such as macaroons, have a tendency to stick to parchment paper. To prevent this, use aluminum foil, which makes it very easy to remove the cookies after they're baked.

Cocoa Wafers

These crunchy wafers are great to have on hand for making sandwich cookies. If you want to do so, use White Chocolate Cream Filling or Ganache (see Chapter 9). Wafers are just as good served dusted with confectioners' sugar.

Preparation time: *15 minutes*

Baking time: *18 minutes*

Yield: *3½ dozen*

¾ cup all-purpose flour	½ cup (1 stick) unsalted butter, softened
½ teaspoon baking soda	⅔ cup light brown sugar
⅓ cup unsweetened natural cocoa powder	2 egg whites
¼ teaspoon salt	1 teaspoon vanilla extract

1 Preheat the oven to 325°. Line a cookie sheet with parchment paper.

2 Sift together the flour, baking soda, cocoa powder, and salt. Set aside briefly.

3 Using a mixer, beat the butter in a large mixing bowl, about 2 minutes. Add the brown sugar and blend until smooth. In a small bowl, blend the egg whites and vanilla and add to the butter mixture. Scrape down the sides of the bowl with a rubber spatula.

4 Add the dry ingredients from Step 2 in three stages, stopping to scrape down the sides of the bowl after each addition. Blend thoroughly.

5 If you're using a cookie press, chill the dough for 30 minutes. Assemble the cookie press and insert the dough in the cylinder. Choose the disk or template and attach it to the press. Hold the cookie press perpendicular to the cookie sheet, about ¼ inch above it. Press down on the handle to release the dough. Repeat to release all the dough. Refill the cookie press as needed with the remaining dough. If using a pastry bag, hold it 1 inch above the cookie sheets and pipe out round circles of dough about 1 inch in diameter. To use a pastry bag, fit a 12- or 14-inch pastry bag with a pastry tube that has a ½-inch plain round opening (#5). Fill the bag partway with the dough. On the cookie sheet, pipe out 1-inch-thick mounds, leaving 2 inches between them.

6 Bake for 18 to 20 minutes, until set. Remove the cookie sheet from the oven and transfer the cookies to racks to cool. Store in an airtight container at room temperature for up to a week. Freeze for longer storage.

Per serving: *Calories 43 (From Fat 21); Fat 2g (Saturated 1g); Cholesterol 6mg; Sodium 33mg; Carbohydrate 6g (Dietary Fiber 0g); Protein 1g.*

Nut Wafers

These wafers are the perfect accompaniment to ice cream or fresh fruit. If you can't decide which nuts to use, try a blend of two or all three. Grind the nuts extremely fine so they're the consistency of flour. Doing so will prevent them from getting stuck in the disk of the cookie press or the tip of the pastry bag.

Preparation time: *15 minutes*

Baking time: *10 minutes*

Yield: *3½ dozen*

½ cup toasted hazelnuts, walnuts, or sliced almonds (see Chapter 4 for information on toasting nuts)

1¼ cups all-purpose flour

¾ cup (1½ sticks) unsalted butter, softened

½ cup sugar

1 egg

1¼ teaspoons vanilla extract

⅛ teaspoon salt

Confectioners' sugar for garnish

1 Preheat the oven to 350°. Line a cookie sheet with parchment paper.

2 Place the nuts and ¼ cup of the flour in the bowl of a food processor fitted with the steel blade. Pulse until the nuts are finely ground, about 30 seconds. If you don't have a food processor, grind the nuts with 1 tablespoon of flour in a clean coffee grinder or use the fine side of a grater to shave them.

3 Using a mixer, beat the butter in a large mixing bowl until light and fluffy, about 1 minute. Add the sugar and continue beating for 1 more minute. Blend in the egg, vanilla, and salt. Add the remaining flour in two stages, blending well after each addition. Fold the nuts into the mixture.

4 If you're using a cookie press, chill the dough for 15 minutes. Assemble the cookie press and insert the dough in the cylinder. Choose the disk or template and attach it to the press. Hold the cookie press perpendicular to the cookie sheet, about ¼ inch above it. Press down on the handle to release the dough. Repeat to release all the dough. Refill the cookie press as needed with the remaining dough. If using a pastry bag, hold it 1 inch above the cookie sheet and pipe out round circles of dough about 1 inch in diameter. To use a pastry bag, fit a 14-inch pastry bag with a pastry tube that has a ½-inch plain round (#5) opening and fill partway with the wafer dough. Pipe out 2-inch fingers of the dough onto the cookie sheet, leaving 1 to 2 inches between the wafers.

5 Bake for 10 to 11 minutes, until the edges of the wafers are golden. Remove the cookie sheet from the oven and transfer the cookies from the parchment to cooling racks. Dust the tops of the wafers with confectioners' sugar before serving. Store the wafers in an airtight container at room temperature for up to 5 days. Freeze for longer storage.

Per serving: Calories 65 (From Fat 40); Fat 4g (Saturated 2g); Cholesterol 14mg; Sodium 9mg; Carbohydrate 6g (Dietary Fiber 0g); Protein 1g.

Chapter 12

Hand-Formed Cookies

Hand-formed cookies take their name from how they're made, like many other types of cookies. This type of cookie is formed into a ball or other shape by hand before baking. These are some of the easiest cookies to make. Making hand-formed cookies is a great way to get family and friends involved. Many of these cookies are thought of as comfort food because many people grew up eating them. But others are new and will become old favorites after you've savored them. These are definitely hands-on cookies!

Handling Hand-Formed Cookies

Although these cookies are great fun for children to make because they can really get their hands into them, encourage them to handle the dough as little as possible when shaping these cookies so that the cookies don't turn out tough.

Hand-formed cookies are made with a butter-rich dough that is easier to handle if chilled briefly — about 15 minutes — before shaping. Chilled dough also spreads less when baked. Don't skip chilling the dough, even if you're in a hurry. Doing so will make working with it too difficult and frustrating.

To keep the cookie dough from sticking to your hands as you work with it, lightly moisten your hands with cool water. Doing so cools down the temperature of your hands and keeps the dough from sticking to them.

Familiar Favorites

The three cookies in this section are everyone's favorites. You can't go wrong with any of them or all three. The only problem will be making enough of them. They seem to disappear off the cooling racks!

Classic Sugar Cookies

All bakers should have sugar cookies in their repertoire; these cookies are hard to resist for bakers and eaters. They're the cookies I most remember eating as a child. I loved them then and still do. They're perfect with a glass of milk or a cup of hot tea.

Preparation time: *1 hour 20 minutes; includes chilling*

Baking time: *10 minutes*

Yield: *About 3 dozen*

½ cup (1 stick) unsalted butter, softened

½ cup confectioners' sugar, sifted

½ cup sugar

1 egg at room temperature

½ cup canola oil

1 teaspoon vanilla extract

2½ cups all-purpose flour

½ teaspoon baking soda

½ teaspoon cream of tartar

½ teaspoon ground nutmeg, preferably freshly ground or grated

¼ teaspoon salt

⅓ cup pearl sugar (see Chapter 3) or granulated sugar

1 Using a mixer, beat the butter in a large mixing bowl until it's fluffy, about 1 minute. Add the confectioners' sugar and sugar and mix together until smooth. In a small bowl, mix together the egg, oil, and vanilla and blend into the butter mixture thoroughly. Stop occasionally and scrape down the sides and bottom of the bowl with a rubber spatula.

2 In a separate bowl, blend together the flour, baking soda, cream of tartar, nutmeg, and salt. Add to the butter mixture in four stages, blending well after each addition. Cover the bowl tightly with plastic wrap and chill for at least 1 hour.

3 Preheat the oven to 350°. Line a baking sheet with parchment paper. Place the pearl sugar or granulated sugar in a small bowl. Pinch off walnut-size pieces of the dough and roll into balls. Flatten the balls to disks, about ¼ inch thick, and dip in the sugar. Transfer the cookies to the baking sheet, leaving 2 inches between them.

4 Bake for 10 minutes, until golden and set. Remove the cookie sheet from the oven and transfer the cookies to racks to cool. Store the cookies in an airtight container at room temperature for up to 1 week. Freeze for longer storage.

Per serving: *Calories 107 (From Fat 52); Fat 6g (Saturated 2g); Cholesterol 13mg; Sodium 36mg; Carbohydrate 13g (Dietary Fiber 0g); Protein 1g.*

Gingersnaps

These yummy cookies are great year-round, but their full-bodied flavor seems to taste best when it's cold outside. The use of both ground and crystallized ginger makes the flavor really sing.

Preparation time: *45 minutes*

Baking time: *12 minutes*

Yield: *About 4 dozen*

2¼ cups all-purpose flour

1 teaspoon baking soda

2 teaspoons ground ginger

1¼ teaspoons ground cinnamon

½ teaspoon ground cloves

¼ teaspoon salt

2 tablespoons finely minced crystallized ginger

¾ cup (1½ sticks) unsalted butter, softened

¾ cup sugar

1 egg at room temperature

⅓ cup dark molasses

½ cup sugar (for rolling the cookies)

1 Sift the flour with the baking soda, ground ginger, cinnamon, and cloves. Add the salt and crystallized ginger and toss to blend well.

2 Using a mixer, beat the butter in a large mixing bowl, about 1 minute. Add the sugar and mix together until smooth. Add the egg and molasses and blend thoroughly. Stop occasionally and scrape down the sides and bottom of the bowl with a rubber spatula.

3 Add the dry ingredients from Step 1 in three stages, blending well after each addition. Cover the mixing bowl with plastic wrap and chill the dough in the refrigerator for 30 minutes.

4 If your oven is electric, place an oven rack on the upper shelf of the oven. In a gas oven, place the oven rack on the center shelf. In either case, preheat the oven to 350°. Line a cookie sheet with parchment paper. Place the ½ cup sugar in a small bowl. Remove the bowl of cookie dough from the refrigerator. Dampen your hands with cold water. Pinch off pieces of the dough the size of a walnut, roll them into balls, and roll in the sugar. Place the balls on the baking sheet, leaving 2 inches between them.

5 Bake the cookies for 12 minutes, until the cookies are firm and the tops are cracked. Remove the cookie sheet from the oven and transfer the cookies to racks to cool completely. Store in an airtight container at room temperature for up to 5 days. Freeze for longer storage.

Tip: *Baking these cookies on the upper rack in an electric oven exposes them to more intense heat and thus helps create some of the crackle on top.*

Per serving: *Calories 61 (From Fat 22); Fat 2g (Saturated 1g); Cholesterol 10mg; Sodium 33mg; Carbohydrate 9g (Dietary Fiber 0g); Protein 1g.*

Snickerdoodles

You may have eaten snickerdoodles as a child, but they're good enough to love at any age. They're definitely one of my childhood favorites.

Preparation time: *10 minutes*

Baking time: *8 minutes*

Yield: *2 dozen*

½ cup (1 stick) unsalted butter, softened

¾ cup plus 3 tablespoons sugar

1 egg at room temperature

½ teaspoon vanilla extract

1⅓ cups all-purpose flour

Pinch of salt

½ teaspoon baking soda

1 teaspoon cream of tartar

2½ teaspoons ground cinnamon

1 Preheat the oven to 350°. Line a cookie sheet with parchment paper. Using a mixer, beat the butter in a large mixing bowl until light and fluffy, about 2 minutes. Add the ¾ cup sugar and mix together until smooth. Add the egg and vanilla and blend well.

2 Blend together the flour, salt, baking soda, and cream of tartar. Add to the butter mixture in three to four stages, blending well after each addition.

3 Combine the 3 tablespoons sugar and cinnamon in a small bowl. Break off walnut-size pieces of the dough, roll into balls, and coat with the sugar-cinnamon mixture. Place the balls on the cookie sheet, with 2 inches between them. Bake for 8 to 10 minutes, until the cookies are set and slightly cracked on top. Remove the cookie sheet from the oven and transfer to racks to cool. Store in an airtight container at room temperature for up to 1 week. Freeze for longer storage.

Per serving: Calories 91 (From Fat 37); Fat 4g (Saturated 2g); Cholesterol 19mg; Sodium 36mg; Carbohydrate 13g (Dietary Fiber 0g); Protein 1g.

Keeping the Balls Rolling

All cookie making is fun, but rolling cookie dough into balls can be a real kick. There's something about going around and around with the dough between your hands that makes you feel like you're up to something very special. There's no great skill involved here. Just roll them until you're happy with the shape (see Figure 12-1). When rolling them, you may find that your hips start to move, so you may want to put on a little music as you make these cookies.

You can make a variety of sizes, but try to bake the same sizes together so that they bake evenly

ROLLING DOUGH INTO BALLS

Figure 12-1:
Rolling
dough into
little balls.

PULL OFF A PIECE OF
DOUGH. ROLL IT BETWEEN
YOUR PALMS UNTIL IT
FORMS A BALL.

Coconut Butter Balls

These cookies are so tender that they practically melt in your mouth.

Preparation time: *1 hour 10 minutes; includes chilling*

Baking time: *24 minutes*

Yield: *1½ dozen*

1 cup all-purpose flour	*1 cup (2 sticks) unsalted butter, softened*
2 tablespoons cornstarch	*1 teaspoon vanilla extract*
½ cup confectioners' sugar	*1 to 1¼ cups shredded coconut*

1 Combine the flour, cornstarch, and confectioners' sugar in the work bowl of a food processor fitted with the steel blade. Pulse briefly to blend. Cut the butter into small pieces and add with the vanilla. Pulse until the mixture forms a soft dough, about 2 minutes. Wrap the dough tightly in plastic and chill for at least 1 hour. (To mix the dough without a food processor, place the butter in the bowl of a mixer and beat until fluffy, about 1 minute. Sift the confectioners' sugar and add. Cream the two together, stopping occasionally to scrape down the sides of the bowl. Add the vanilla and blend until smooth. Sift together the flour and cornstarch and add to the butter mixture in three stages. Stop and scrape down the sides of the bowl after each addition. Blend until smooth. Form the dough into a disk and wrap tightly in plastic. Chill for at least 1 hour.)

2 Preheat the oven to 300°. Line a cookie sheet with parchment paper. Place the coconut in a shallow bowl. Break off quarter-size pieces of the dough, roll into 1-inch diameter balls, and roll the balls in the coconut. Place the balls on the cookie sheet, with 2 inches between them.

3 Bake for 24 minutes, until the edges are golden. Remove the cookie sheet from the oven and transfer the cookies to racks to cool. Store in an airtight container at room temperature for up to 5 days. Freeze for longer storage.

Per serving: Calories 67 (From Fat 47); Fat 5g (Saturated 3g); Cholesterol 12mg; Sodium 7mg; Carbohydrate 5g (Dietary Fiber 0g); Protein 0g.

Cardamom-Orange Nut Balls

Cardamom is one of my favorite spices because it adds an intriguing depth to flavors. Here I combine it with fresh orange zest, which gives these cookies a unique citrusy flavor. To be sure that the cardamom is fresh, buy whole cardamom pods from a shop that carries spices in bulk. Crack the pods to remove the seeds and grind them just before use.

Preparation time: *15 minutes*

Baking time: *20 minutes*

Yield: *About 4 dozen*

1½ cups sliced or slivered almonds	*1 cup (2 sticks) unsalted butter, chilled*
2 cups all-purpose flour	*2 teaspoons vanilla extract*
½ cup sugar	*Finely minced zest of 1 large orange*
1 teaspoon ground cardamom	*Confectioners' sugar for garnish*
⅛ teaspoon salt	

1 Preheat the oven to 350°. Place the almonds in a cake pan or pie plate and toast for 5 minutes. Shake the pan and continue to toast until golden, about 5 more minutes. Remove from the oven and cool. Lower the oven temperature to 325°. Line a cookie sheet with parchment paper.

2 Place the almonds, flour, sugar, cardamom, and salt in the work bowl of a food processor fitted with a steel blade. Pulse briefly to blend. Cut the butter into small pieces and pulse until cut into tiny pieces. Add the vanilla and orange zest and process the dough until it wraps itself around the blade, 30 seconds to 1 minute. (To mix the dough without a food processor, grind the almonds finely with 1 tablespoon of the sugar in a blender or in a clean coffee grinder. Beat the butter in a mixing bowl until fluffy, about 1 minute. Add the remaining sugar and cream together. Blend in the vanilla and orange zest and beat until smooth. Combine the cardamom with the flour and salt and add to the butter mixture in three stages, stopping to scrape down the sides of the bowl after each addition. Mix until thoroughly blended.)

3 Pinch off quarter-size pieces of the dough and roll them into balls about 1 inch in diameter. Place the balls on the cookie sheet, leaving 1 inch of space between them.

4 Bake until golden and set, about 20 minutes. Remove the cookie sheet from the oven and transfer the cookies to racks to cool. Lightly dust the cookies with confectioners' sugar. Store the cookies between layers of wax paper in an airtight container at room temperature for up to a week. Freeze for longer storage.

Per serving: Calories 79 (From Fat 49); Fat 5g (Saturated 3g); Cholesterol 10mg; Sodium 7mg; Carbohydrate 7g (Dietary Fiber 1g); Protein 1g.

Finding out more about cardamom

Cardamom is one of the world's costliest spices because the pods are handpicked from their stems. Inside of the oval pods are between 12 and 20 three-sided seeds, which are ground to release their tangy flavor and aroma. In hot weather, store cardamom in a tightly sealed jar in the refrigerator to maintain its freshness.

Hazelnut Chocolate Balls

These little gems will melt in your mouth. They're reminiscent of chocolate truffles but pack more crunch. These look very elegant when presented in paper candy cups.

Preparation time: *1 hour; includes chilling*

Baking time: *10 minutes*

Yield: *2½ dozen*

4 ounces high-quality bittersweet or semisweet chocolate, finely chopped

6 tablespoons (¾ stick) unsalted butter, softened

1 cup confectioners' sugar, sifted

1¼ cups toasted, skinned, and finely ground hazelnuts (see Chapter 4)

Confectioners' sugar for garnish

1 Melt the chocolate in the top of a double boiler over hot water. Stir often with a rubber spatula to ensure even melting. Set aside to cool slightly.

2 Using a mixer, beat the butter until light and fluffy, about 1 minute. Add the confectioners' sugar and mix together until smooth. Add the melted chocolate and blend until creamy. Scrape down the sides of the bowl frequently with a rubber spatula. Add the hazelnuts and blend well.

3 Cover the mixture with plastic wrap and chill for at least 30 minutes.

4 Line a cookie sheet with parchment paper. Preheat the oven to 300°. Pinch off pieces of the dough and roll into ½-inch balls. Place the balls on the cookie sheet, with 1 inch between them.

5 Bake for about 10 minutes, until set. Remove the cookie sheet from the oven and transfer the cookies to racks to cool. When the cookies are cool, dust the tops with confectioners' sugar. Store in an airtight container at room temperature for up to 5 days. Freeze for longer storage.

Per serving: Calories 62 (From Fat 41); Fat 5g (Saturated 2g); Cholesterol 5mg; Sodium 0mg; Carbohydrate 5g (Dietary Fiber 0g); Protein 1g.

Dressy Cookies

Sometimes you're looking for a cookie that is more on the elegant side. You want it to be easy to make and not take too much time. It must also, of course, taste great. The following cookies fit the bill perfectly. Their shape, texture, and eye appeal make them stand out from the crowd. And the crowds will most definitely go for them.

Hazelnut Crescents

These cookies are so delicate and delicious that they practically melt in your mouth. Who can resist that? To make delicious variations, you can replace the hazelnuts with other nuts such as almonds or walnuts. These cookies are perfect for an afternoon tea party or when you want to serve something special. For another crescent cookie recipe, see the Almond-Vanilla Crescents in Chapter 15.

Preparation time: *50 minutes; includes chilling*

Baking time: *18 minutes*

Yield: *About 5 dozen*

1 cup (2 sticks) unsalted butter, softened	*½ teaspoon salt*
½ cup sugar	*2 cups all-purpose flour*
1 egg yolk at room temperature	*1 teaspoon vanilla extract*
1½ cups toasted, skinned, and finely ground hazelnuts (see Chapter 4 for information on toasting nuts)	*½ teaspoon almond extract*

1 Preheat the oven to 350°. Using a mixer, beat the butter in a large mixing bowl until light and fluffy, about 2 minutes. Add the sugar and mix together until smooth. Add the egg yolk and blend. Stir in the hazelnuts and beat the mixture well.

2 Mix the salt with the flour and add in three batches, mixing thoroughly, stopping to scrape down the sides of the bowl with a rubber spatula after each addition. Blend in the vanilla and almond extracts thoroughly.

3 Wrap the dough in plastic wrap and chill for at least 30 minutes, or until the dough is firm but pliable.

4 Line a cookie sheet with parchment paper. Dust your hands with flour and pinch off about 1 tablespoon of the dough. Roll the dough into crescent shapes (see Figure 12-2) and place on the cookie sheet with 1 inch between them.

5 Bake for 18 minutes, until golden. Remove the cookie sheet from the oven; leave the cookies on the cookie sheet for at least a minute, and then transfer the cookies to racks to cool. Store in an airtight container at room temperature for up to 5 days. Freeze for longer storage.

Per serving: *Calories 62 (From Fat 39); Fat 4g (Saturated 2g); Cholesterol 12mg; Sodium 20mg; Carbohydrate 5g (Dietary Fiber 0g); Protein 1g.*

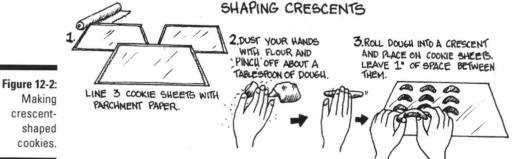

Figure 12-2: Making crescent-shaped cookies.

SHAPING CRESCENTS

1. LINE 3 COOKIE SHEETS WITH PARCHMENT PAPER.

2. DUST YOUR HANDS WITH FLOUR AND PINCH OFF ABOUT A TABLESPOON OF DOUGH.

3. ROLL DOUGH INTO A CRESCENT AND PLACE ON COOKIE SHEETS. LEAVE 1" OF SPACE BETWEEN THEM.

Hazelnut Crisscross Cookies

These cookies come from my good friend Jan Meyers. They're satisfying and have a rich flavor and crumbly texture that are similar to the finest shortbread. Even if you like to bake more than one sheet of cookies at a time, in this recipe it's best to bake only one sheet at a time.

Preparation time: *15 minutes*

Baking time: *18 minutes*

Yield: *About 4 dozen*

1¾ cups raw shelled hazelnuts, or 1 cup finely ground, toasted hazelnuts (see Chapter 4 for information on toasting nuts)

½ cup sugar

2 cups all-purpose flour

¼ teaspoon baking soda

1 cup (2 sticks) unsalted butter at room temperature, cut into small pieces

1 tablespoon vanilla extract

1 egg yolk at room temperature

1 Preheat the oven to 350°. If working with raw shelled hazelnuts, spread the hazelnuts in a single layer in a large cake pan. Toast for 15 minutes, until the skins split and the nuts are golden. Remove and transfer to a kitchen towel. Wrap the towel around the nuts and leave for 10 minutes. Rub the nuts in the towel or between your hands to remove most of the skins. Place the nuts in the work bowl of a food processor fitted with a steel blade or in a blender or a clean coffee grinder. Add 2 tablespoons of the sugar and pulse until the nuts are finely ground, about 2 minutes. Transfer the ground nuts to a bowl.

2 Combine the flour, baking soda, and butter in the work bowl of a food processor fitted with the steel blade. Pulse until the butter is cut into tiny pieces, about 1 minute. Add the ground hazelnuts and the remaining sugar and process briefly until well blended. In a small bowl, combine the vanilla and the egg yolk and add to the dry mixture. Process until the dough forms a ball, about 1 minute. (To mix the dough without a food processor, beat the butter in the bowl of a mixer until fluffy, about a minute. Add the sugar, and cream together well. In a small bowl, combine the vanilla and egg yolk and add to the butter mixture. Stop and scrape down the sides of the bowl, and mix until smooth. Combine the flour and baking soda and add to the butter mixture in three stages, stopping to scrape down the sides of the bowl with a rubber spatula after each addition. Mix thoroughly. Add the hazelnuts and blend well.)

3 Line a cookie sheet with parchment paper. Break off walnut-size pieces of the dough and roll into balls. Place the balls on the baking sheet, with 2 inches between them. Dip a fork into flour and use it to lightly flatten each ball. Use the fork to press into the cookies a second set of lines that intersect the first.

4 Bake for 18 to 20 minutes, until golden and set. Remove the cookie sheet from the oven and transfer the cookies to racks to cool. Use a metal spatula to lift the cookies from the baking sheets when cool. Store in an airtight container at room temperature for up to 1 week. Freeze for longer storage.

Tip: *You can occasionally find chopped hazelnuts in the supermarket. Save some time and effort in Step 1 by grinding the chopped hazelnuts with the sugar.*

Per serving: *Calories 73 (From Fat 44); Fat 5g (Saturated 2g); Cholesterol 15mg; Sodium 7mg; Carbohydrate 6g (Dietary Fiber 0g); Protein 1g.*

Almond Jam Slices

These cookies are inspired by cookies I ate in pastry shops in Germany and Austria. The jam glistens against the cookie, making each slice look like a special jewel.

Preparation time: *1 hour; includes chilling*

Baking time: *15 minutes*

Yield: *About 4 dozen*

¾ cup (1½ sticks) unsalted butter, softened

⅔ cup sugar

1 egg at room temperature

1 teaspoon vanilla extract

1 teaspoon almond extract

½ cup finely ground almonds

1½ cups all-purpose flour

½ teaspoon baking powder

⅓ cup apricot or raspberry jam or preserves

1 Using a mixer, beat the butter in a large mixing bowl until light and fluffy, about 1 minute. Add the sugar and mix together until smooth. In a small bowl, combine the egg with the vanilla and almond extracts. Add to the butter mixture and blend well.

2 In a separate bowl, mix together the almonds, flour, and baking powder. Add to the butter mixture in three stages, blending well after each addition. Cover the mixture and chill for 30 minutes.

3 Line a cookie sheet with parchment paper. Divide the dough into four equal pieces. On a lightly floured work surface, roll each piece into a log about 10 to 12 inches long and ¾ inch wide. Place all of the rolls on the cookie sheet, leaving space between them. Use your finger and press a groove about ¼ inch deep in the center of each roll, down the entire length of the roll. Chill again for 30 minutes. Preheat the oven to 350°. Spread a heaping tablespoon of jam into the center groove of each roll.

4 Bake for 15 to 20 minutes, until golden and set. Remove the cookie sheet from the oven and transfer to a rack to cool. Slice each roll on the diagonal into 1-inch-wide cookies. Store in a single layer in an airtight container at room temperature for up to 2 days.

Per serving: *Calories 75 (From Fat 41); Fat 5g (Saturated 2g); Cholesterol 12mg; Sodium 7mg; Carbohydrate 8g (Dietary Fiber 0g); Protein 1g.*

Biscotti

Biscotti means "twice baked." *Bis* is the Italian prefix meaning "twice," and *còtto* means "baked." The second baking is what makes biscotti very crunchy and dry. They're meant to be dunked into coffee, tea, or milk. Their firm texture makes them great keepers — up to 3 weeks in an airtight container at room temperature. In recent years, biscotti have become wildly popular in the United States with the proliferation of upscale coffee establishments. The Italians have been enjoying them practically forever.

To make shaping biscotti easier and to prevent the dough from sticking to your hands, dust your hands with flour first.

Anise Biscotti

These biscotti are crisp and not too sweet. Anise, the classic flavor for biscotti, has a sweet licorice flavor that is distinct but not overpowering. These are basic biscotti from which several variations can be made. Biscotti keep very well and travel well, too.

Preparation time: 15 minutes

Baking time: 50 minutes; includes resting

Yield: About 3 dozen

2 cups all-purpose flour	*2 eggs at room temperature, lightly beaten*
2 teaspoons baking powder	*½ cup (1 stick) unsalted butter, melted*
Pinch of salt	*1 teaspoon anise extract*
¾ cup sugar	*¼ cup anise seed*

1 Preheat the oven to 350°. Line a cookie sheet with parchment paper.

2 Sift together the flour and baking powder. In a large mixing bowl using a mixer, combine the flour mixture with the salt and sugar and blend together by mixing at low speed for 30 seconds. Add the eggs, melted butter, and anise extract and mix well. Add the anise seed and mix for 30 seconds, until well blended.

3 Divide the dough in half. Take one half and pat it out onto a lined cookie sheet to form a mound about 8 inches long, 2 inches wide, and ¾ inch thick (see Figure 12-3). Keep the remaining dough covered with plastic wrap in the refrigerator.

4 Bake for 25 minutes, until golden and set. Remove the cookie sheet from the oven and let stand for 15 minutes. Transfer the log to a cutting board. Slice each mound on the diagonal into ½-inch-thick slices. Place the slices on their sides. Return the cookie sheet to the oven and bake for another 10 to 15 minutes, until the biscotti are firm. Remove the cookie sheet from the oven and transfer the cookies to racks to cool. Store in an air-tight container at room temperature. Freeze for longer storage.

Per serving: *Calories 71 (From Fat 27); Fat 3g (Saturated 2g); Cholesterol 19mg; Sodium 29mg; Carbohydrate 10g (Dietary Fiber 0g); Protein 1g.*

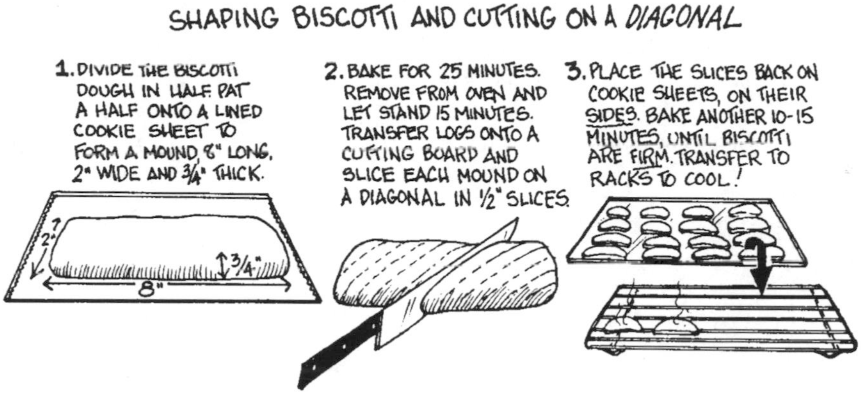

SHAPING BISCOTTI AND CUTTING ON A *DIAGONAL*

Figure 12-3:
Shaping biscotti and cutting on the diagonal.

1. DIVIDE THE BISCOTTI DOUGH IN HALF. PAT A HALF ONTO A LINED COOKIE SHEET TO FORM A MOUND, 8" LONG, 2" WIDE AND 3/4" THICK.

2. BAKE FOR 25 MINUTES. REMOVE FROM OVEN AND LET STAND 15 MINUTES. TRANSFER LOGS ONTO A CUTTING BOARD AND SLICE EACH MOUND ON A DIAGONAL IN 1/2" SLICES.

3. PLACE THE SLICES BACK ON COOKIE SHEETS, ON THEIR SIDES. BAKE ANOTHER 10-15 MINUTES, UNTIL BISCOTTI ARE FIRM. TRANSFER TO RACKS TO COOL!

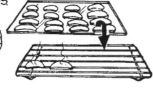

Biscotti variations

You can make different flavors of biscotti simply by changing a few ingredients in the Anise Biscotti recipe in this chapter.

✔ **Anise-Almond Biscotti:** Add 2 teaspoons vanilla extract and 1½ cups sliced almonds to the dough when adding the anise seeds.

✔ **Hazelnut Biscotti:** Eliminate the anise seeds. Add 2 teaspoons vanilla extract and

1 cup toasted (see Chapter 4), skinned, and coarsely chopped hazelnuts to the dough after mixing in the eggs and butter.

✔ **Ginger Biscotti:** Eliminate the anise seeds. Add 2 teaspoons ground ginger and ½ cup finely diced crystallized ginger to the flour before mixing it with the other ingredients.

Chocolate Biscotti

This recipe is a truly superb version of biscotti — the kind you can send as special gifts or serve at elegant gatherings.

Preparation time: *15 minutes*

Baking time: *53 minutes; includes resting*

Yield: *About 3 dozen*

½ cup (1 stick) unsalted butter, softened

1½ cups all-purpose flour

½ cup unsweetened Dutch-processed cocoa powder

2 teaspoons baking soda

Pinch of salt

¾ cup sugar

2 eggs

1 teaspoon vanilla extract

½ teaspoon almond extract

½ teaspoon chocolate extract (optional)

2 ounces (½ cup) bittersweet or semisweet chocolate chopped into small chunks, or ½ cup chocolate chips

1½ cups sliced almonds

1 Preheat the oven to 350°. Line a cookie sheet with parchment paper.

2 Melt the butter in a small saucepan or in the microwave.

3 In a large mixing bowl, sift together the flour, cocoa powder, baking soda, and salt. Add the sugar and stir to blend well.

4 In a separate bowl, whisk the eggs with the vanilla and almond extracts and chocolate extract (if desired). Add to the dry ingredients along with the melted butter. Using a mixer, blend the mixture on low speed until thoroughly combined. Blend in the chocolate chunks or chips and the almonds.

5 Divide the dough in half. Shape each into a log about 8 inches long x 2 inches wide x ¾ inch high. Center a log on the cookie sheet. Keep the remaining dough covered with plastic in the refrigerator, or you can bake two logs on one sheet if you want.

6 Bake for 22 to 24 minutes, until set. Remove the cookie sheet from the oven and rest for 15 minutes. Lower the oven temperature to 325°.

7 Transfer the log to a cutting board. Cut the log on the diagonal into ½-inch-thick slices and place the slices on their sides. Bake for 16 to 18 minutes, until firm. Remove the cookie sheet from the oven and transfer the cookies to racks to cool. Store in an airtight container at room temperature for up to 3 weeks. Freeze for longer storage.

Per serving: Calories 97 (From Fat 50); Fat 6g (Saturated 2g); Cholesterol 19mg; Sodium 78mg; Carbohydrate 11g (Dietary Fiber 1g); Protein 2g.

Cornmeal Almond Biscotti

The extra crunch in these biscotti comes from the addition of cornmeal. To add an extra flavor element, I like to use sambuca, an Italian liqueur that has a hint of licorice flavor.

Preparation time: *15 minutes*

Baking time: *55 minutes; includes resting*

Yield: *About 3 dozen*

1¼ cups whole unblanched almonds

2¼ cups all-purpose flour

½ cup yellow cornmeal

¼ teaspoon salt

1½ teaspoons baking powder

3 tablespoons anise seed

½ cup (1 stick) unsalted butter, softened

1 cup sugar

2 eggs at room temperature

1 tablespoon sambuca, or 2 teaspoons vanilla extract

1 Preheat the oven to 350°. Toast the almonds in a shallow pan for 10 minutes, until golden. Remove, cool, and chop coarsely. Lower the oven temperature to 325°. Line a cookie sheet with parchment paper.

2 Combine the flour, cornmeal, salt, baking powder, and anise seed in a large bowl.

3 Using a mixer, beat the butter in a large mixing bowl until light and fluffy, about 2 minutes. Add the sugar and mix together until smooth. In a small bowl, blend the eggs and sambuca together and add to the butter mixture. Stop occasionally and scrape down the sides of the bowl with a rubber spatula. Blend well. Add the dry ingredients from Step 2 in three stages, blending well. Stir in the chopped almonds.

4 Dust your hands with flour. Divide the dough into fourths. Shape each piece of dough into a log about 8 inches long x 2 inches wide x ¾ inch high. Place two logs on the cookie sheet, leaving a few inches of space between them. Bake for 30 to 35 minutes, until the edges are golden. Remove and cool for 15 minutes.

5 Transfer each log to a cutting board. Cut the logs on the diagonal into ½-inch-thick slices and place the slices on their sides on the cookie sheet. Bake for 10 to 12 minutes more, until firm. Remove the cookie sheet from the oven and transfer the cookies to racks to cool. Store in an airtight container at room temperature for up to 3 weeks. Freeze for longer storage.

Per serving: Calories 114 (From Fat 50); Fat 6g (Saturated 2g); Cholesterol 19mg; Sodium 36mg; Carbohydrate 14g (Dietary Fiber 1g); Protein 2g.

Chocolate-dipped biscotti

You can dip any biscotti in chocolate. And you can use any type of chocolate you prefer: white, milk, semisweet, or bittersweet. You can make chocolate-dipped biscotti by using one of the biscotti recipes in this chapter and then following these steps:

1. Take 8 ounces chocolate, chop it into matchstick-size pieces, and set aside one-third of it.

2. Melt the remaining two-thirds chocolate in the top of a double boiler over hot water, stirring frequently with a rubber spatula to ensure even melting.

3. Remove the double boiler from the heat, remove the top pan of the double boiler, and thoroughly dry the bottom and sides of the pan. Stir in the remaining chocolate in three batches, making sure that each batch is completely melted before adding the next.

4. When all the chocolate has been added, the chocolate will be ready for dipping. To test that it is not too hot, place a dab below your lower lip. It should feel comfortable, not too hot or too cool. If it's too hot, add a little more finely chopped chocolate until it feels comfortable. To hold the chocolate at the same temperature, place it over a shallow pan with water that is slightly warmer.

5. To dip the biscotti, line a cookie sheet with parchment or wax paper. Hold a cookie between your fingers and dip into the chocolate about halfway up the bar or along one end. Remove the cookie from the chocolate and let the excess drip off. To help remove the excess chocolate, tap the cookie very lightly against the side of the pan.

6. Place the cookie on the cookie sheet. When the cookie sheet is full, place it in the refrigerator for 10 minutes to set the chocolate.

Chapter 13

Molded Cookies

Molded cookies are made by using a couple different methods. Some molded cookies, like madeleines, are baked in the molds and then turned out while warm so they keep their designs. Molded cookies also can be made by pressing or rolling the dough into a floured mold and then tapping the mold out on a firm surface before baking. These cookies have embossed designs that give them extra eye appeal.

Cookie molds are made of wood, ceramic, or metal and are used to imprint decorative designs into cookie dough. They're available in a wide variety of shapes and sizes. Springerle cookies can also be molded by using a special type of rolling pin, described later in this chapter.

Keep your eye out for interesting cookies molds at antique stores and swap meets.

When your cookie molds are not being used for baking, they make great kitchen decorations. Hang them on the walls or display them on shelves. Keeping them out so you can see them is a great way to get inspired to bake. Cookie molds also make nice gifts for people who bake. Include a cookie mold in a basket of ingredients with a recipe for a specific cookie. This almost guarantees that you'll receive cookies in return. What could be better than that?

Keeping Your Shape

There are three types of molded cookies: those formed by pressing a shape or mold onto the dough to imprint the design, those made by fitting the dough into the mold and tapping it out before baking, and those baked in the mold. Molded cookies that are formed by imprinting the design on the dough and those that are shaped in the mold and turned out before baking are made from dough that is similar in texture to pie dough. That is, the dough is firm and easy to roll out. Madeleines are made from a thin dough that is baked in the molds. Springerle cookies, made by imprinting designs onto the dough, need to stand at room temperature for as long as 24 hours before they're baked so the designs set in the dough and won't spread in a hot oven. The dough for speculaas needs to be chilled for several hours before it's formed and baked so it's easy to work with and not too soft.

For cookies shaped in a mold and tapped out before baking, generously flour the mold and the surface of the dough before pressing the dough into the mold. Doing so helps keep the dough from sticking in the mold. Loosen one corner of the dough from the mold, using your fingertips. Holding the mold at a 45-degree angle towards a hard surface, such as a countertop or wood cutting board, tap the mold firmly but gently to release the cookie dough. Tapping the mold too hard can actually make the dough stick in the mold. If this happens, carefully remove it by using your fingertips and a rubber spatula. Knead the dough briefly and let it stand for about 20 minutes at room temperature to dry. Flour the mold and dough and press the dough into the mold. Once you get the hang of doing this, you'll be turning out cookies like a pro!

Don't tap the cookie mold so hard that it breaks.

Madeleines: Proust's Favorite Cookies

Madeleines are so special they made their mark in French history and literature. The Duke of Lorraine served them at his court in the 18th century. They are said to take their name from Madeleine, the girl who brought them to the Duke's court. Nineteenth-century novelist Marcel Proust wrote about how unforgettable the ones he ate as a child were. How can you go wrong? They resemble a small cake with a light, delicate texture but are consumed like a cookie, in two or three bites. Madeleines are perfect for afternoon tea. They take on the air of elegance because of their beautiful shell shape, which is imprinted on them as they bake.

Madeleines are made in a madeleine pan — a flat rectangular pan made of tinned-steel or aluminum with shell-shaped indentations that give madeleines a characteristic ribbed scallop-shell shape. Madeleine pans come in a variety of sizes. The most common pan has 12 indentations, each measuring 3 inches long x 1¾ inches wide x ½ inch deep. Other madeleine pans have as few as 8 or as many as 24 indentations. Madeleines are baked in the pans and turned out to cool shortly after coming from the oven.

You can bake madeleines in mini-muffin tins if you don't have madeleine pans. They won't look as attractive but will taste the same.

This chapter contains several recipes for madeleines. Basic madeleines are the classic ones that you can find in France in any pastry shop. They're very adaptable and are easy to vary by adding other ingredients, such as spices, nuts, and citrus, to the recipe. I love madeleines so much that I created recipes for dark chocolate, white chocolate, and almond variations. These recipes are different from the basic recipe, so it's important to follow the proportions of ingredients in each recipe when making them. In order to balance out texture and consistency in the baked madeleines, each recipe contains different amounts of eggs, flour, sugar, and butter. They're all delicious, so I highly recommend that you make each recipe — just not at the same time!

Spray madeleine pans with a nonstick coating or use a pastry brush to lightly coat them with butter. Then dust with flour and shake out the excess.

Basic Madeleines

This is a classic recipe for madeleines from which a number of variations can easily be created.

Specialty tools: *Two 12-cavity madeleine pans*

Preparation time: *15 minutes*

Baking time: *10 minutes*

Yield: *2 dozen*

4 eggs

¼ teaspoon salt

⅔ cup sugar

1 teaspoon vanilla extract

1 cup all-purpose flour

½ cup (1 stick) unsalted butter, melted and cooled

1 teaspoon lemon zest, finely minced

1 Preheat the oven to 400°. Spray the cavities of two 12-cavity madeleine pans with non-stick cooking spray and set aside briefly.

2 Using a mixer, beat the eggs with the salt in a large mixing bowl until they're foamy. Gradually add the sugar and whip the mixture at medium-high speed for about 5 minutes, until the mixture is pale colored and holds a slowly dissolving ribbon when the beater is lifted. Add the vanilla extract and blend in well.

3 Fold the flour into the mixture in three stages. Fold in the melted butter in three stages. Blend in the lemon zest.

4 Transfer the mixture to a 2-cup liquid measuring cup. Pour the batter into each cavity of the pans, filling them three-fourths full. (See Figure 13-1.) Place the pans on baking sheets. Bake for 10 minutes, until the madeleines are golden and spring back when touched.

5 Remove the cookie sheets from the oven and turn the madeleine pans upside down on cooling racks. Gently shake the pans to remove the madeleines. Cool completely on the racks. Store in an airtight container at room temperature for up to 3 days. Freeze for longer storage.

Per serving: Calories 87 (From Fat 42); Fat 5g (Saturated 3g); Cholesterol 46mg; Sodium 35mg; Carbohydrate 46g (Dietary Fiber 0g); Protein 2g.

MAKING MADELEINES

1. TRANSFER THE MIXTURE TO A 2 CUP LIQUID MEASURE. POUR THE BATTER INTO EACH CAVITY OF THE PANS, FILLING THEM 3/4 FULL.

2. PLACE THE PANS ON A BAKING SHEET. BAKE FOR 10 MINUTES UNTIL THEY ARE GOLDEN AND SPRING BACK WHEN TOUCHED.

3. REMOVE PANS FROM OVEN. TURN UPSIDE DOWN ON RACK. GENTLY SHAKE THE PAN TO REMOVE THE MADELEINES. COOL COMPLETELY ON RACKS.

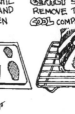

Figure 13-1:
Making
madeleines.

Whipping adds air to the batter, causing it to increase its volume. When a mixture is whipped until it becomes thick and pale, it is at the ribbon stage, shown in Figure 13-2. The thick batter forms a ribbonlike pattern when it's held above the bowl and drops back onto the surface. Whipping to this stage provides body and substance to the mixture by trapping air within it, which helps it rise as it bakes. You see this happen when cream or egg whites are whipped to soft peaks.

⊱Ribbon Stage⊰

or

Figure 13-2:
Determining
the ribbon
stage.

when you lift the beater out of the mixture it forms a ribbonlike pattern!

Draw a line in the middle of the mixture with your finger. If it stays, you're at ribbon stage!

Dark Chocolate Madeleines

This madeleine is the perfect treat for chocolate lovers. It's made with either bitter-sweet or semisweet chocolate. The bittersweet chocolate has a little less sugar than semisweet chocolate, giving it a deeper flavor. You can use whichever chocolate you prefer without having to adjust the ingredients in this recipe.

Specialty tools: *Two 12-cavity madeleine pans*

Preparation time: *25 minutes; includes time to melt chocolate*

Baking time: *12 minutes*

Yield: *2 dozen*

2½ ounces (½ cup) bittersweet or semisweet chocolate, finely chopped

6 tablespoons (¾ stick) unsalted butter, cut into pieces

2 eggs

⅓ cup sugar

⅛ teaspoon salt

½ cup all-purpose flour

½ teaspoon vanilla extract

1 Melt the chocolate and the butter together in the top pan of a double boiler over hot water. Stir often with a rubber spatula to ensure even melting.

2 Preheat the oven to 350°. Spray the cavities of two 12-cavity madeleine pans with non-stick cooking spray.

3 Using a mixer, whip the eggs and sugar on medium-high speed in a large mixing bowl until the mixture is very thick and holds a slowly dissolving ribbon as the beater is lifted, about 5 minutes.

4 In a separate mixing bowl, blend the salt into the flour and add to the eggs in three stages. Stop and scrape down the sides of the bowl with a rubber spatula after each addition. Add the chocolate and butter mixture and blend in thoroughly. Blend in the vanilla.

5 Transfer the mixture to a 2-cup liquid measuring cup. Pour the batter into each cavity of the pans, filling them three-fourths full. Bake for 12 to 15 minutes, until the madeleines are set and the tops spring back when lightly touched.

6 Remove the cookie sheets from the oven and turn the madeleine pans upside down onto cooling racks. Gently shake the pans to remove the madeleines. Cool completely on the racks. Store in an airtight container at room temperature for up to 3 days. Freeze for longer storage.

Per serving: *Calories 68 (From Fat 39); Fat 4g (Saturated 3g); Cholesterol 26mg; Sodium 18mg; Carbohydrate 6g (Dietary Fiber 0g); Protein 1g.*

White Chocolate Madeleines

For this recipe, buy white chocolate that is made with cocoa butter, which comes from the cocoa bean. Many people bake with and eat so-called white chocolate that's made with too much sugar and another vegetable fat other than cocoa butter, giving the chocolate a chalky texture. Seek out good-quality white chocolate, and your extra effort will be rewarded when you bite into one of these.

Specialty tools: *Two 12-cavity madeleine pans*

Preparation time: *25 minutes; includes time to melt chocolate*

Baking time: *12 minutes*

Yield: *3½ dozen*

4 ounces top-quality white chocolate, finely chopped	⅔ cup sugar
¾ cup (1½ sticks) unsalted butter	¼ teaspoon salt
4 eggs	1 cup all-purpose flour

1 Melt the white chocolate and butter together in the top of a double boiler over hot water. Stir often with a rubber spatula to ensure even melting.

2 Preheat the oven to 350°. Spray the cavities of two 12-cavity madeleine pans with non-stick cooking spray.

3 Using a mixer, whip the eggs and sugar on medium-high speed in a large mixing bowl until the mixture is very thick and holds a slowly dissolving ribbon as the beater is lifted, about 5 minutes.

4 In a separate mixing bowl, blend the salt into the flour and add to the egg mixture in three stages. Stop and scrape down the sides of the bowl with a rubber spatula after each addition. Add the white chocolate and butter mixture and blend in thoroughly.

5 Transfer the mixture to a 2-cup liquid measuring cup. Pour the batter into each cavity of the pans, filling them three-fourths full. Place the madeleine pans onto cookie sheets. Bake for 12 to 15 minutes, until the madeleines are set and golden.

6 Remove the cookie sheets from the oven and turn the madeleine pans upside down onto cooling racks. Let them stand for 5 minutes and gently shake the pans to remove the madeleines. Cool completely on the racks. Store in an airtight container at room temperature for up to 3 days. Freeze for longer storage.

Per serving: Calories 75 (From Fat 43); Fat 5g (Saturated 3g); Cholesterol 30mg; Sodium 23mg; Carbohydrate 7g (Dietary Fiber 0g); Protein 1g.

Almond Madeleines

I love the chewy texture that almond paste contributes to cookies. It easily explains why this is my favorite version of madeleines. When the texture of the batter is soft, as it is in this recipe, chilling it before pouring into the molds makes it easier to handle. The softness of the batter comes from the extra egg and the almond paste. Be sure to use almond paste, not marzipan, which has more sugar than almond paste.

Specialty tools: *Two 12-cavity madeleine pans*

Preparation time: *30 minutes*

Baking time: *8 minutes*

Yield: *2 dozen*

¾ cup (1½ sticks) unsalted butter

7-ounce roll of almond paste, cut into small pieces

1 cup sugar

5 eggs, lightly beaten

1 teaspoon almond extract

1 cup all-purpose flour

1 teaspoon baking powder

½ cup sliced almonds

1 Spray the cavities of two 12-cavity madeleine pans with nonstick cooking spray and set aside briefly.

2 Melt the butter in a small saucepan over low heat or on low power in a microwave oven. Using a mixer, beat the almond paste and sugar together on low speed in a large mixing bowl. Add the eggs and the almond extract. Beat the mixture until light and fluffy, about 3 minutes.

3 In a separate mixing bowl, sift the flour and baking powder together and gently fold the dry ingredients into the egg mixture. Fold in the melted butter in three stages. Refrigerate the mixture for 15 minutes before baking.

4 Preheat the oven to 425°. Place the madeleine pans on cookie sheets. Transfer the mixture to a 2-cup liquid measuring cup. Pour the batter into each cavity of the pans, filling them three-fourths full. Sprinkle the sliced almonds over the cookies.

5 Bake for 8 minutes, until golden. Remove the cookie sheets from the oven, turn the madeleine pans upside down on cooling racks, and gently shake to remove the madeleines. Cool completely on the racks. Store in an airtight container at room temperature for up to 3 days. Freeze for longer storage.

Per serving: Calories 169 (From Fat 92); Fat 10g (Saturated 4g); Cholesterol 60mg; Sodium 31mg; Carbohydrate 17g (Dietary Fiber 1g); Protein 3g.

Basic Madeleine recipe variations

The Basic Madeleine recipe lends itself to many scrumptious variations, as found in the following list:

✔ **Spicy Madeleines:** Blend together 1 teaspoon ground cinnamon, ½ teaspoon ground ginger, and ¼ teaspoon freshly grated nutmeg and add to the batter with the flour.

✔ **Double-Ginger Madeleines:** Add 2 teaspoons ground ginger and ½ cup finely diced crystallized ginger to the batter after folding in the butter.

✔ **Nut Madeleines:** Add ½ cup toasted, finely chopped nuts to the batter after folding in the butter.

✔ **Lemon Madeleines:** Add 1 teaspoon lemon extract and the finely minced zest of 2 large lemons to the batter after folding in the butter.

✔ **Orange Madeleines:** Add 1 teaspoon orange extract and ½ cup finely chopped candied orange peel to the batter after folding in the butter.

Making Spectacular Speculaas

Speculaas are spice cookies claimed by both Holland and Belgium as holiday classics. Traditionally they are made with decorative molds, but they're easy to make with any cookie cutter. They also can be cut into bars. Due to their crisp texture, they can be made in advance because they keep very well.

Speculaas molds are made in a variety of images, such as animals (birds, cats, and swans, for example), St. Nicholas, angels, knights, and other figures. They are traditionally made of carved wood and are collectors' items. Modern versions are easier to find these days than the antique ones. Many cookware shops, catalogs, and Web sites carry them seasonally for the winter holidays. Just as with other cookie molds, speculaas molds make beautiful kitchen decorations.

Speculaas take their name from the Dutch word for mirror. The molds used to make the cookies are designed to "mirror" images of the world.

To care for speculaas molds, use a large pastry brush to remove any excess flour left in them. If any dough is stuck to the mold, use your finger or a rubber spatula to remove it. Don't use any sharp instruments, which could scratch or cut the mold. Then wipe them out with a damp, soft cloth and dry thoroughly. Never immerse speculaas molds in water, which could cause them to warp.

Shaping speculaas is a lot of fun. After the dough is mixed and chilled, chunks are pinched off and rolled into golf-ball-size pieces. Each ball of dough is pressed or rolled with a rolling pin firmly into a prepared mold. Apply enough pressure so that the dough spreads out, filling the entire mold, including all crevices. This ensures that the design of the mold is imprinted onto the dough. Hold the mold at an angle and firmly tap it against a hard surface to release the dough. Gently transfer the cookie to a baking sheet. If there is excess dough around the rim of the design, use a small sharp knife to carefully cut out the shape. Use a large pastry brush to remove any excess flour left on the cookies.

Lightly dust speculaas and springerle molds with flour before pressing the dough into them.

Speculaas

This recipe for speculaas is a classic that I collected during a Christmas holiday trip to Belgium. If you don't have molds to make these, you can use ceramic cookie molds found in many cookware shops and catalogs. Even without molds, you can still make these cookies by cutting them into rectangles or using cookie cutters. Simply roll out the dough between lightly floured sheets of wax paper to a large rectangle about ¼-inch thick. Trim the edges of the dough evenly. Use a ruler to mark rectangles 2 inches long x 3 inches wide. Transfer the rectangles to the lined baking sheets, leaving 1 inch of space between them. Gather any scraps together and chill briefly if they're soft. Roll out the dough and cut into rectangles. Repeat with the remaining half of the dough. If using cookie cutters, dip them in flour occasionally to keep them from sticking.

Specialty tools: *Speculaas molds or cookie cutters. If making bars, you need a ruler.*

Preparation time: *20 minutes*

Baking time: *9 minutes*

Yield: *3½ dozen*

2 cups all-purpose flour	*½ cup finely ground almonds*
1 teaspoon baking powder	*½ cup plus 1 tablespoon (1⅛ sticks) unsalted butter, softened*
1¼ teaspoons ground cinnamon	
½ teaspoon ground cardamom	*¼ cup superfine sugar*
½ teaspoon ground cloves	*⅓ cup light brown sugar*
¼ teaspoon ground nutmeg, preferably freshly ground or grated	*1 egg*
	Zest of 1 large lemon, finely minced or grated
¼ teaspoon salt	*½ cup sliced or slivered almonds*

1 Preheat the oven to 350°. Line a cookie sheet with parchment paper. Sift together the flour, baking powder, cinnamon, cardamom, and cloves and toss with the nutmeg, salt, and ground almonds.

2 Using a mixer, beat the butter in a large mixing bowl until soft and fluffy, about 1 minute. Add the superfine sugar and brown sugar and mix together until smooth. In a small bowl, lightly beat the egg and add to the mixture. Blend in the lemon zest. Stop occasionally and scrape down the sides of the bowl with a rubber spatula.

3 Add the dry ingredients from Step 1 in three to four stages, blending well after each addition. Divide the dough in half. Form each half into a flat disk, wrap in plastic wrap, and refrigerate for 2 to 3 hours. Keep one half refrigerated while working with the other half.

4 Prepare the cookie molds by dusting them with flour. Pinch off large pieces of dough and roll each into a golf-ball-size piece. (See Figure 13-3.) Place a ball of dough in the center of the cookie mold and firmly press or roll out the dough into the mold. Then lightly tap the mold on a countertop to release the cookie. Place the cookies on the cookie sheet. Sprinkle a few sliced or slivered almonds on each cookie and press gently so they will stick.

5 Bake the cookies for 9 to 11 minutes, until the cookies are golden and set. Remove the cookie sheet from the oven and transfer the cookies to racks to cool. Store the cookies in an airtight container at room temperature for up to 3 months.

Per serving: Calories 80 (From Fat 45); Fat 5g (Saturated 2g); Cholesterol 12mg; Sodium 25mg; Carbohydrate 8g (Dietary Fiber 1g); Protein 2g.

Figure 13-3:
Making
Speculaas.

Springing into Springerle

Springerle are classic German Christmas cookies flavored with anise seeds. They originated in Swabia, a historic region of Germany, in the 15th century. Springerle are usually made by imprinting designs on the dough with an engraved rolling pin or carved wooden molds. They are then left to dry overnight at room temperature before baking so the dough will hold the design, which is raised and stands out from the dough. These cookies are traditionally crisp and eggshell colored.

A springerle rolling pin is a type of wooden rolling pin that has designs carved into it. These designs protrude from the rolling pin and imprint the dough as the pin rolls. To prevent sticking, dust the top of the dough and the rolling pin lightly with flour before rolling the dough. Each design on the rolling pin is contained within a rectangle or square shape. After rolling the dough, cut along the lines to separate the cookies into the imprinted rectangles or squares.

Never put your springerle rolling pin in the dishwasher. It could crack or warp and become uneven.

To care for your springerle rolling pin, use a large pastry brush to remove any excess flour that may have collected in the designs. If any dough is stuck to the pin, use your finger or a rubber spatula to remove it. Don't use a knife or any other sharp tools, which could scratch or cut the pin. Wipe off the rolling pin with a damp, soft cloth and dry thoroughly. Store rolling pins on a flat surface, either in a drawer or on a cabinet shelf.

Shaping springerle, shown in Figure 13-4, is as easy as can be. It's all in the imprinted rolling pin or molds. After the dough is mixed, it's rolled out on a flat surface with a regular rolling pin. Then the springerle rolling pin is rolled over the surface of the dough, imprinting its designs. If a mold is used, it is pressed onto the dough to leave its design. After either of these is used, separate the rectangles or squares of dough with a sharp knife and transfer the cookies to a baking sheet. Springerle need to air-dry for at least 12 hours before they're baked to ensure that the designs will hold their shape as they bake.

The typical designs on springerle rolling pins and molds are items found in nature, such as birds and flowers. Often a large heart holds smaller designs of birds or flowers inside of it. I've seen some molds with a small cornucopia and one with a sailboat. Antique springerle molds and rolling pins can be hard to obtain. However, you can find modern ones at some cookware shops and through catalogs and Web sites (see Appendix B for sources).

Cookie stamps

Cookie stamps are a great way to imprint designs onto cookie dough. Here's how to use cookie stamps:

1. **Roll the cookie dough into a small ball about the size of a walnut.**

2. **Place the ball of cookie dough onto a parchment-paper-lined or greased and floured cookie sheet.**

3. **Place the cookie stamp on top of the ball of cookie dough and press firmly and evenly to flatten out the ball of dough.**

If the cookie stamp sticks to the dough, lightly dip it in flour and then shake it off to remove any excess.

You can use cookie stamps to make the Coconut Butter Balls, Cardamom-Orange Nut Balls, and Classic Sugar Cookies, all in Chapter 12; the Springerle and Speculaas in this chapter; and the Lebkuchen in Chapter 14.

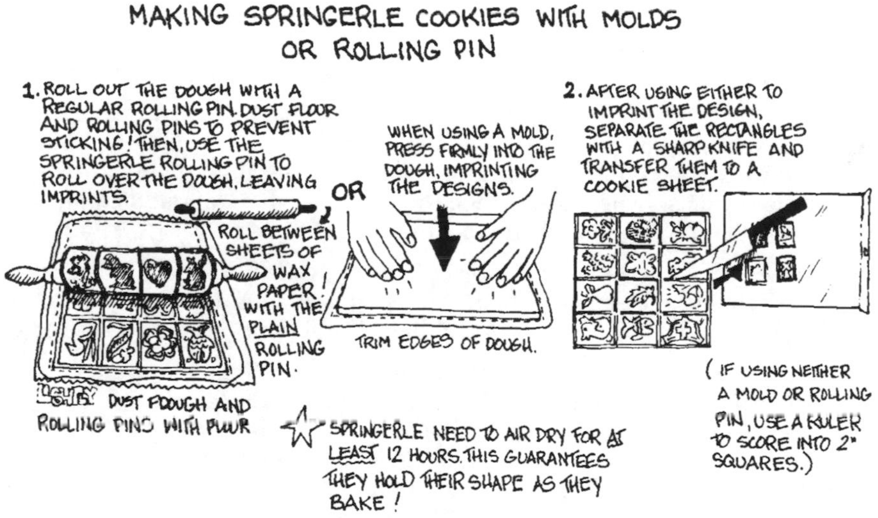

Figure 13-4: Making Springerle cookies with molds or a rolling pin.

MAKING SPRINGERLE COOKIES WITH MOLDS OR ROLLING PIN

1. ROLL OUT THE DOUGH WITH A REGULAR ROLLING PIN. DUST FLOUR AND ROLLING PINS TO PREVENT STICKING! THEN, USE THE SPRINGERLE ROLLING PIN TO ROLL OVER THE DOUGH, LEAVING IMPRINTS.

ROLL BETWEEN SHEETS OF WAX PAPER! WITH THE PLAIN ROLLING PIN.

DUST DOUGH AND ROLLING PINS WITH FLOUR

WHEN USING A MOLD, PRESS FIRMLY INTO THE DOUGH, IMPRINTING THE DESIGNS.

OR

TRIM EDGES OF DOUGH.

SPRINGERLE NEED TO AIR DRY FOR AT LEAST 12 HOURS. THIS GUARANTEES THEY HOLD THEIR SHAPE AS THEY BAKE!

2. AFTER USING EITHER TO IMPRINT THE DESIGN, SEPARATE THE RECTANGLES WITH A SHARP KNIFE AND TRANSFER THEM TO A COOKIE SHEET.

(IF USING NEITHER A MOLD OR ROLLING PIN, USE A RULER TO SCORE INTO 2" SQUARES.)

Springerle

Springerle are crisp cookies that can be made as much as 3 months in advance because their flavor improves with age. If you don't own a springerle rolling pin or molds, you can still make these cookies by cutting the dough into squares.

Specialty tools: *Regular rolling pin, springerle rolling pin or springerle molds. If making bars, you need a ruler.*

Preparation time: *15 minutes, plus 24 hours rest time*

Baking time: *16 minutes*

Yield: *3 dozen*

1 tablespoon unsalted butter, for the pans

2 teaspoons anise seed

2 eggs

2 cups confectioners' sugar, sifted

1 teaspoon anise extract, or 1 tablespoon dark rum

Zest of 1 medium lemon, finely minced or grated

2 cups all-purpose flour

1 teaspoon baking powder

1 teaspoon anise seed, crushed

1 Line a cookie sheet with parchment paper and butter the paper. Scatter a teaspoon of anise seed over the cookie sheet.

2 Using a mixer, whip the eggs on medium-high speed in a large mixing bowl until frothy. Slowly add the confectioners' sugar and whip together until the mixture is pale and holds a slowly dissolving ribbon when the beater is lifted, about 8 minutes. Add the extract or rum and lemon zest and blend thoroughly.

3 Sift together the flour and baking powder and toss with the crushed anise seed. Add the dry ingredients to the egg mixture in three to four stages, blending well after each addition. Stop occasionally to scrape down the sides of the bowl with a rubber spatula.

4 Using a regular rolling pin, roll out the dough between lightly floured sheets of wax paper to form a large rectangle about ¼-inch thick. Trim the edges of the dough evenly. Use a springerle rolling pin to imprint the cookies and use a sharp knife to separate them. Transfer the cookies to the cookie sheet, leaving 1 inch between the cookies. If using springerle molds, dust the molds with flour and firmly press the mold onto the dough and pull it off. Transfer the cookies to the cookie sheet. If using neither a springerle rolling pin nor molds, use a ruler to score the cookies into 2-inch squares and proceed.

5 Let the cookies rest overnight uncovered at room temperature. The next day, preheat the oven to 300°. Bake the cookies for 16 to 18 minutes, until set. Remove the cookie sheet from the oven and place on a cooling rack. When the cookies are completely cooled, store them, along with any loose anise seed from the baking sheets, in an airtight container at room temperature for up to 3 months.

Per serving: *Calories 55 (From Fat 6); Fat 1g (Saturated 0g); Cholesterol 13mg; Sodium 14mg; Carbohydrate 11g (Dietary Fiber 0g); Protein 1g.*

Part V

Cookies of Distinction

In this part . . .

If you're looking for a special cookie, this is the place to be. Here you find a variety of cookies that not only are delicious but also look fabulous. Cookies with an international flair, holiday cookies, chocolate cookies, big cookies, cookies for kids, and cookies to help you stay slim and trim are in this part. I have selected many of my personal favorites that are easy and quick to prepare and have a track record of high satisfaction.

Chapter 14

International Specialties

In This Chapter

▷ Getting acquainted with international cookies

▷ Discovering the tasty appeal of cookies from other cultures

Recipes in This Chapter

▷ Husar Rounds
▷ Mexican Wedding Cakes
▷ Chinese Almond Cookies
▷ Pinolate (Italian Pine Nut Cookies)
▷ Walnut Mandelbrot
▷ Pizzelles
▷ Bizochitos

*J*ust about every cuisine of the world has a well-known and beloved cookie. Because so many of these international cookies are so popular in the United States, you may be surprised to learn that some of these cookies really did originate in other countries. Biscotti, pizzelles, and rugelach, for example, are all native to other countries but have become favorites in the United States.

Cookies Are Everywhere!

Some cookies are named for their countries of origin, such as Mexican Wedding Cakes and Greek Butter Cookies. Many holiday cookies, such as those found in Chapter 15, are also international classics. They're usually made only once a year, so people look forward to making them. These cookies often have baking rituals, emotional connections, and fond family memories attached to them. Many of them are heirloom recipes.

Most cultures have their favorites, such as Husar Rounds from Austria and Pinolate from Italy. International cookies cross over into many of the other cookie categories in this book, such as rolled cookies or molded cookies. Examples include Sables, the French classic rolled cookies found in Chapter 6, and the Madeleines from France, Speculaas from Holland and Belgium, and Springerle from Germany, all molded cookie recipes found in Chapter 13.

The United Nations of Cookies

There are so many great cookies in the world that selecting cookies for this chapter wasn't easy. The ones you find here, I will have to admit, are my personal favorites and include cookie recipes from Europe, Mexico, and Asia. These cookies will probably be familiar to you because they're popular in the United States as well as in their countries of origin. When I get a request for international cookies, these are the ones I make. You don't have to wait for a particular occasion to serve them. They're perfect anytime. And it's always gratifying when someone says, "This is just like the cookie I ate in (Italy or Germany or wherever the cookie originated)."

Husar Rounds

These Austrian specialties are similar to thumbprint cookies. They have an indentation in the center that holds apricot or raspberry preserves. When I was traveling in Austria several years ago, these became one of my favorite cookies. I was able to obtain the recipe by asking a lot of questions of some of the Austrian bakers in the pastry shops I visited.

Preparation time: *25 minutes, plus 12 hours rest time*

Baking time: *10 minutes*

Yield: *5 dozen*

½ cup plus 2 tablespoons (1¼ sticks) unsalted butter, softened	*2½ cups all-purpose flour*
½ cup plus 1 tablespoon sugar	*¾ cup toasted, skinned, and finely ground hazelnuts*
2 egg yolks	*1 cup apricot or raspberry preserves*
½ teaspoon vanilla extract	*Confectioners' sugar for garnish*

1 Using a mixer, beat the butter in a large mixing bowl until light and fluffy, about 1 minute. Add the sugar and mix together until smooth.

2 In a separate bowl, gently whisk the egg yolks with the vanilla and add to the butter mixture, blending well. Scrape down the sides of the bowl frequently during mixing.

3 Stir in the flour and the hazelnuts and beat until thoroughly mixed. Wrap the dough in plastic wrap and chill overnight.

4 Preheat the oven to 350°. Line a cookie sheet with parchment paper. Break off 1-inch pieces of the dough and shape into balls. With your finger, make a deep indentation in the center. Place on the lined cookie sheets, leaving 1 inch between the cookies. Bake for 10 minutes, until golden. Remove the cookie sheet from the oven and transfer the cookies to cooling racks.

5 Dust the cookies lightly with confectioners' sugar. Put a dab of preserves in the center of each cookie, being careful not to ovefill. Store in a single layer in an airtight container at room temperature for up to 4 days.

Tip: *To toast hazelnuts, place them in a single layer in a shallow pan with a lip, such as a jelly roll pan. Toast them in a preheated 350° oven for 15 to 18 minutes. You'll be able to tell they're ready because you'll smell their appetizing aroma, the skins will split open, and the nuts will be light golden brown. Remove the baking pan from the oven and transfer the warm hazelnuts to a kitchen towel. Wrap the towel around the nuts and let them steam for about 10 minutes. Then rub the nuts in the towel to help remove the skins.*

Per serving: *Calories 80 (From Fat 38); Fat 4g (Saturated 1g); Cholesterol 12mg; Sodium 3mg; Carbohydrate 10g (Dietary Fiber 1g); Protein 1g.*

A brief history of cookies

The exact origin of cookies isn't really known. One thought is that small cookielike cakes come from Persia, where sugar was cultivated in the seventh century. Some food historians say that cookies come from Greece, where little flat cakes were made from mixtures of flour and honey many hundreds of years ago. Other food historians speculate that cookies are derived from hard, baked pieces of dough that traveled with sailors and soldiers in medieval times. And some say that French petit fours (translating to "little ovens") are the forerunners of elegant or fancy cookies. Petit fours were baked at the end of the day when the ovens were turned off to cool. The lower temperatures were just right for these small cookielike cakes.

Mexican Wedding Cakes

These familiar buttery gems are served at festive occasions in Mexico. The cookies are of Arab origin and are found in many other countries of the world under different names. They're a close cousin to Kourambiedes, also known as Greek Butter Cookies (see Chapter 15). Sometimes they have nuts, as they do here, but other recipes leave the nuts out.

Preparation time: *20 minutes*

Baking time: *20 minutes*

Yield: *2½ dozen*

1 cup (2 sticks) unsalted butter, softened	*2⅓ cups all-purpose flour*
2 cups confectioners' sugar	*Pinch of salt*
2 teaspoons vanilla extract	*1 cup pecans, finely chopped*

1 Preheat the oven to 350°. Line a cookie sheet with parchment paper.

2 Using a mixer, beat the butter in a large bowl until light and fluffy, about 1 minute. Add ½ cup of the confectioners' sugar and mix together until smooth. Blend in the vanilla.

3 Stir the flour, salt, and pecans together. Add to the mixture in three stages and blend thoroughly. Break off walnut-size pieces of the dough and shape into balls. Place on the cookie sheet, leaving 1 inch of space between the cookies. Bake for 20 to 25 minutes, until golden and set. Let the cookies cool for 3 to 4 minutes on the cookie sheet.

4 Sift ¾ cup of the confectioners' sugar onto another cookie sheet. Transfer the cookies to the cookie sheet with the sugar and sift the remaining ¾ cup confectioners' sugar over them. Let the cookies cool completely and then roll them in the confectioners' sugar. Store in the confectioners' sugar in an airtight container at room temperature for up to a week.

Per serving: Calories 141 (From Fat 79); Fat 9g (Saturated 4g); Cholesterol 17mg; Sodium 6mg; Carbohydrate 15g (Dietary Fiber 1g); Protein 1g.

Chinese Almond Cookies

Classic Chinese almond cookies are made with lard. I make these with butter, which sacrifices some of the tenderness but benefits the flavor. My good friend Lily Loh makes these for Christmas and other festive occasions. To make Chinese Five-Spice Almond Cookies, a variation of these cookies, add 1 teaspoon of five-spice powder to the flour before adding it to the dough.

Preparation time: *12 minutes*

Baking time: *13 minutes*

Yield: *2½ dozen*

1 cup all-purpose flour	*½ teaspoon vanilla extract*
¼ cup baking powder	*½ teaspoon almond extract*
½ cup (1 stick) unsalted butter, softened	*¼ cup blanched whole almonds*
⅔ cup sugar	*¼ cup water*
1 egg yolk at room temperature	

1 Preheat the oven to 350°. Line a cookie sheet with parchment paper.

2 In a mixing bowl, combine the flour and baking powder. Using a mixer, beat the butter in a large bowl until light and fluffy, about 1 minute. Add the sugar and mix together until smooth. In a small bowl, gently whisk the egg yolk with the vanilla and almond extracts and add to the mixture, blending well. Add the dry ingredients to the butter mixture in three stages and blend thoroughly.

3 Break off walnut-size pieces of the dough and shape into balls. Place on the cookie sheet, leaving an inch of space between the cookies. Place an almond in the center of each cookie and gently press the balls into rounds.

4 Gently brush the tops of the cookies with water. The water acts as a glaze and helps the top of the cookies brown and develop their characteristic crackly texture. Bake for 13 to 15 minutes, until golden and set. Remove the cookie sheet from the oven and cool on a rack for a few minutes. Use a metal spatula to transfer the cookies to racks to cool completely. Store in an airtight container at room temperature for up to a week. Freeze for longer storage.

Per serving: *Calories 49 (From Fat 25); Fat 3g (Saturated 1g); Cholesterol 11mg; Sodium 109mg; Carbohydrate 11g (Dietary Fiber 0g); Protein 1g.*

Pinolate (Italian Pine Nut Cookies)

These classic Italian cookies showcase Italy's famous pine nuts. They're chewy inside and crisp outside, similar to a macaroon. I first ate pinolate (pea-no-LAH-tay), which is also spelled "pignolati," many years ago when I traveled in Italy.

Preparation time: *10 minutes*

Baking time: *15 minutes*

Yield: *2 dozen*

2 cups finely ground almonds

1½ cups sugar

3 egg whites at room temperature

¼ teaspoon almond extract

2 to 3 cups pine nuts

1 Place an oven rack in the upper third of the oven. Preheat the oven to 375°. Line a cookie sheet with parchment paper.

2 Using a mixer, combine the ground almonds and sugar in a large bowl. Stir to blend. Add the egg whites and almond extract and blend thoroughly. The dough will be sticky.

3 Place the pine nuts in a shallow bowl. Roll walnut-size spoonfuls of the dough into balls. Roll the balls in the pine nuts and press in the nuts gently with your fingertips. Place the balls on the lined cookie sheet, leaving 2 inches space between the cookies.

4 Bake for 15 minutes, until the cookies and nuts are golden. Remove the cookie sheet from the oven and use a metal spatula to transfer the cookies to racks to cool. Store in an airtight container at room temperature for up to one week. Freeze for longer storage.

Per serving: Calories 144 (From Fat 91); Fat 10g (Saturated 1g); Cholesterol 0mg; Sodium 4mg; Carbohydrate 11g (Dietary Fiber 2g); Protein 5g.

Walnut Mandelbrot

I grew up eating these Eastern European cookies, which are one of my mother's specialties. She always has a fresh batch waiting when I visit her. Mandelbrot are crispy twice-baked cookies, like Italian biscotti, but they have a classic cinnamon-sugar coating.

Preparation time: *3½ hours; includes chilling*

Baking time: *40 minutes; includes resting*

Yield: *About 4 dozen*

3 cups all-purpose flour	*1 cup sugar*
1 teaspoon baking powder	*3 eggs*
1 teaspoon baking soda	*2 teaspoons vanilla extract*
1 cup (2 sticks) unsalted butter, softened	*½ cup roughly chopped walnuts*
2 tablespoons unflavored vegetable oil	

Garnish

2 teaspoons sugar

1 teaspoon cinnamon

1 Sift together the flour, baking powder, and baking soda. Line a cookie sheet with parchment paper.

2 Using a mixer, beat the butter until light, about 1 minute. Add the oil and mix together until smooth. Add the sugar and beat until fluffy, about 1 minute.

3 In a separate bowl, lightly beat the eggs with the vanilla and add to the butter mixture. Beat until well combined, about 2 minutes. Add the dry ingredients from Step 1 in three or four stages, blending well after each addition. Stir in the walnuts. Divide the dough in two and wrap each piece in plastic. Chill for at least 3 hours, until firm.

4 Preheat the oven to 325°. Work with one half of the dough while keeping the other in the refrigerator. Divide each half of the dough into three equal pieces. Shape each piece into a log about 8 inches long and 2 to 3 inches wide. Place three logs on the cookie sheet, leaving at least 2 inches between the logs. Combine the sugar and cinnamon for the garnish in a small bowl and toss to blend. Sprinkle the tops of each log evenly with the mixture. Bake for 20 to 23 minutes, until golden. Remove the cookie sheet from the oven and cool on a rack for 10 minutes.

5 Use a serrated-edge knife to cut each strip into ½-inch-wide slices. Arrange the slices on their sides on the cookie sheet. Return to the oven and bake for another 10 minutes, until crisp. Remove the cookie sheet from the oven and transfer the cookies to racks to cool. Store the cookies in an airtight container at room temperature for up to a week. Freeze for longer storage.

Per serving: Calories 97 (From Fat 50); Fat 6g (Saturated 3g); Cholesterol 24mg; Sodium 39mg; Carbohydrate 11g (Dietary Fiber 0g); Protein 1g.

Mandelbrot variations

Making variations of the Walnut Mandelbrot recipe in this chapter is easy. All you do is add one or two ingredients to the main recipe. Here are some of my favorite variations:

✔ **Lemon Mandelbrot:** Reduce the vanilla extract to 1 teaspoon. Add 1 teaspoon lemon extract and the zest of 2 large lemons, finely minced, to the batter when adding the vanilla extract.

✔ **Orange Mandelbrot:** Substitute orange extract and orange zest for the lemon extract and lemon zest.

✔ **Cranberry Mandelbrot:** Add ½ cup chopped dried cranberries to the batter when adding the walnuts.

✔ **Dried Cherry Mandelbrot:** Add ½ cup chopped dried sour cherries to the batter when adding the walnuts.

✔ **Chocolate Chip Mandelbrot:** Add ½ cup chocolate chips to the batter when adding the walnuts.

✔ **Raisin Mandelbrot:** Add ½ cup raisins to the batter when adding the walnuts.

Pizzelles

Pizzelles are classic Italian wafer cookies. They're baked on a specially designed iron that imprints them with a lacy design (for more information on the iron, see Chapter 2). Pizzelle irons are available in the cookware section of department stores, in cookware shops, and through mail order catalogs. Some pizzelle irons have a double design, enabling you to make two at one time. Pizzelles are very versatile and can be formed into different shapes while warm. You can make them into cones for ice cream, roll them into cylinders, or fit them into cups to make a lacy container for ice cream, sorbet, or mousse. They're also great to use as wafers for ice cream sandwiches. Or make a sandwich with a filling of whipped cream or store-bought lemon curd and fresh strawberries or raspberries.

Specialty tool: *Pizzelle iron*

Preparation time: *20 minutes*

Baking time: *1 minute*

Yield: *2½ dozen*

½ cup plus 2 tablespoons (1¼ sticks) unsalted butter

2 cups all-purpose flour

1 teaspoon baking powder

2 eggs

¾ cup sugar

1 teaspoon anise extract

1 teaspoon vanilla extract

Unflavored vegetable oil to brush the pizzelle iron

1 Melt the butter in a small saucepan over medium heat. Combine the flour and baking powder in a medium bowl.

2 Using a mixer, whip the eggs in a large bowl until frothy. Add the sugar and beat until the mixture is very thick and holds a slowly dissolving ribbon as the beater is lifted, about 5 minutes. Add the melted butter and blend well. Stir in the anise and vanilla extracts. Add the dry ingredients from Step 1 in three stages, blending well after each addition.

3 Follow the instructions for the pizzelle iron you're using (see Figure 14-1). Heat the iron and brush the grids lightly with the vegetable oil before baking the first pizzelle. Pour a generous teaspoon of batter in the center of each pattern on the pizzelle baker. Close the iron and bake for approximately 1 minute, until golden. Use a flexible-blade spatula to remove each pizzelle from the iron. Lay flat to cool on a rack or immediately shape as desired and then cool. Store in an airtight container at room temperature for up to 4 days. Freeze for longer storage.

Per serving: Calories 93 (From Fat 42); Fat 5g (Saturated 3g); Cholesterol 25mg; Sodium 18mg; Carbohydrate 11g (Dietary Fiber 0g); Protein 1g.

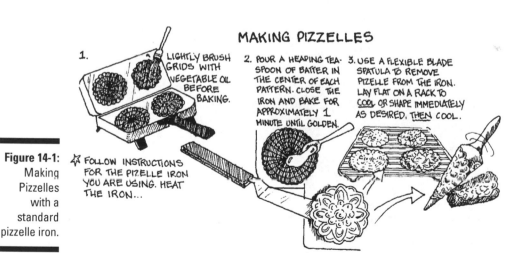

Figure 14-1: Making Pizzelles with a standard pizzelle iron.

Pizzelles with pizzazz

To add extra flavor to basic pizzelles and to make variations, all you have to do is substitute one ingredient for another. Here's a list of some delicious variations. Use a flavor in the pizzelles that complements the filling you plan to use. Orange and lemon go very well with fresh fruit. Here's where you can get creative!

- **Orange Pizzelles:** Eliminate the anise extract. Add 1 teaspoon orange extract and the finely minced zest of 1 large orange.

- **Lemon Pizzelles:** Eliminate the anise extract. Add 1 teaspoon lemon extract and the finely minced zest of 1 large lemon.

- **Cinnamon Pizzelles:** Eliminate the anise extract. Add 1 teaspoon ground cinnamon when adding the flour.

- **Cardamom Pizzelles:** Eliminate the anise extract. Add 1 teaspoon ground cardamom when adding the flour.

- **Five-Spice Pizzelles:** Eliminate the anise extract. Add 1 teaspoon ground five-spice powder when adding the flour.

- **Chocolate Pizzelles:** Reduce the flour to 1¾ cups and add ¼ cup unsweetened cocoa powder, sifted after measuring, to the flour.

Bizochitos

These anise-flavored holiday cookies are found throughout the Southwestern United States and in Mexico. The traditional shape is a fleur-de-lis, but you can cut the cookies into any shape you choose.

Specialty tools: *3-inch fleur-de-lis cookie cutter (or other variety)*

Preparation time: *20 minutes*

Baking time: *10 minutes*

Yield: *3½ dozen*

2 cups all-purpose flour

2 teaspoons anise seed, crushed

½ teaspoon baking powder

⅛ teaspoon salt

¾ cup plus 2 tablespoons (1¾ sticks) unsalted butter, softened

⅔ cup sugar

1 egg

1 teaspoon vanilla extract

Zest of 1 large lemon, finely minced

Decoration

2 teaspoons sugar

1 teaspoon ground cinnamon

1 Preheat the oven to 375°. Line a cookie sheet with parchment paper.

2 In a mixing bowl, combine the flour, anise seed, baking powder, and salt.

3 Using a mixer, beat the butter in a large bowl until fluffy, about 1 minute. Add the ⅔ cup sugar and mix together until smooth. In a small bowl, mix the egg with the vanilla and the lemon zest. Add to the butter mixture and blend well. Add the dry ingredients in three stages, blending well after each addition.

4 Divide the dough in half. Work with one portion while keeping the other refrigerated. Roll out each section of dough between sheets of floured wax paper until the dough is about ⅛-inch thick. If the dough is soft, transfer it to a cookie sheet and chill in the freezer for 15 minutes. Gently peel off both pieces of wax paper. Use a 3-inch cutter to cut out shapes. Transfer them to the cookie sheet, leaving 1 inch between the cookies.

5 Mix the 2 teaspoons sugar and the cinnamon together in a small bowl. Sprinkle on top of the cookies, taking care not to sprinkle the mixture on the cookie sheet.

6 Bake for 10 to 12 minutes, until golden and set. Remove the cookie sheet from the oven and transfer the cookies to cooling racks. Store in an airtight container at room temperature for up to a week. Freeze for longer storage.

Per serving: Calories 71 (From Fat 36); Fat 4g (Saturated 2g); Cholesterol 15mg; Sodium 14mg; Carbohydrate 8g (Dietary Fiber 0g); Protein 1g.

Chapter 15

Cookies to Celebrate the Holidays

In This Chapter

▶ Celebrating the holidays with traditional cookies

▶ Making your holiday cookies look their best

▶ Sampling cookies from around the world

Holiday time is cookie time. Cookies are a tradition during most holiday celebrations. I can't imagine attending a holiday celebration that doesn't offer cookies. For one thing, everybody expects to have cookies and you wouldn't want to disappoint anyone. Also, cookies accent a celebration by providing sweet treats that are easy to handle. And, for the maker of the cookies, it's a whole lot simpler to make cookies than to put together elaborate desserts.

Several different types of cookies can be made for holidays and celebrations. Actually, I like to make an assortment of cookies for various holidays and celebrations. Butter cookies are a favorite for holidays. They can be made in many different shapes and decorated in a wide variety of ways. Cookies made with spices and sugar cookies are also favorites.

Try to match the cookies to the particular occasion. Sugar cookies are perfect for this because they lend themselves to being shaped and decorated to match a seasonal or celebration theme. Also, think about who will be at the celebration and what you think they might like. However, it's easy to please with cookies, so don't worry too much about it.

Holiday Baking Tips

There's always way too much to do during the holiday season. I like to think of cookie baking as one of my favorite stress relievers. Homemade cookies are wonderful holiday gifts. You can accomplish two things at once (baking and gift making) if you plan to give cookies as gifts, and you don't have to go to the mall to do it! Wrapping and packaging cookies is part of the gift, as well. Keep your eyes open for interesting plates, tins, or other containers (see Chapter 23 for packaging ideas).

To make holiday baking easy, stay organized. Make a list of the people you plan to give cookies to. Then make a list of the cookies you want to bake. I like to give an assortment of three or four cookies as a holiday gift. A cookie exchange is a great way to get together with friends and acquire a variety of cookies.

One of the nice parts of baking is that many recipes can be made in steps. You can mix the dough one day and bake it another. If you really want to get a jump-start on holiday cookie baking, you can mix and freeze many cookie doughs. Then all you'll have to do is bake and decorate the cookies when the season draws closer.

Some recipes for holiday cookies can be made a month or more in advance, giving the cookies time to mellow. Read over the recipes you plan to bake to see which ones you can prepare in advance and then make a list of the order for baking the cookies. Finally, make a shopping list of ingredients and any equipment you might need. Following these steps will alleviate some pressure and worry and make holiday baking fun.

Holiday Cookies from Around the World

There are traditional cookies made for Christmas, many of which originated in countries around the world (see Chapter 14 for international cookies). Macaroons are always made for Passover (see Chapter 5). Cookies that work well to celebrate many holidays such as Halloween, Chanukah, Valentine's Day, and Easter are rolled sugar cookies (see Chapter 6) cut into particular shapes and decorated in the spirit of the day (see Chapter 21 for decorating ideas). And, of course, most chocolate and chocolate-dipped cookies (see Chapter 16 for recipes and Chapter 20 for chocolate decorating ideas) are ideal for Valentine's Day. Ischl Tartlets (see Chapter 9) cut into heart shapes are perfect for Valentine's Day, as well.

In general, cookies for holiday celebrations have a tradition behind them or are made and decorated in shapes appropriate for each particular holiday. Of course, you can start your own family traditions and make a particular cookie that is served at your holiday celebrations. Don't forget to show off your holiday cookies to their best advantage. After all, it is a special occasion.

Kourambiedes (Greek Butter Cookies)

These classic cookies are always part of the Greek Christmas holiday celebrations, which is celebrated on the Gregorian calendar and comes after December 25. Kourambiedes (koo-rah-bee-YAY-dehs) are so tender that they practically melt in the mouth. Rosewater, an optional ingredient in these cookies, is used often in Greek and Turkish cuisine. It has a distinct yet delicate flavor. Buy edible-quality rosewater, which is available at many cookware shops, at shops that specialize in Middle Eastern ingredients, or through mail-order catalogs.

Preparation time: *15 minutes*

Baking time: *11 minutes*

Yield: *About 4 dozen*

1 cup (2 sticks) unsalted butter, softened

3½ cups confectioners' sugar, sifted

1 egg yolk

2 tablespoons brandy or cognac

1 teaspoon vanilla extract

2½ to 2¾ cups all-purpose flour

1 teaspoon baking powder

2 to 3 tablespoons rosewater (optional)

1 Preheat the oven to 350°. In a large mixing bowl, beat the butter with a mixer until fluffy, about 5 minutes. Gradually add ½ cup of the confectioners' sugar and blend in the egg yolk, the brandy or cognac, and vanilla extract. Stop and scrape down the sides of the bowl with a rubber spatula a few times during the mixing.

2 Sift together the flour and baking powder and then add to the butter mixture in four or five batches, making sure that each batch is well blended before adding the next. Stop and scrape down the sides of the bowl with a rubber spatula a few times, as necessary.

3 Line a cookie sheet with parchment paper. Break off walnut-size pieces of the cookie dough and roll by hand into balls or half-moon or **S** shapes. Place the rolled cookies on the cookie sheet, leaving 1 inch between them.

4 Bake the cookies for 11 to 12 minutes, until golden.

5 Remove the cookie sheet from the oven and transfer to a cooling rack. Lightly sprinkle the cookies with the rosewater (if desired). To do this, pour the rosewater into a small bowl. Dip the tips of your fingers into the rosewater and sprinkle it over the tops of the cookies. Or put the rosewater in a clean plastic spray bottle and spray the tops of the cookies. Cool the cookies until just warm. Place 1½ cups of the remaining confectioners' sugar on a baking sheet. Remove the cookies from the parchment paper and place the cookies on the confectioners' sugar. Sift more confectioners' sugar on top of them. Cool completely and then roll the cookies in the confectioners' sugar on the cookie sheet. Store in the confectioners' sugar in an airtight container at room temperature for 1 week.

Per serving: *Calories 87 (From Fat 36); Fat 4g (Saturated 2g); Cholesterol 15mg; Sodium 9mg; Carbohydrate 12g (Dietary Fiber 0g); Protein 1g.*

Cocoa Brownie Balls

These brownies are dressed up and decorated with confectioners' sugar, which makes them look like snowflakes. They flatten out a bit as they bake and become cakey cookies. They're a hit with everyone and are perfect for the holiday season.

Preparation time: *4¼ hours; includes chilling*

Baking time: *8 minutes*

Yield: *4 dozen*

1 cup all-purpose flour	*1 cup sugar*
1 teaspoon baking powder	*2 eggs, lightly beaten*
⅛ teaspoon salt	*1 teaspoon vanilla extract*
¼ cup plus 1 tablespoon (5 tablespoons) unsalted butter	*1 cup finely chopped walnuts*
½ cup (scant) natural cocoa powder, sifted	*1 cup confectioners' sugar, sifted*

1 Combine the flour, baking powder, and salt in a mixing bowl and set aside.

2 Melt the butter in a 1-quart heavy saucepan over low heat. Stir in the cocoa powder and blend until smooth. Remove from heat and stir in the sugar. Using a mixer, combine the cocoa powder mixture with the eggs in a large mixing bowl and blend well. Blend in the vanilla. Add the flour mixture in three stages, blending well after each addition. Stir in the walnuts. Cover the bowl tightly with plastic wrap and chill for at least 4 hours or overnight.

3 Preheat the oven to 400°. Line a cookie sheet with parchment paper. Place the confectioners' sugar in a small bowl. Roll teaspoonfuls of the dough into balls and roll the balls in confectioners' sugar. Place the balls on the cookie sheet, leaving 2 inches between them.

4 Bake for 8 to 9 minutes, until set. Remove the cookie sheet from the oven and transfer the cookies from the parchment paper to cooling racks. Store in an airtight container at room temperature for up to a week. Freeze for longer storage.

Per serving: *Calories 66 (From Fat 29); Fat 3g (Saturated 1g); Cholesterol 12mg; Sodium 17mg; Carbohydrate 9g (Dietary Fiber 1g); Protein 1g.*

Spritz Cookies

Buttery Spritz Cookies are as much fun to make as they are to eat. You can make several different shapes of spritz cookies with a cookie press merely by changing the decorative plate at one end and then pressing the dough through. If you don't have a cookie press, use a pastry bag fitted with a large star-shaped tube (#4). See Chapter 11 for more information on pressed cookies.

Specialty tools: *Cookie press or pastry bag fitted with a large star-shaped tube (#4)*

Preparation time: *30 minutes*

Baking time: *10 minutes*

Yield: *4 dozen*

1 cup (2 sticks) unsalted butter, softened	1 teaspoon vanilla extract
½ cup sugar	Pinch of salt
1 egg	3 cups all-purpose flour

1 Line a cookie sheet with parchment paper.

2 Using a mixer, beat the butter in a large mixing bowl until fluffy, about 2 minutes. Add the sugar and mix together until smooth. In a separate bowl, lightly whisk the egg with the vanilla and add to the butter mixture. Stir to blend well. Combine the salt with the flour and add in three stages, blending well after each addition. Chill the dough for 30 minutes.

3 Preheat the oven to 350°. Transfer the dough to the cookie press and press cookies out onto the cookie sheet, leaving 1 inch between them. Bake for 10 minutes, until golden. Remove the cookie sheet from the oven and transfer the cookies from the parchment paper to cooling racks. Store in an airtight container at room temperature for up to a week. Freeze for longer storage.

Vary It! *You can make some delicious variations of Spritz Cookies by adding different flavorings like spices, chocolate, and citrus to the basic cookie dough. For Anise Spritz, add 1 tablespoon crushed anise seed to the flour mixture. For Chocolate Spritz, add 3 ounces melted and cooled semisweet chocolate to the butter mixture. For Orange Spritz, add 1 tablespoon finely minced orange zest to the butter mixture.*

Per serving: *Calories 72 (From Fat 36); Fat 4g (Saturated 2g); Cholesterol 15mg; Sodium 5mg; Carbohydrate 8g (Dietary Fiber 0g); Protein 1g.*

Almond-Vanilla Crescents

These delicate crescent-shaped butter cookies are Austrian specialties. You can make Hazelnut-Vanilla Crescents by substituting toasted and finely ground hazelnuts for the almonds. For another crescent cookie recipe, see the Hazelnut Crescents in Chapter 12.

Preparation time: *20 minutes*

Baking time: *12 minutes*

Yield: *2½ dozen*

1¼ cups all-purpose flour

½ cup finely ground almonds

⅓ cup superfine sugar

Pinch of salt

½ cup (1 stick) unsalted butter, cold

2 egg yolks

1 teaspoon vanilla extract

Confectioners' sugar for garnish

1 Preheat the oven to 350°. Line a cookie sheet with parchment paper.

2 In the work bowl of a food processor fitted with the steel blade, combine the flour, ground almonds, sugar, and salt. Pulse briefly to blend. Cut the butter into small pieces and add to the flour mixture. Pulse until the butter is cut into very tiny pieces, about 15 to 20 pulses.

(To use a mixer and mixing bowl, soften the butter to room temperature. Beat the butter in the mixing bowl until fluffy, about 2 minutes. Add the sugar, and cream together well. Combine the flour, ground almonds, and salt. Add to the butter mixture in four stages, blending well after each addition.)

3 In a separate bowl, lightly whisk the egg yolks with the vanilla and add to the flour mixture. Process or mix until the dough forms a ball, about 1 minute.

4 Pinch off walnut-size pieces and roll on a lightly floured surface into ¼-inch-thick ropes about 4 inches long. Bend the ropes into crescent shapes and place them on the cookie sheet, leaving 2 inches between them.

5 Bake for 12 to 15 minutes, until golden and set. Remove the cookie sheet from the oven and transfer the cookies to racks to cool. Dust the crescents heavily with confectioners' sugar. Store in an airtight container at room temperature for up to a week. Freeze for longer storage.

Per serving: Calories 86 (From Fat 53); Fat 6g (Saturated 2g); Cholesterol 22mg; Sodium 6mg; Carbohydrate 7g (Dietary Fiber 1g); Protein 2g.

Moravian Molasses Spice Cookies

These heirloom cookies are typical of those made by descendants of the Moravians. Moravia is a historic area located in the eastern part of the Czech Republic. The unsulphured or robust flavor molasses gives these cookies their characteristic deep brown color and full-bodied flavor. If you can't find this type of molasses at the grocery store, check with the local health food store. The trick to making these crisp is to roll the dough as thin as possible (see Chapter 6 for tips on making rolled cookies). Chill the dough in between steps to make it easier to handle.

Specialty tools: *Rolling pin; a 2½-inch round fluted-edge cookie cutter or daisy-shaped cookie cutter*

Preparation time: *4 hours; includes chilling*

Baking time: *8 minutes*

Yield: *4 to 5 dozen*

1⅓ cups all-purpose flour	¼ teaspoon salt
1¼ teaspoons baking soda	½ cup (1 stick) unsalted butter, softened
1 teaspoon ground ginger	½ cup light brown sugar
1 teaspoon ground cinnamon	1 teaspoon vanilla extract
½ teaspoon ground cloves	½ cup unsulphured or robust flavor molasses
¼ teaspoon nutmeg, preferably freshly grated	

1 In a mixing bowl, combine the flour, baking soda, ginger, cinnamon, cloves, nutmeg, and salt.

2 Using a mixer, beat the butter in a large mixing bowl until fluffy, about 2 minutes. Add the brown sugar and mix together until smooth. Add the vanilla and molasses and beat until well blended. Form the dough into a disk and wrap tightly in plastic. Chill until firm, at least 3 hours or overnight.

3 Preheat the oven to 350°. Line a cookie sheet with parchment paper. Divide the dough into equal thirds. Work with one portion while keeping the others refrigerated.

4 Roll out each section of dough between sheets of floured wax paper until the dough sections are about ⅟₁₆-inch thin. Transfer the covered dough to a cookie sheet and chill in the freezer for 15 minutes. Gently peel off both pieces of wax paper. Use a 2½-inch round fluted-edge cutter or daisy-shaped cutter to cut out shapes (see Figure 15-1). Transfer the shapes to the cookie sheet, leaving 1 inch between them.

5 Bake for 8 minutes. Remove the cookie sheet from the oven and transfer the cookies from the parchment paper to cooling racks. Store in an airtight container at room temperature for up to a month. Freeze for longer storage.

Per serving: *Calories 45 (From Fat 18); Fat 2g (Saturated 1g); Cholesterol 5mg; Sodium 41mg; Carbohydrate 7g (Dietary Fiber 0g); Protein 0g.*

ROLLING AND CUTTING OUT MORAVIAN MOLASSES SPICE COOKIES

Figure 15-1:
Rolling and cutting out Moravian Molasses Spice Cookies.

1. ROLL OUT DOUGH BETWEEN SHEETS OF WAX PAPER UNTIL DOUGH SECTIONS ARE ABOUT 1/16" THIN

WOW! THAT'S THIN!

2. TRANSFER THE COVERED DOUGH TO A COOKIE SHEET AND CHILL IN FREEZER FOR 15 MINUTES.

BRRR

GENTLY PEEL OFF BOTH SIDES OF WAX PAPER.

USE A 2½" ROUND, FLUTED EDGE CUTTER OR DAISY SHAPE TO CUT OUT SHAPES.

TRANSFER TO COOKIE SHEETS, LEAVE 1" OF SPACE BETWEEN THEM.

Lebkuchen

These classic honey and spice cookies are rolled cookies (see Chapter 6 for tips on making rolled cookies) that are traditionally served in Germany during the Christmas holiday season. You can make Lebkuchen (LAYB-koo-kuhn) up to 3 months in advance, so you save time during the busier days around Christmas.

Specialty tools: *Rolling pin*

Preparation time: *3¼ hours; includes chilling*

Baking time: *12 minutes*

Yield: *About 5 dozen*

3⅔ cups all-purpose flour	½ teaspoon crushed anise seed
1 teaspoon baking powder	Zest of 1 large lemon, finely minced
1 teaspoon baking soda	½ cup (1 stick) unsalted butter, cut into small pieces
¼ teaspoon salt	⅔ cup honey
2 teaspoons ground cinnamon	
1 teaspoon ground cardamom	½ cup superfine sugar
1 teaspoon ground ginger	½ cup light brown sugar
1 teaspoon ground cloves	1 cup finely ground almonds
¾ teaspoon ground mace	1 egg

1 Sift together the flour, baking powder, and baking soda, and toss with the salt. Separately, sift together the cinnamon, cardamom, ginger, cloves, and mace, and toss with the anise seed and lemon zest.

2 In a 2-quart heavy-bottomed saucepan, combine the butter, honey, superfine sugar, and brown sugar and warm over low heat, stirring frequently with a wooden spoon, until the butter is melted and the sugar is dissolved, about 5 minutes.

3 Remove the saucepan from the heat. Using a mixer, blend the butter mixture with the spice mixture in a large mixing bowl. Add the ground almonds in two stages, blending well. Add the flour mixture in four stages, blending well after each addition. Stop occasionally and scrape down the sides of the bowl with a rubber spatula. Stir in the egg and blend thoroughly.

4 Gather the dough into a large rectangle and wrap tightly in plastic wrap. Refrigerate for at least 3 hours or overnight.

5 Preheat the oven to 350°. Line a cookie sheet with parchment paper. Cut the chilled dough in half and keep one half in the refrigerator while rolling out the other half.

6 Roll out the dough between lightly floured sheets of wax paper to a large rectangle about 9 inches x 15 inches and ¼-inch thick. Trim the edges of the dough evenly. Use a ruler to mark rectangles 2½ inches long x 1½ inches wide. Transfer the rectangles to the lined cookie sheet, leaving 1 inch between them. Gather any scraps together, reroll, and cut. Repeat with the remaining half of the dough.

7 Bake for 12 minutes. Remove the cookie sheet from the oven and use an offset spatula to transfer the cookies to cooling racks to cool completely. Store in an airtight container at room temperature for up to 3 months.

Per serving: Calories 95 (From Fat 37); Fat 4g (Saturated 1g); Cholesterol 8mg; Sodium 39mg; Carbohydrate 13g (Dietary Fiber 1g); Protein 2g.

Chapter 16

Chocolate Indulgences

In This Chapter

▶ Reveling in the luxury of chocolate

▶ Knowing the origin of chocolate and cocoa

▶ Satisfying your chocolate desires

The first thing you should know about chocolate cookies is that they go fast — real fast — so make plenty! The second thing, which you probably know already, is that chocolate adds a richness that sets these cookies apart from others. When you eat chocolate cookies, you're in for an extra-special treat. Chocolate not only tastes good but also makes you feel good. Chocolate contains some naturally occurring properties that react with chemicals in our brains to mimic the feelings of euphoria we experience when in love. This explains why chocolate is so closely associated with romance and especially with Valentine's Day. It's also why we turn to chocolate when we're feeling low. It's no wonder that chocolate lovers are so passionate about their chosen flavor. Chocolate as an ingredient has almost magical qualities. It is very malleable and can be used in many different ways: chopped, melted, as chips, or as cocoa powder.

Phenylethylamine is a chemical that is naturally in our bodies and is also a component of chocolate. It helps open synapses in the brain to allow easy release of seratonin, which is an endorphin — a "feel good" chemical. It provides a mood lift that creates positive energy — the type of feeling we experience after vigorous exercise.

Life without Chocolate? No Way!

I can't imagine living without chocolate, and I know I'm far from alone. There are more chocolate lovers in the world than just about any other type of person I can think of. In fact, I've met only a handful of people who say they aren't in love with chocolate. I can't imagine why.

Since I'm the curious sort, I like to know where chocolate and cocoa come from. How do these magical substances get to be the way they are when we buy them in the store? Chocolate and cocoa really do grow on trees — well, sort of. Not to put a damper on chocolate's romantic image, but there's a lot of science and a bit of alchemy behind chocolate's transformation from a pod on a tree to the lush, delicious food we love. Armed with this information, you will be a fount of knowledge for other chocolate lovers.

Dubbed "food of the gods" by the Swedish naturalist Linnaeus in 1753, chocolate and cocoa have been beloved for hundreds of years. It would be hard to imagine making cookies without chocolate in some form. Both chocolate and cocoa come from cacao beans grown on trees in tropical climates throughout the world.

The cacao beans are fermented, dried, roasted, and winnowed (cracked open), leaving the inner nibs, or cocoa seeds. These are ground to a thick paste, called chocolate liquor (not alcoholic). More than half of this paste is made up of cocoa butter, with the rest being tiny particles of the ground nibs. The cocoa butter is separated out, leaving presscake, which is used to make cocoa powder and various types of chocolate. Cocoa butter is used not only by the food industry to make chocolate but also by the pharmaceutical and cosmetic industries to make such things as suntan oil.

If the presscake is to become natural cocoa powder, the presscake is sifted through several stages of fine mesh. Natural cocoa powder has no added ingredients. It has a bitter flavor, so it is best used in baked goods where its flavor is mellowed when combined with other ingredients.

If the presscake is Dutch-processed — a procedure developed by the Dutchman Coenraad Van Houten that gives the process its name — it is treated with an alkaline substance, which mellows the flavor, deepens the color, and makes the final product more easily dispersible in liquid. Dutch-processed cocoa is used most often where it's not mixed with other ingredients, such as to decorate baked goods and candies. This allows its mellow flavor to be thoroughly enjoyed.

If the presscake is to become chocolate, varying amounts of cocoa butter are added to it, along with sugar, vanilla, and other ingredients, depending on the type of chocolate. The mass is then refined through steel rollers and conched, the process that drives off volatile oils and makes smooth, melt-in-the-mouth chocolate. Then the chocolate is tempered, a process that stabilizes the mixture so it stays shiny and evenly colored with no white streaks or dots. Finally, the chocolate is molded into whatever shape it is to take, such as slabs, bars, squares, coins, or chips.

The flavor of chocolate complements and combines well with other flavors. Chocolate goes very well with many fruit flavors, such as strawberry, raspberry, cherry, apricot, and banana. Dried fruits, such as dates, raisins, and figs are also good with chocolate. Vanilla and chocolate are natural partners. Chocolate marries wonderfully with coffee to make mocha. Chocolate even works well with citrus, such as lemon and orange. Mint and chocolate are a classic combination, as are coconut and chocolate. Many nuts take well to chocolate. Try almonds, hazelnuts, walnuts, peanuts, macadamia nuts, pistachio nuts, and Brazil nuts. Certain spices, like cinnamon, nutmeg, cloves, and ginger, work magic when combined with chocolate. Some people even love chili with chocolate. About the only flavors that don't work well with chocolate are those that are salty and bitter.

So Go Ahead, Indulge Yourself

The recipes in this chapter use a variety of forms of chocolate and a variety of techniques. Some simply use chopped chocolate, and others use a combination of chocolate and either natural or Dutch-processed cocoa powder. These are examples of some of the myriad chocolate cookies in the world, and some of my personal favorites. They also vary from easy to a bit more complicated, so you can choose how much time and energy you'd like to devote to baking chocolate cookies. You can even get into dipping in chocolate if you make the recipe for Florentines. You might call this chapter a "Concentration of Chocolate Cookies." There are several other chocolate cookie recipes in the book, categorized by the techniques used to make them, their origins, or their special qualities. Chapters 5 and 15 have recipes for cookies with chocolate in them, and Chapters 3 and 20 contain more information on chocolate.

Chocolate Drops

These tasty cookies are a snap to make, which is good, because they disappear quickly. You can make a variation of the above recipe — Chocolate Nut Drops — by adding ½ cup finely ground or minced walnuts or pecans to the dough after adding the dry ingredients. Proceed to shape and bake the same as Chocolate Drops.

Preparation time: *20 minutes*

Baking time: *12 minutes*

Yield: *4 dozen*

8 ounces bittersweet or semisweet chocolate, finely chopped

½ cup (1 stick) unsalted butter, cut into small pieces

½ cup superfine sugar

3 eggs

1½ teaspoons vanilla extract

1¾ cups all-purpose flour

½ cup natural cocoa powder

Pinch of salt

1¼ cups confectioners' sugar, for garnish

1 Melt the chocolate and butter together in the top of a double boiler over hot water. Stir often with a rubber spatula or a whisk to ensure even melting. Remove the top pan of the double boiler and thoroughly dry the bottom and sides. Transfer the mixture to a large mixing bowl. Stir in the sugar and blend well. Add the eggs one at a time, stirring after each addition. Blend in the vanilla.

2 Sift together the flour, cocoa powder, and salt. Add to the chocolate mixture in four stages, blending well after each addition. Cover the mixture tightly with plastic wrap and chill for 1 hour.

3 Preheat the oven to 350°. Line a cookie sheet with parchment paper. Place 1 cup of the confectioners' sugar in a small bowl.

4 Pinch off walnut-size pieces of the dough and roll into balls. Roll each ball in the confectioners' sugar to coat completely. Arrange the balls on the cookie sheet, with 2 inches between them. Bake for 12 to 14 minutes, until firm.

5 Remove the cookie sheet from the oven and transfer the cookies to cooling racks. Dust the tops of the cookies with the remaining confectioners' sugar. Store in an airtight container at room temperature for up to a week. Freeze for longer storage.

Per serving: Calories 85 (From Fat 36); Fat 4g (Saturated 2g); Cholesterol 19mg; Sodium 8mg; Carbohydrate 11g (Dietary Fiber 1g); Protein 1g.

Chocolate-Peanut Butter Coins

I find that I can't stop eating these delicious cookies once I start. They're just too tasty!
I like to use a natural-style or freshly ground peanut butter in this recipe.

Preparation time: *15 minutes*

Baking time: *10 minutes*

Yield: *4 dozen*

½ cup (1 stick) unsalted butter, softened

1 cup light brown sugar

1 egg

1 teaspoon vanilla extract

1½ cups all-purpose flour

½ cup natural cocoa powder

½ teaspoon baking soda

Pinch of salt

½ cup creamy peanut butter

1 Using a mixer and mixing bowl, beat the butter until fluffy, about 2 minutes. Add the
sugar and mix together until smooth. In a small bowl, stir the egg with the vanilla and
add to the butter mixture, blending well.

2 Sift together the flour, cocoa powder, baking soda, and salt and add to the mixture in
three stages, blending well after each addition. Add the peanut butter and blend well.

3 Divide the dough in half. Place each piece on a large rectangle of wax paper and roll
each into a cylinder about 10 inches long and 1 inch thick. Wrap the cylinders in the
wax paper, wrap again in plastic wrap, and chill for at least 2 hours, until firm. The cylinders can be frozen at this point. If frozen, defrost overnight in the refrigerator before
using.

4 Preheat the oven to 350°. Line a cookie sheet with parchment paper. Cut each cylinder
into ¼-inch-thick slices. Place on the cookie sheet, with 2 inches between them.

5 Bake for 10 minutes or until firm. Remove the cookie sheets from the oven and transfer
the cookies from the parchment to cooling racks to cool. Store in an airtight container
at room temperature up to a week. Freeze for longer storage.

Vary It! *For even more of a chocolate indulgence, try dipping these cookies in chocolate.*

Per serving: *Calories 68 (From Fat 32); Fat 4g (Saturated 2g); Cholesterol 10mg; Sodium 32mg; Carbohydrate 8g
(Dietary Fiber 1g); Protein 1g.*

Mocha Pretzels

These classic German cookies are shaped to look like the popular salty snacks, but taste much different. Decorate with coarse decorating or crystal sugar to mimic the look of salt.

Preparation time: 1 hour and 20 minutes; includes chilling

Baking time: 11 minutes

Yield: 2 dozen

2 ounces bittersweet or semisweet chocolate, finely chopped

2½ cups all-purpose flour

⅓ cup unsweetened Dutch-processed cocoa powder

2 teaspoons instant espresso powder

¼ teaspoon salt

¾ cup plus 2 tablespoons (1¾ sticks) unsalted butter, softened

¾ cup superfine sugar

1 large egg

2 teaspoons vanilla extract

Garnish

1 egg white mixed with 2 teaspoons water

¼ cup crystal sugar

1 Melt the chocolate in the top of a double boiler over hot water. Stir often with a rubber spatula to ensure even melting. In a separate bowl, mix together the flour, cocoa powder, espresso powder, and salt.

2 Using a mixer and mixing bowl, beat the butter until fluffy, about 2 minutes. Add the sugar and mix together until smooth. Add the melted chocolate and blend well. In a small bowl, combine the egg with the vanilla and add to the butter mixture, blending well. Add the dry ingredients from Step 1 in three stages, blending well after each addition.

3 Shape the dough into a log about 2 inches wide. Wrap tightly in plastic and chill for at least 1 hour, until firm.

4 Preheat the oven to 350°. Line a cookie sheet with parchment paper. Cut the log into 24 equal pieces, each about ½ inch thick. Work with one piece of the dough at a time, while keeping the other pieces in the refrigerator. Roll each piece into a ball and then into a rope about 12 inches long and the same thickness as a pencil. Twist the ends up and over, crossing each other, and secure them at the base, forming a pretzel shape. See Figure 16-1, which includes instructions for making multiple sheets of mocha pretzels.

5 Brush the top of each cookie with the egg white mixture and sprinkle with crystal sugar. Use a flat metal spatula to transfer the cookies to the cookie sheet, leaving 2 inches between them. Bake for 11 to 12 minutes, until firm. Remove the cookie sheet from the oven and transfer the cookies from the parchment to cooling racks. Store in an airtight container at room temperature for up to a week. Freeze for longer storage.

Per serving: Calories 160 (From Fat 72); Fat 8g (Saturated 5g); Cholesterol 27mg; Sodium 31mg; Carbohydrate 20g (Dietary Fiber 1g); Protein 2g.

SHAPING MOCHA PRETZELS

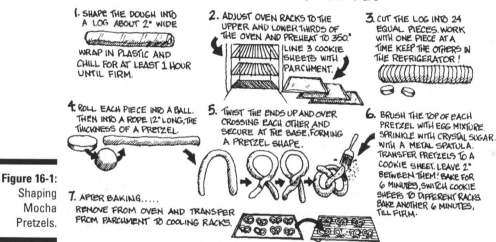

1. SHAPE THE DOUGH INTO A LOG ABOUT 2" WIDE. WRAP IN PLASTIC AND CHILL FOR AT LEAST 1 HOUR UNTIL FIRM.

2. ADJUST OVEN RACKS TO THE UPPER AND LOWER THIRDS OF THE OVEN AND PREHEAT TO 350°. LINE 3 COOKIE SHEETS WITH PARCHMENT.

3. CUT THE LOG INTO 24 EQUAL PIECES. WORK WITH ONE PIECE AT A TIME. KEEP THE OTHERS IN THE REFRIGERATOR!

4. ROLL EACH PIECE INTO A BALL. THEN INTO A ROPE 12" LONG, THE THICKNESS OF A PRETZEL.

5. TWIST THE ENDS UP AND OVER CROSSING EACH OTHER AND SECURE AT THE BASE, FORMING A PRETZEL SHAPE.

6. BRUSH THE TOP OF EACH PRETZEL WITH EGG MIXTURE. SPRINKLE WITH CRYSTAL SUGAR. WITH A METAL SPATULA, TRANSFER PRETZELS TO A COOKIE SHEET. LEAVE 2" BETWEEN THEM! BAKE FOR 6 MINUTES, SWITCH COOKIE SHEETS TO DIFFERENT RACKS. BAKE ANOTHER 6 MINUTES, TILL FIRM.

7. AFTER BAKING..... REMOVE FROM OVEN AND TRANSFER FROM PARCHMENT TO COOLING RACKS.

Figure 16-1: Shaping Mocha Pretzels.

Cocoa Spice Drops

Cloves give these cookies an intriguing flavor. These are light and soft and seem to melt in the mouth.

Preparation time: *15 minutes*

Baking time: *8 minutes*

Yield: *About 4 dozen*

2½ cups all-purpose flour

¼ cup natural cocoa powder

1 tablespoon baking powder

½ teaspoon baking soda

Pinch of salt

1 teaspoon ground cloves

½ teaspoon ground cinnamon

½ teaspoon nutmeg, preferably freshly grated

2 eggs

¾ cup sugar

½ cup whole or 2-percent milk

½ cup (1 stick) unsalted butter, melted and cooled

1 Preheat the oven to 350°. Line a cookie sheet with parchment paper.

2 In a medium mixing bowl, combine the flour, cocoa powder, baking powder, baking soda, salt, cloves, cinnamon, and nutmeg. Toss the mixture to blend.

3 Using a mixing bowl and mixer, whip the eggs until frothy. Add the sugar and continue to whip until the mixture holds a slowly dissolving ribbon as the beater is lifted, about 2 minutes. Pour in the milk and melted butter and blend thoroughly. Add the dry ingredients from Step 2 in three stages, blending well after each addition.

4 Drop heaping teaspoonfuls of the batter onto the cookie sheet, leaving 2 inches between the cookies. Bake for 8 to 10 minutes, until set. Remove the cookie sheet from the oven and transfer the cookies from the parchment to cooling racks. Store the cookies between layers of wax paper in an airtight container at room temperature for up to a week. Freeze for longer storage.

Per serving): *Calories 47 (From Fat 17); Fat 2g (Saturated 1g); Cholesterol 12mg; Sodium 35mg; Carbohydrate 7g (Dietary Fiber 0g); Protein 1g.*

Chocolate Fudge Brownies

Nothing beats a fudgy brownie when you're in the mood for chocolate! These are some of the best brownies I've ever eaten, so they're definitely worth making from scratch. When you make brownies from scratch, you're in charge of choosing the ingredients, rather than having to settle for what you get. You can choose to use fabulous chocolate, excellent-quality butter, and fresh nuts. All that combined makes brownies that are out of this world. A word of caution: You may have to hide the batch or eat your share before anyone else knows you've baked these. They're *that* good! If you prefer cakelike brownies instead, see the recipe for Very Rich Cakelike Brownies in Chapter 8.

Preparation time: *15 minutes*

Baking time: *30 minutes*

Yield: *25*

4 ounces bittersweet chocolate, finely chopped

½ cup (1 stick) unsalted butter, cut into small pieces

1½ cups sugar

1 tablespoon instant espresso powder dissolved in 1 tablespoon water

2 teaspoons vanilla extract

2 eggs

¾ cup all-purpose flour

1 cup walnuts, finely chopped

1 Generously butter and flour the inside of an 8-inch square baking pan. Preheat the oven to 350°.

2 Melt the chocolate and butter together in the top of a double boiler over hot water, stirring frequently with a rubber spatula to ensure even melting.

3 Remove the top pan from the double boiler and thoroughly dry the bottom and sides of the pan. Transfer the mixture to a mixing bowl. Stir in the sugar in three batches, blending thoroughly after each addition, and blend in the espresso and vanilla. Stir in the eggs, blending well.

4 Add the flour to the mixture in three batches, blending thoroughly after each addition. Stir in the walnuts.

5 Pour the batter into the prepared pan. Bake for 30 minutes, until a toothpick inserted 2 inches from the edge still has moist crumbs clinging to it. Remove the pan from the oven and cool completely on a rack.

6 Cut the brownies into squares, five rows in each direction. They'll keep up to 4 days at room temperature stored in an airtight container or for a week in a tightly covered container in the refrigerator. The brownies can also be frozen for up to 4 months. If frozen, defrost them for 24 hours in the refrigerator before serving.

Per serving: *Calories 161 (From Fat 83); Fat 9g (Saturated 4g); Cholesterol 28mg; Sodium 6mg; Carbohydrate 18g (Dietary Fiber 1g); Protein 2g.*

Mocha Walnut Coins

I love the combination of the flavors of mocha and walnut. They seem to be made for each other. These cookies are perfect for afternoon coffee or tea. They're also great to pack for a picnic.

Preparation time: *1¼ hours; includes chilling*

Baking time: *15 minutes*

Yield: *About 4 dozen*

1 cup (2 sticks) unsalted butter, softened

½ cup sugar

2 teaspoons instant espresso powder

2 teaspoons vanilla extract

1¾ cup all-purpose flour

¼ cup unsweetened natural cocoa powder

Pinch of salt

½ cup walnuts, finely chopped

1 Using a mixing bowl and mixer, beat the butter until fluffy, about 2 minutes. Add the sugar and mix together until smooth.

2 In a small bowl, mix the espresso powder and vanilla together and add to the butter mixture. Scrape down the sides of the bowl and blend well. Toss together the flour, cocoa powder, and salt and add to the butter mixture in three stages, blending well after each addition. Stir in the walnuts, blending well.

3 Divide the dough into two equal portions. Place each piece on a large rectangle of wax paper and roll each into a cylinder about 13 inches long and 1½ inches thick. Wrap the cylinders in the wax paper, wrap again in plastic wrap, and chill for 1 hour, until firm. The cylinders can be frozen at this point. If frozen, defrost overnight in the refrigerator before using.

4 Preheat the oven to 350°. Line a cookie sheet with parchment paper. Cut each chilled cylinder into slices between ¼ and ½ inch thick. Place the slices on the cookie sheet, leaving 1 inch between them.

5 Bake for 15 to 18 minutes, until firm. Remove the cookie sheet from the oven and transfer the cookies from the parchment to cooling racks. Store in an airtight container at room temperature for up to a week. Freeze for longer storage.

Per serving: Calories 55 (From Fat 34); Fat 4g (Saturated 2g); Cholesterol 8mg; Sodium 3mg; Carbohydrate 5g (Dietary Fiber 0g); Protein 1g.

Mocha Hazelnut Fingers

Hazelnuts give a sophisticated edge to these very delicate cookies. These are perfect to serve for afternoon tea or as part of an assortment of cookies.

Specialty tools: *12- or 14-inch pastry bag with a large pastry tube containing a ½-inch plain opening (#5).*

Preparation time: *20 minutes*

Baking time: *13 minutes*

Yield: *2½ dozen*

1 cup (2 sticks) unsalted butter, softened

½ cup confectioners' sugar

2 teaspoons instant espresso powder

1¼ cups all-purpose flour

¼ cup unsweetened Dutch processed cocoa powder

½ cup toasted and finely ground hazelnuts (see Chapter 4)

1 Preheat the oven to 350°. Line a cookie sheet with parchment paper.

2 Using a mixing bowl and mixer, beat the butter until fluffy, about 2 minutes. Add the confectioners' sugar and mix together until smooth. Add the espresso powder, blending well.

3 Sift together the flour and cocoa powder and add to the mixture in three stages, blending well after each addition. Reserve 2 tablespoons of the hazelnuts and add the rest to the mixture, blending well.

4 Fit a 12- or 14-inch pastry bag with a large pastry tube with a ½-inch plain opening (#5). Pipe out finger shapes about 3 inches long x ½ inch wide onto the cookie sheet, leaving 2 inches between them. Sprinkle the tops of the cookies with the reserved hazelnuts.

5 Bake for 13 to 15 minutes, until firm. Remove the cookie sheet from the oven and transfer the cookies from the parchment paper to cooling racks. Store in an airtight container at room temperature for up to a week. Freeze for longer storage.

Per serving: Calories 89 (From Fat 63); Fat 7g (Saturated 4g); Cholesterol 17mg; Sodium 1mg; Carbohydrate 6g (Dietary Fiber 0g); Protein 1g.

Florentines

These old-world favorites are true confections, a cross between a cookie and a candy. They're first cooked and then baked in a standard-size muffin pan. They are fairly thin and flat looking, kind of like a Frisbee, but much, much tastier. After these are baked, their bottoms are spread with melted chocolate. Although preparing these delicacies requires several steps, you won't regret the extra time, especially when you see the satisfied smiles on the faces of family and friends lucky enough to sample these.

Specialty tools: 2 muffin pans — 12 cups each; decorating comb (or fork)

Preparation time: 30 minutes

Baking time: 10 minutes

Yield: 20

3 tablespoons unflavored vegetable oil or nonstick cooking spray

½ cup plus 2 tablespoons (1¼ sticks) unsalted butter, cut into small pieces

⅔ cup sugar

2 tablespoons honey

¼ cup heavy cream

2 cups sliced almonds

⅔ cup finely diced candied orange peel

2 tablespoons all-purpose flour

8 ounces bittersweet or semisweet chocolate for garnish

1 Preheat the oven to 350°. Lightly oil or spray two jelly roll pans and 20 2½ inch metal rings, or the cups of two muffin pans (12 cups each).

2 In a 2-quart heavy saucepan, combine the butter, sugar, honey, and cream. Cook over medium heat until the mixture reaches 248° on a candy thermometer, stirring constantly with a wooden spoon, about 15 minutes. Immediately add the almonds, candied orange peel, and flour and stir vigorously until thoroughly blended, about 1 minute. Remove from the heat.

3 Put a generous tablespoon of the mixture in each muffin cup. Dip the back of a spoon in cold water and press each mound to flatten. Bake for about 10 minutes, until golden. Remove the muffin pans from the oven and cool on a rack for 5 minutes. Oil the bottom of another jelly roll pan. Place it over the top of the muffin tin and invert the tin to release the confections.

4 While the Florentines cool, chop the chocolate into matchstick-size pieces and set aside one-third of them. Melt the remaining two-thirds in the top of a double boiler over hot water, stirring frequently with a rubber spatula to ensure even melting.

5 Remove the double boiler from the heat, remove the top pan of the double boiler, and thoroughly dry the bottom and sides of the pan. Stir in the remaining chocolate in three batches, making sure that each batch is completely melted before adding the next.

6 When all the chocolate has been added, the chocolate will be ready for dipping. To test that it is not too hot, place a dab below your lower lip. It should feel comfortable, not too hot or too cool. If it's too hot, add a little more finely chopped chocolate until it feels comfortable. To hold the chocolate at the same temperature, place it over a shallow pan with water that is slightly warmer.

7 To coat the Florentines, line two cookie sheets with parchment or wax paper. To dip the bottom of the cookie in chocolate, hold a cookie flat (horizontally) between your fingers and dip the bottom into the chocolate. Remove the cookie from the chocolate and let the excess drip off. To help remove excess chocolate, very lightly tap the cookie against the side of the pan. Place the cookie onto the cookie sheet, chocolate side up. After dipping four cookies, use a decorating comb or a fork to make a wavy pattern in the chocolate. When the cookie sheet is full, place it in the refrigerator for 10 minutes to set the chocolate. Store in a single layer in an airtight container at room temperature for up to a week.

Per serving: Calories 246 (From Fat 158); Fat 18g (Saturated 7g); Cholesterol 20mg; Sodium 9mg; Carbohydrate 21g (Dietary Fiber 2g); Protein 3g.

Chapter 17

Big Cookies

People in the United States like big things, so big cookies hold a special appeal for them. Who can resist biting into a big cookie, knowing that a treat of this dimension will offer longer-lasting enjoyment?

People of all ages like big cookies, but kids seem to love them the most. Big cookies started showing up in bakeries several years ago, and they're still going strong. One of the great things about baking big cookies is that you save steps. Because you're baking fewer cookies, you save some time and labor.

Big cookies can easily substitute for a cake. Next time you have a birthday party, bake a batch of big cookies rather than a cake. I'm sure that your guests will enjoy having their own individual treat! You can even get creative by decorating big cookies for the occasion and placing a candle in the center.

Another good thing about big cookies is that they keep well and can travel well, too, so they're great to take to a potluck gathering or on a picnic or to pack in a lunch box.

Big cookies may last longer than small, individual cookies, too. You can eat a little and save the rest for another time.

Thinking Big

By big cookies, I don't mean cookies that are the size of the Empire State Building. And I don't mean cookies that are the size of a cake. I'm talking about cookies that are 4 to 5 inches in diameter, which is a pretty good size cookie. Yet, cookies this size are still an easy size for the home cook to bake and store, and they're more fun to bake than regular size cookies because they can be formed so quickly.

Plan in advance of baking big cookies to make sure that you have enough cookie sheets and cooling racks to make the process easy. Also set aside enough space to hold the cooling racks while still leaving room to work.

Leave at least 3 inches between big cookies when placing them on a cookie sheet. If they don't have enough space, they spread into each other, making one super-giant cookie.

Giving Your Small Cookies Growth Hormones

Some cookie recipes seem naturally destined for bigger things. For example, most drop cookies can easily be made into big cookies. Simply scoop out bigger portions. Chocolate Chip Cookies, White Chocolate Macadamia Nut Cookies, and Peanut Butter Cookies (see Chapter 5) are all good candidates for big cookies. Some rolled cookies (see Chapter 6) can become big cookies, too, by cutting them out with larger cookie cutters. Refrigerator cookies (see Chapter 7) can be enlarged by rolling the dough into larger (thicker) logs before chilling and cutting. Simply cut bar cookies (see Chapter 8) larger to make them bigger, but be careful that they don't crumble.

If you adapt a cookie recipe and make big cookies, keep in mind that you will have fewer cookies.

However, not all cookies lend themselves to larger proportions. Many cookies are hard to handle if they get big, and besides, they need to bake at different times and temperatures than regular-size cookies. In some cases, bigger cookies bake unevenly. I wouldn't bake big biscotti for this reason. Sandwich cookies become gigantic if made big — they would be just too darn big to get your mouth around. After all, you don't want to make the cookie-eating experience unpleasant! Who wants to eat a baseball-size cookie, anyway? Eating several small ball-shaped cookies is more fun than eating one big one. And it would be disrespectful to fiddle with the size of some traditional cookies, such as the international specialties found in Chapter 14 and the holiday cookies in Chapter 15.

Increase the baking time if you make cookies bigger than their standard size. Generally, you need to add at least 25 percent more time. Use your timer and check the cookies for doneness before removing them from the oven.

No, You Don't Need an Airplane Hangar

One of the main considerations about big cookies is finding containers large enough to hold them. Standard-size cookie jars or tins may be too small. But don't let that stop you. Visit a store that sells containers for just about everything in the world to find storage solutions. Wide-mouth plastic jars with lids that seal tightly are good candidates. Don't stack too many layers of cookies on top of each other, or the bottom layer may suffer damage. Another way to store big cookies is to place them on a jelly roll pan and cover tightly with aluminum foil. You can also store them in gallon-size zipper-type plastic bags. These seal well and don't take up a lot of space.

Stack cookies no more than three layers deep in their storage container. Too many layers puts a lot of weight on the bottom layer, causing it to crack or crumble. Put sheets of wax paper between the cookie layers to keep them from sticking together.

Ginger Molasses Giants

I love these chewy, spice-filled cookies. They're great with a glass of milk or a cup of tea. This recipe uses two unusual ingredients — crystallized ginger and cardamom. A candied form of fresh, young ginger, crystallized ginger is processed and rolled in sugar. It's available in many specialty food shops and health food stores, either in bulk or prepackaged. Crystallized ginger will last up to a year in the pantry, as long as you store it in an airtight container. It's also easy to cut into small pieces with kitchen scissors. Ginger chips are small pieces of crystallized ginger, about the size of chocolate chips, and are sold in small cans. Cardamom has a fresh lemony flavor and aroma. It works very well with the crystallized ginger in this recipe.

Preparation time: *15 minutes*

Baking time: *15 minutes*

Yield: *16*

½ cup sugar

¾ cup (1½ sticks) unsalted butter, softened

¼ cup light brown sugar

½ cup molasses

2¼ cups all-purpose flour

2 teaspoons baking soda

1¼ teaspoons ground ginger

½ teaspoon ground cardamom

½ teaspoon ground cinnamon

¼ teaspoon nutmeg, preferably freshly ground

Pinch of salt

2 tablespoons ginger chips or finely chopped crystallized ginger

1 egg

1 Preheat the oven to 350°. Line a cookie sheet with parchment paper. Place ¼ cup sugar in a small bowl.

2 Using a mixer and mixing bowl, beat the butter until fluffy, about 1 minute. Add the remaining ¼ cup sugar and the brown sugar and mix together until smooth. Scrape down the sides of the bowl, add the molasses, and blend well.

3 Sift together the flour, baking soda, ground ginger, cardamom, cinnamon, nutmeg, and salt. Add to the butter mixture in three stages, blending well after each addition. Stop and scrape down the sides of the bowl occasionally. Stir in the ginger chips. Lightly beat the egg and add. Blend thoroughly.

4 Scoop out large spoonfuls (about 2 tablespoons each) and roll into balls. Drop the balls in the bowl of sugar and toss to coat completely. Place the balls on the cookie sheet, leaving 3 inches between them. Chill for 15 minutes.

5 Bake for 15 minutes, until the tops are cracked. Remove the cookie sheet from the oven and transfer the cookies from the parchment paper to cooling racks. Store in an airtight container at room temperature for up to 5 days. Freeze for longer storage.

Per serving: *Calories 215 (From Fat 82); Fat 9g (Saturated 6g); Cholesterol 37mg; Sodium 178mg; Carbohydrate 31g (Dietary Fiber 1g); Protein 2g.*

Giant Pecan O's

These not only will melt in your mouth but also will melt the heart of anyone lucky enough to eat them. Shaping these cookies takes a little more time because you have to first shape them into a rope and then form the rope into an O. Once you get the hang of it, though, shaping them goes quickly.

Preparation time: *1½ hours; includes chilling*

Baking time: *20 minutes*

Yield: *16*

1 cup shelled pecans	*½ cup confectioners' sugar, sifted*
2 cups all-purpose flour	*2 teaspoons vanilla extract*
1 cup (2 sticks) unsalted butter, softened	*Confectioners' sugar for garnish*

1 Place the pecans and ½ cup flour in the bowl of a food processor fitted with the steel blade. Pulse until the nuts are finely ground, about 2 minutes. Add the remaining 1½ cups flour and pulse to blend well.

2 Using a mixer and mixing bowl, beat the butter until fluffy, about 2 minutes. Add the ½ cup confectioners' sugar and mix together until smooth. Blend in the vanilla thoroughly. Add the flour and nut mixture in three stages, blending well after each addition.

3 Line a cookie sheet with parchment paper. Divide the dough into 16 even portions. Roll each portion into a ball. On a flat surface, roll each ball into a rope abut 6 inches long. Shape each rope into an O on the cookie sheets, pressing the ends together so they stick. Leave 3 inches between the cookies. Chill in the refrigerator for at least 1 hour.

4 Preheat the oven to 350°. Bake the cookies for 20 minutes, until the bottoms of the cookies are golden. Remove the cookie sheet from the oven and transfer the cookies from the parchment paper to cooling racks. Dust the cookies heavily with confectioners' sugar. Store in an airtight container at room temperature for up to 5 days. Freeze for longer storage.

Per serving: *Calories 219 (From Fat 149); Fat 17g (Saturated 8g); Cholesterol 31mg; Sodium 2mg; Carbohydrate 16g (Dietary Fiber 1g); Protein 2g.*

Cocoa Walnut Giants

Cocoa gives these cookies a rich, deep flavor that blends beautifully with the brown sugar and walnuts. You can use other nuts if you'd like to be adventurous. Try whole, unblanched almonds — the ones with the skins left on. I like the way they add both color and a bit more flavor than the ones without the skins. Macadamia nuts work well here, too. You can even experiment with peanuts.

Preparation time: *20 minutes*

Baking time: *20 minutes*

Yield: *28*

1 cup (2 sticks) unsalted butter, softened

1 cup light brown sugar

1¼ cups sugar

2 eggs

1 teaspoon vanilla extract

¾ cup cocoa powder

2½ cups all-purpose flour

1 teaspoon baking soda

1¼ cups walnuts, coarsely chopped

1 Preheat the oven to 350°. Line a cookie sheet with parchment paper.

2 Using a mixer and mixing bowl, beat the butter until fluffy, about 1 minute. Add the brown sugar and sugar and mix together until smooth. In a small bowl, lightly beat the eggs with the vanilla and add to the butter mixture. Scrape down the sides of the bowl and blend well.

3 Sift together the cocoa powder, flour, and baking soda. Add to the butter mixture in three stages, blending well after each addition. Stir in the walnuts.

4 Scoop out large spoonfuls (about 2 tablespoons each) and roll into balls. Place the balls on the cookie sheet, leaving 3 inches between them. Bake for 20 minutes, until set. Remove the cookie sheet from the oven and transfer the cookies from the parchment paper to cooling racks. Store in an airtight container at room temperature for up to 5 days. Freeze for longer storage.

Per serving: Calories 355 (From Fat 162); Fat 18g (Saturated 8g); Cholesterol 58mg; Sodium 95mg; Carbohydrate 47g (Dietary Fiber 2g); Protein 5g.

Oatmeal Raisin Walnut Giants

These are my all-time favorites. They're a giant version of cookies I grew up eating and still love. They're also one of my most requested cookies by friends and family of all ages.

Preparation time: *20 minutes*

Baking time: *20 minutes*

Yield: *About 3 dozen*

1 cup (2 sticks) unsalted butter, softened	*2¼ cups all-purpose flour*
1½ cups sugar	*Pinch of salt*
2 eggs	*1 teaspoon baking soda*
2 teaspoons vanilla extract	*1¼ cups raisins*
1¾ cups old-fashioned rolled oats	*1 cup roughly chopped walnuts*

1 Preheat the oven to 325°. Line a cookie sheet with parchment paper.

2 Using a mixer and mixing bowl, beat the butter until fluffy, about 2 minutes. Add the sugar and mix together until smooth. In a small bowl, lightly beat the eggs with the vanilla and add to the butter mixture. Blend well. Add the oats and blend thoroughly.

3 Sift together the flour, salt, and baking soda. Add to the butter mixture in three stages, blending well after each addition. Stir in the raisins and walnuts.

4 Scoop out large spoonfuls (about 2 tablespoons each) and roll into balls. Place the balls on the cookie sheet, leaving 3 inches between them. Bake for 20 to 22 minutes, until the cookies are golden and set. Remove the cookie sheet from the oven and transfer the cookies from the parchment paper to cooling racks. Store in an airtight container at room temperature for up to 5 days. Freeze for longer storage.

Per serving: Calories 329 (From Fat 142); Fat 16g (Saturated 7g); Cholesterol 51mg; Sodium 88mg; Carbohydrate 44g (Dietary Fiber 2g); Protein 5g.

Chapter 18

Cookies Are for Kids

Children and cookies go together naturally. Children love to participate in cookie making because they have a great time, keep busy, learn, and have sweet rewards at the end. Involving children in cookie baking also is a good way for them to learn new skills in a fun and nurturing setting. They learn math from measuring and weighing ingredients. They find out about patience by letting the cookies bake until they're done and then letting them cool before eating. In addition, children get a lesson on follow-through — how to do a project from start to finish. Cookie baking also teaches children something about concentration — they come to understand that if they focus on the task, they'll have something delicious to eat at the end. Working with others and sharing are other good skills that children can learn from baking cookies. By doing things for others at an early age, such as making cookies for Grandpa, children gain some idea of what it means to be an active member of society, even if they don't appreciate that lesson at the time.

Cookie baking offers rewards other than the cookies themselves. Children derive a sense of accomplishment when they realize they're eating cookies they've created from start to finish. They also may experience feelings of pride as they share those cookies with family members. Another reward is the opportunity for children to express their creativity through cutting cookies in different shapes or decorating them. Dexterity, gained from working with different kitchen tools, is another benefit children derive from baking cookies — which are the perfect size for those little hands. But one of the best rewards of making cookies is having the great memories of helping Mom or Grandma in the kitchen to look back on when they're older.

Here are some good ways to get kids involved in cookie baking:

- Set aside one day a month as cookie-baking day. Let the kids pick the recipes and help with various stages of preparation and baking.

- Keep a variety of cookie cutters on hand for rainy days. Nothing beats baking cookies when the weather is bad.

- Plan a cookie-baking party. The kids can invite their friends, and everyone can help plan which recipes to bake, choose the cookie cutters, and set up the stations for mixing, rolling, cooling, and decorating. Set up packaging materials so that everyone can take home cookies they've baked. This is a great way to celebrate a birthday or other special occasion.

- Bake cookies as gifts for Mother's Day, Father's Day, and birthday celebrations for family members and friends.

- Contribute cookies to the school bake sale or make treats to share with classmates or scout groups.

Nearly All Ages Can Help Bake Cookies

Children of different ages can get involved in different stages of cookie baking. If they start young enough, by the time they're 11 or 12 they can bake cookies completely on their own. Won't it be fun when your children surprise you with a freshly baked batch of your favorite cookies?

The following list offers some guidelines for when to allow your children to handle different tasks:

- Children as young as 3 years old can get involved in cookie baking. Let the young ones help by adding premeasured ingredients to the bowl, choosing cookie cutters, and even stirring the mixture.

- At 5 years old, kids can participate in activities, such as breaking eggs, rolling dough into balls, dropping batter from a spoon, arranging cookies on the cookie sheets, and helping with simple decorations.

- At 7 years and older, children can learn to read recipes and measure ingredients, roll dough, cut out cookies and arrange them on cookie sheets, and learn about using the oven and timers.

- Over the age of 11, most children are capable of baking cookies on their own with a little supervision and occasional help, especially if they participated in cookie baking when they were younger.

You can involve your kids in baking recipes found in other chapters of this book. Start with easy recipes and work up to the more challenging ones as you see progress.

Baking Safely with Kids

Safety is the number one priority when baking with children. Always stress the importance of putting safety first. Talk with your children about what the cookie-baking experience will be like and explain to them precautions they need to follow to make it a safe and fun time. By following these tips you will have a great time in the kitchen and know that everyone involved will be safe.

- Don't allow children to climb on the oven door or touch hot oven racks or hot cookie sheets.

- Always use dry potholders to touch hot pans or pot handles.

- Never put fingers in the mixing bowl, especially when the mixer is turned on. Also, don't put spatulas in the beaters when the mixer is on.

- Don't eat the batter after eggs have been added and don't use cracked eggs. Salmonella bacteria is a concern in raw eggs, and cracked eggs may hold the bacteria. ***Note:*** Cookie baking is a great opportunity to teach safe food handling and good kitchen habits to kids.

- Wash hands with soap and warm water before beginning and wash hands often as you work in the kitchen.

- Keep your work space clean. Wash utensils and put them away after using them.

- Always dry your hands thoroughly before turning on a switch or putting a plug into an electrical outlet.

- Don't leave the kitchen while working on a recipe. Stay focused and keep working on your baking project from start to finish. It's too easy to get sidetracked and forget to go back to the kitchen.

- Don't cut any ingredients while holding them in your hands. Cut ingredients only on a cutting board.

- Don't run or play rough games in the kitchen. Always walk rather than run and be aware of your surroundings.

Switching the cookie sheets on oven racks should always be done by an adult or older child who is carefully using potholders.

Peanut Butter and Jelly Disks

Who doesn't love a peanut butter and jelly sandwich? These cookies have the same great flavor, but they are even better than the sandwich. Kids love to help make and eat these cookies.

Preparation time: *15 minutes*

Baking time: *12 minutes*

Yield: *3½ dozen*

1¼ cups all-purpose flour	*⅓ cup sugar*
1 teaspoon baking soda	*⅔ cup chunky peanut butter*
Pinch of salt	*1 teaspoon vanilla extract*
½ cup (1 stick) unsalted butter, softened	*1 egg*
⅔ cup light brown sugar	*About ¾ cup jelly, jam, or preserves*

1 Combine the flour, baking soda, and salt in a mixing bowl. Set aside. Using a mixer and mixing bowl, beat the butter until fluffy, about 1 minute. Add the brown sugar and sugar and mix together until smooth. Add the peanut butter, scrape down the sides of the bowl, and blend well. In a small bowl, lightly beat the vanilla into the egg to blend and add to the butter mixture and blend well. Add the dry ingredients in three stages to the peanut butter mixture, scraping down the sides of the bowl after each addition. Mix until smooth. Cover the bowl with plastic wrap and chill for 45 minutes to an hour, until firm but still pliable.

2 Preheat the oven to 350°. Line a cookie sheet with parchment paper.

3 Pinch off walnut-size pieces of the dough and roll into balls. Place the balls on the cookie sheet, with 2 inches between them. With your thumb, press a deep indentation into the center of each cookie. Place about ½ teaspoon of jelly, jam, or preserves into the thumbprint in each cookie.

4 Bake for 12 to 14 minutes, until the cookies are golden and set. Remove the cookie sheet from the oven and transfer the cookies from the parchment paper to cooling racks. Store the cookies between layers of wax paper in an airtight container at room temperature for up to 3 days.

Per serving: Calories 88 (From Fat 39); Fat 4g (Saturated 2g); Cholesterol 11mg; Sodium 57mg; Carbohydrate 11g (Dietary Fiber 0g); Protein 2g.

Butterscotch Nut Squares

These quick and easy cookies are favorites. In this recipe, children learn about using a square baking pan and about greasing the pan before baking. Either buy the nuts already chopped or have an adult or older child (over the age of 11) chop the nuts. Almonds or hazelnuts also work well in this recipe.

Preparation time: *15 minutes*

Baking time: *15 minutes*

Yield: *3 dozen*

2 tablespoons (¼ stick) unsalted butter	*¼ teaspoon baking soda*
2 eggs	*Pinch of salt*
1 cup light brown sugar	*1 teaspoon vanilla extract*
⅓ cup all-purpose flour	*1 cup roughly chopped walnuts or other nuts*

1 Preheat the oven to 350°. Melt 1 tablespoon of the butter in a small saucepan over medium heat and pour it into an 8-inch square pan. Swirl it around to coat the bottom and sides of the pan. Add the remaining tablespoon of butter to the warm pan and let it melt.

2 Beat the eggs lightly in a mixing bowl. Add the brown sugar and blend well. Stir in the flour, baking soda, and salt and mix well. Add the vanilla and the nuts and blend together. Add the remaining butter and mix well.

3 Pour the mixture into the pan. Bake for 15 minutes, until golden and set. Remove the pan from the oven and transfer it to a cooling rack. Cut the bars into 1⅓-inch squares, six in each direction. Store the bars in an airtight container at room temperature for up to 4 days. Freeze for longer storage.

Per serving: Calories 59 (From Fat 28); Fat 3g (Saturated 1g); Cholesterol 14mg; Sodium 19mg; Carbohydrate 7g (Dietary Fiber 0g); Protein 1g.

Gingerbread People

Kids love to get involved in making gingerbread people. They love to eat them, too. These are great cookies to make with a group because there's something for everyone to do. They can help with rolling the dough, cutting, and decorating. If you want to make cookie ornaments, poke a hole near the top before baking. When cool, string a decorative ribbon through the hole.

Specialty tools: *Gingerbread people cookie cutters*

Preparation time: *1½ hours; includes chilling*

Baking time: *10 minutes*

Yield: *Twelve 6-inch or fourteen 5-inch cookies*

3 cups all-purpose flour

1 teaspoon baking soda

¼ teaspoon salt

1 cup light brown sugar

2 teaspoons ground cinnamon

1 tablespoon ground ginger

½ teaspoon ground cloves

½ teaspoon nutmeg, preferably freshly grated

Zest of 1 large orange

¾ cup (1½ sticks) unsalted butter

½ cup unsulphured molasses

1 egg

Decorations: Currants or raisins, crystallized ginger chips, cinnamon candies such as Red Hots (optional)

Royal Icing (see Chapter 20) colored with paste food coloring or powder food coloring (optional)

1 In the work bowl of a food processor fitted with the steel blade, combine the flour, baking soda, salt, brown sugar, cinnamon, ginger, cloves, nutmeg, and orange zest. Pulse briefly to blend. Cut the butter into small pieces and add to the dry ingredients. Pulse until the butter is cut into very tiny pieces. Add the molasses and egg and process until the mixture forms a ball, about 30 seconds. Wrap the dough tightly in plastic and chill until firm, about 1 hour.

(To make the dough with a mixer and mixing bowl, soften the butter to room temperature and beat until soft and fluffy, about 1 minute. Add the brown sugar and blend together well. Lightly beat the egg and add to the mixture along with the molasses and orange zest. Stop and scrape down the sides of the bowl with a rubber spatula to blend evenly. Combine the flour with the baking soda, salt, cinnamon, ginger, cloves, and nutmeg. Add to the mixture in the mixing bowl in three stages, blending well after each addition. Proceed with the same instructions given for using the food processor.)

2 Preheat the oven to 350°. Line a cookie sheet with parchment paper.

3 Divide the dough in half and roll each half on a lightly floured surface or between sheets of lightly floured wax paper to about ⅛-inch thick. Gently peel off the wax paper and use a gingerbread person cookie cutter to cut out the dough. Transfer the cookie people to the cookie sheet, leaving 2 inches between them. If using decorations, press raisins, ginger chips, or Red Hots into the shapes to form faces and buttons on the bodies.

4 Bake for 10 to 12 minutes, until firm. Remove the cookie sheet from the oven and transfer the cookies from the parchment paper to cooling racks.

5 If using the Royal Icing to decorate the cookies, wait until they're completely cool. Color the icing with paste or powder food coloring. Place the icing into a parchment paper pastry cone and snip off a small opening at the pointed end. Pipe the icing onto the cookies and leave to set until firm. Store in an airtight container at room temperature for up to a week. Freeze for longer storage.

Per serving (based on 12 cookies): Calories 331 (From Fat 111); Fat 12g (Saturated 7g); Cholesterol 49mg; Sodium 173mg; Carbohydrate 52g (Dietary Fiber 1g); Protein 4g.

Trail Mix Cookies

These are lots of fun for kids to make. Use any type of commercial trail mix. If you have none on hand, making your own trail mix is easy. Use any combination of whole unblanched almonds, walnuts, Brazil nuts, macadamia nuts, coconut chips or flakes, raisins, dried cranberries, dried cherries, or other dried fruit.

Preparation time: *30 minutes*

Baking time: *10 minutes*

Yield: *4 dozen*

2½ cups all-purpose flour	¾ cup sugar
1 teaspoon baking soda	1 teaspoon vanilla extract
¼ teaspoon salt	½ teaspoon almond extract
1 cup (2 sticks) unsalted butter, softened	2 eggs
1 cup light brown sugar	2 cups trail mix

1 Combine the flour, baking soda, and salt in a mixing bowl.

2 Using a mixer and mixing bowl, beat the butter until fluffy, about 2 minutes. Add the brown sugar, sugar, vanilla extract, and almond extract and mix together until smooth.

3 Add the eggs one at a time, stopping to scrape down the sides of the bowl with a rubber spatula after each addition. Blend in the flour mixture in three stages and stir in the trail mix. Cover the bowl tightly with plastic wrap and chill for 30 minutes.

4 Line a cookie sheet with parchment paper. Scoop out walnut-sized mounds of the cookie dough and place on the cookie sheet, leaving 2 inches between them. Chill the cookies for 30 minutes.

5 Preheat the oven to 375°.

6 Bake for 10 to 12 minutes, until golden. Remove the cookie sheet from the oven and transfer the cookies from the parchment paper to the cooling racks. Store the cookies in an airtight container at room temperature for up to a week. Freeze for longer storage.

Per serving: Calories 120 (From Fat 54); Fat 6g (Saturated 3g); Cholesterol 19mg; Sodium 59mg; Carbohydrate 16g (Dietary Fiber 0g); Protein 2g.

Hermits

Hermits is a funny name for a tasty cookie. These were named after people who like to be by themselves. They got their name from their quality of keeping very well. But they're so good that they disappear quickly.

Preparation time: *30 minutes*

Baking time: *12 minutes*

Yield: *3½ dozen*

2 cups all-purpose flour

1 teaspoon baking soda

¼ teaspoon salt

½ cup plus 2 tablespoons (1¼ sticks) unsalted butter, softened

1 cup light brown sugar

2 teaspoons ground cinnamon

2 teaspoons ground ginger

½ teaspoon ground cloves

¼ teaspoon nutmeg, preferably freshly grated

2 teaspoons instant espresso powder

1 egg

¼ cup dark molasses

¾ cup raisins

¾ cup walnuts, roughly chopped

1 Preheat the oven to 375°. Line a cookie sheet with parchment paper.

2 Sift together the flour, baking soda, and salt. Using a mixer and mixing bowl, beat the butter until fluffy, about 2 minutes. Add the brown sugar and mix together until smooth. Stir in the cinnamon, ginger, cloves, nutmeg, and espresso powder and blend well.

3 In a small bowl, stir the egg and molasses together and add to the butter mixture. Blend well. Add the sifted dry ingredients from Step 2 in three stages, blending well after each addition. Stir in the raisins and walnuts.

4 Scoop out walnut-size mounds of the dough and place on the cookie sheet, leaving 2 inches between the cookies. Bake for 12 to 15 minutes, until the cookies are golden and set. Remove the cookie sheet from the oven and transfer the cookies from the parchment paper to cooling racks. Store the cookies in an airtight container at room temperature for up to a week. Freeze for longer storage.

Per serving: Calories 94 (From Fat 37); Fat 4g (Saturated 2g); Cholesterol 12mg; Sodium 50mg; Carbohydrate 14g (Dietary Fiber 1g); Protein 1g.

Chapter 19

Slender Cookies

In This Chapter

▶ Understanding why fat is used in cookies

▶ Making your cookies lean

▶ Retaining the texture and flavor

▶ Adding spice to your cookies

*E*ating cookies can fit into a healthy lifestyle. You just need to be aware of the total amount of fat in your daily diet. By watching what you eat and trimming fat here and there, you don't have to deprive yourself of eating anything, especially cookies. If you choose cookies with fat, however, the easiest way to lower your fat intake is to eat fewer of them. A couple delicious cookies, nibbled slowly, go a long way toward satisfying a cookie craving. You don't have to eat the whole batch. You can also step up your exercise program to help burn the calories off.

If the cookies that you choose to consume are lowfat, all the better. This chapter provides you with a number of delicious recipes that have a minimum of fat. It also takes a look at why fat is used in cookies and how to replace it with other ingredients and still make scrumptious cookies. After all, who wants to eat cookies that taste like cardboard?

Where Fat in Cookies Comes From and What It Does

You may think that the fat in your cookie recipes comes only from butter, margarine, shortening, or oil. Most of it does, but fat is also found in other ingredients. Egg yolks contain fat, as do nuts and dairy products.

Fats are categorized as either saturated or unsaturated, depending on their chemical makeup and their source. Saturated fats come primarily from animal fats and are in solid form at room temperature. Saturated fats, such as butter and lard, contain cholesterol, which has given them a bad reputation. Unsaturated fats come primarily from plants, seeds, and vegetables and are liquid at room temperature. Unsaturated fats are considered to be the "good" fats; that is, they don't contain cholesterol.

Recent research has shed new light on the fat dilemma. Margarine, for instance, used to be thought of as a good substitute for butter. Margarine is a hydrogenated fat made by forcing pressurized hydrogen gas through liquid fat (oil) to transform it to a solid. This process turns the unsaturated fat into a saturated one, thereby removing its "good" qualities. Furthermore, new studies have shown that stearic acid, which is one of the primary fats in butter, does not raise serum cholesterol. So butter is better for us than we thought — even though it has cholesterol.

The bottom line is that all fats aren't bad for us, but if we can reduce our fat intake and our overall calorie intake, we'll be the leaner and better for it.

Here are some of the roles that fat plays in cookie making:

- **Fat helps cookies rise by creating air pockets in the dough or batter.** When the fat is creamed with sugar, air is trapped between the sugar crystals. This air expands while baking, thereby causing cookies to rise. This is especially true of room-temperature fat when it is creamed with sugar.

- **Fat adds deep flavor to cookies.** Fat tastes good and imparts its flavor to whatever it is added to.

- **Fat tenderizes and helps hold in moisture.** Fats tenderize by softening the stiff texture of proteins such as eggs, milk, and even flour. Fat tends to trap liquid, thereby helping keep dough soft and flexible. Fat can be heated to relatively high temperatures before it evaporates. In the oven, fat eventually turns to steam, helping cookies rise as they bake.

- **Fat adds texture, richness, tenderness, and pleasing mouth-feel.** A cookie made without fat has a drier, more crumbly texture than one made with fat. It also tastes and feels different in the mouth. Fat by its nature is rich and tastes pleasing. It feels smooth in the mouth, imparting an enjoyable experience.

- **Fat makes a more tender product because it limits the development of gluten by coating the gluten strands.** *Gluten* is an elastic protein that is formed when flour is mixed with liquid and then stirred. By limiting its development, the dough is more supple and doesn't become too stretchy.

Lowering the Fat in Cookie Recipes

The challenge to lowering fat is maintaining the flavor and texture of the recipes. Doing this can be tricky. Butter acts a tenderizer, for instance. If it's eliminated from a recipe, the result can be one tough cookie. However, occasionally you can use a small amount of lowfat cream cheese to replace some of the butter and still achieve the same tender results. This is but one of the methods you can use to successfully lower fat in cookies and still maintain their delicious taste and texture.

Be careful when substituting lowfat margarine, margarine spreads, and whipped butter for butter in cookie recipes. Most of these products contain large amounts of water and/or air that will change the proportions of your cookie recipe. As a result, you'll probably not be happy with the outcome.

Using fruit purées to lower fat

One of the easiest ways to lower fat is to replace it. A few fruit-based products on the market have been designed specifically to replace fat and to provide moisture. These are purées of dried fruit, such as plums and apples, mixed with water. Applesauce also works well to replace fat in recipes. Follow these important steps when using fruit-based purées rather than fat:

✔ Start with half the amount of puréed fruit to replace the fat called for in a recipe. You may need to add more if the cookies are too dry.

✔ Keep mixing to a minimum so that less air is incorporated into the batter. Because fruit purée has a different consistency than butter or margarine, it holds air differently. Too much added air will cause the cookies to rise in the oven, but they will deflate as they cool because the fruit purée doesn't have the structure to hold as much air.

✔ Bake the cookies for the least amount of time stated in the recipe. Add more baking time if necessary.

Replacing bad fats with good fats

You can also replace "bad" fats with "good" fats. Instead of using butter or margarine high in saturated fat, use a small amount of oil that is high in unsaturated fat in your cookie recipes. Canola oil is favored because of its healthy qualities. Yes, it's still fat, but it's the good kind. You can also use safflower oil.

Think of butter as an accent flavor rather than a main ingredient. Eliminate most of it from your recipe and use a small amount of canola oil in its place. The result will still be a tasty cookie. Also use parchment paper to line cookie sheets. It has absolutely no fat or calories. Or you can use a nonstick vegetable spray to coat the cookie sheets instead of using parchment paper. Either of these methods will ensure a reduction of the fat in your cookies.

 A good general rule when substituting oil for butter is to use 1 tablespoon of oil in place of 4 tablespoons of butter.

Replacing solid fat with oil may make the cookies slightly flatter, but using some cake flour in place of regular flour can help keep this from happening. Also, reduce the sugar in the recipe by two or three tablespoons, and the finished cookie will be close to the original full-fat one.

Using egg whites to cut fat

Another way to cut fat is to use egg whites in place of whole eggs. Two egg whites are equal to one whole egg. You can easily freeze egg whites so you'll have them on hand when they're needed. Freeze egg whites in ice cube trays. Each cube is one egg white, so it's easy to know how many egg whites you have. Once frozen, transfer the cubes to another container. Defrost only as many egg whites as you need each time. You can also determine the number of egg whites by measuring them in a liquid measuring cup. One-half cup is equal to three large egg whites.

A few other products can be used in place of fresh or defrosted frozen egg whites:

- **Dried egg whites** in a powder form can be found in a sealed can in the baking section of most supermarkets. They're really easy to use. Simply mix some of the powder with water, and you have the equivalent of fresh egg whites. Follow the instructions on the can for the amount of powder to use per egg white. This product has an indefinite shelf life if stored tightly sealed in a cool, dry place.

- **Meringue powder** is a dried egg white product that also contains sugar and gum. It is available at many cake decorating and craft supply shops. Meringue powder is easily mixed with water. Simply follow the instructions on the jar. It has an indefinite shelf life if stored tightly sealed in a cool, dry place.

- **Liquid fresh egg whites** can be found in the refrigerator section of many supermarkets and health food stores. They have been pasteurized and checked for salmonella and will last for up to 4 months in the refrigerator even after they've been opened. If stored in the freezer, they'll last even longer. Simply defrost and bring to room temperature like other frozen egg whites. The only drawback to using these egg whites is that they can't be whipped. Some change occurs to the egg whites during the pasteurization process that changes their ability to hold air.

Reducing fat by cutting down on nuts

A final way to cut fat concerns nuts. Although nuts are delicious, they still have a lot of fat. Cut the amount of nuts in recipes by one-third to one-half and replace some of that with flour. You can also toast the nuts to enhance their flavor. This way, you can still have the nuts and eat them, too.

Maintaining Texture

When manipulating ingredients to make reduced-fat cookies, maintaining the desired texture can sometimes be a problem. Cookies can be too dry, too tough, or too flat compared to their full-fat cousins. Here are a couple tips for dealing with this problem:

- Replace as much as half of the all-purpose flour with cake flour. This product makes cookies softer and more delicate. Start with ½ cup of flour and see what results you obtain.

- Add a little corn syrup to keep the texture pliable. Start with 1 tablespoon and see how that works. Add more if it's needed. Even though corn syrup is a liquid sweetener, it is less sweet than sugar, so adding it in addition to the sugar in the recipe won't make a noticeable difference in the final taste.

Boosting Flavor

Fat tastes good and feels good in the mouth. If you eliminate it from cookie recipes, you have to include something to increase the flavor. Spices are the perfect remedy. By increasing the amount of spices you normally use, the cookies taste richer. Play around with your cookie recipes to see how much spice to use. If you like the flavor of spices as much as I do, experimenting with spices will be easy and lots of fun.

You can also use extracts to add flavor. Try adding extra vanilla. Or use other extracts that complement the main flavor of the cookie, such as almond, lemon, and orange extracts.

Try using dried fruits such as cherries, cranberries, apricots, and pears in place of nuts or chocolate chips. Substitute them in an equal amount to the chocolate chips or nuts. You'll be pleasantly surprised with your creations. To keep the dried fruits from sticking together, dust them with a tablespoon or two of flour and toss lightly.

Chocolate and Cocoa Touches

These cookies make it easy to "have your cookies and eat them too." They taste so good that it will be hard for you or your friends to tell them from full-fat cookies. And there's really no special trick to making these cookies. They simply use a little less of some ingredients and a few different ingredients. Make plenty so that everyone can indulge.

Florentine Bars

Florentines are a true confection, first cooked and then baked. This reduced-fat version is an adaptation of the classic round shape that is coated on the underside with chocolate (see Chapter 16 for the classic recipe). In this recipe, they're made in a square pan, cut into bars, and drizzled with chocolate. Although these look different from the traditional rounds, they're equally delicious.

Preparation time: *25 minutes; includes chilling*

Baking time: *8 minutes*

Yield: *20*

2 tablespoons (¼ stick) unsalted butter, cut into small pieces

2 tablespoons canola oil

¼ cup evaporated lowfat milk

3 tablespoons light corn syrup

⅔ cup sugar

2 cups sliced almonds

½ cup finely chopped candied orange peel (optional)

2 ounces bittersweet or semisweet chocolate, very finely chopped

1 Preheat the oven to 400°. Coat the inside of an 8-inch square baking pan with nonstick cooking spray.

2 Combine the butter, canola oil, evaporated milk, corn syrup, and sugar in a 2-quart heavy saucepan. Cook over medium heat until the butter melts and the mixture begins to boil. Brush down the inside of the pan with a pastry brush dipped in warm water to prevent the sugar from crystallizing.

3 Cook the mixture, stirring often with a long wooden spoon, until it registers 240° on a candy thermometer, about 10 minutes. Remove the pan from the heat and immediately stir in the almonds and candied orange peel, if desired.

4 Turn the mixture out into the baking pan and spread evenly into the corners. Bake for 8 minutes. Remove the pan from the oven and transfer to a rack to cool for 5 minutes.

5 Use a sharp knife to cut the mixture into 20 bars. You may need to cut the bars a few times as they cool so they'll hold the indentations of the knife.

6 For the chocolate, melt two-thirds of it in the top of a double boiler over hot water. Stir often with a rubber spatula. When the chocolate is smooth, remove the top pan of the double boiler, wipe it dry, and place it on a heatproof surface. Stir in the remaining chocolate in two or three batches, letting each melt before adding the next. When all the chocolate is added, dip your finger in it to test the temperature. It should feel comfortable, not too hot or too cool. Or you can use an instant-read thermometer. The temperature should register slightly cooler than body temperature, about 90°.

7 Drizzle the top of the Florentines with chocolate or transfer the chocolate to a parchment paper pastry cone (see Chapters 9 and 20 and Figure 19-1). Fold down the top tightly and snip off a tiny opening at the point. Using a back and forth motion, draw lines across the top of the Florentines in both directions. Chill the pan in the refrigerator for 10 minutes to set the chocolate. Serve the Florentines at room temperature. Store them in a single layer in an airtight container at room temperature for up to 5 days. Freeze for longer storage.

Per serving: Calories 120 (From Fat 71); Fat 8g (Saturated 1g); Cholesterol 4mg; Sodium 10mg; Carbohydrate 11g (Dietary Fiber 1g); Protein 3g.

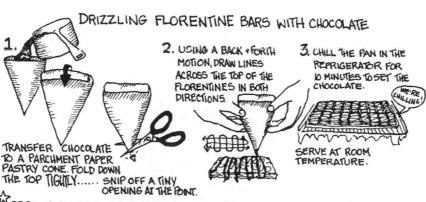

Figure 19-1: Decorating Florentine bars with chocolate.

DRIZZLING FLORENTINE BARS WITH CHOCOLATE

1.

2. USING A BACK + FORTH MOTION, DRAW LINES ACROSS THE TOP OF THE FLORENTINES IN BOTH DIRECTIONS.

3. CHILL THE PAN IN THE REFRIGERATOR FOR 10 MINUTES TO SET THE CHOCOLATE.

WE'RE CHILLING!

TRANSFER CHOCOLATE TO A PARCHMENT PAPER PASTRY CONE. FOLD DOWN THE TOP TIGHTLY...... SNIP OFF A TINY OPENING AT THE POINT.

SERVE AT ROOM TEMPERATURE.

STORE IN A SINGLE LAYER IN AN AIRTIGHT CONTAINER AT ROOM TEMPERATURE FOR UP TO 5 DAYS. FREEZE FOR LONGER STORAGE.

Cocoa Meringue Drops

Looking for a lowfat cookie and a way to use up extra egg whites? Cocoa Meringue Drops are the answer. Their unique texture sets them apart from most other cookies. They're light as air, with a crunchy outside and chewy inside.

Preparation time: *10 minutes*

Baking time: *40 minutes*

Yield: *About 3 dozen*

⅔ cup confectioners' sugar

3 tablespoons unsweetened Dutch-processed cocoa powder

3 egg whites, at room temperature

¼ teaspoon cream of tartar

½ cup sugar

1 Preheat the oven to 300°. Line a cookie sheet with foil, shiny side up.

2 Sift together the confectioners' sugar and cocoa powder.

3 Using a mixer, make the meringue by whipping the egg whites with the cream of tartar in a large bowl on medium speed until frothy. Sprinkle in ¼ cup of the sugar and whip until the egg whites hold firm peaks. Sprinkle on the remaining ¼ cup sugar and blend well.

4 Fold in the cocoa mixture until well blended. Drop mounds (about 2 teaspoons for each mound) of the mixture onto the cookie sheet, leaving 1 inch between the cookies. Bake for 40 minutes, until set. Remove the cookie sheet from the oven and transfer to a cooling rack. Peel the foil off the cookies. Store in an airtight container at room temperature for up to 3 weeks.

Per serving: Calories 20 (From Fat 1); Fat 0g (Saturated 0g); Cholesterol 0mg; Sodium 5mg; Carbohydrate 5g (Dietary Fiber 0g); Protein 0g.

Swiss Cocoa Spice Cookies

These Swiss favorites are light and chewy, made from a delicious mixture of ground almonds, cocoa, chocolate, and spices.

Specialty tools: *Cookie cutters*

Preparation time: *25 minutes; includes chilling*

Baking time: *10 minutes*

Yield: *4½ dozen*

1½ cups finely ground almonds, or 1¼ cups whole almonds, ground to a powder	*4 ounces bittersweet or semisweet chocolate, finely chopped*
1½ cups superfine sugar	*2 egg whites at room temperature*
3 tablespoons unsweetened Dutch-processed cocoa powder	*¼ teaspoon almond extract*
1½ teaspoons ground cinnamon	*Confectioners' sugar for rolling the dough*
½ teaspoon ground cloves	*3 ounces bittersweet or semisweet chocolate, very finely chopped (optional)*

1 Place an oven rack in the upper third of the oven and preheat the oven to 300°. Line a cookie sheet with parchment paper.

2 Combine the ground almonds, sugar, cocoa powder, cinnamon, and cloves in the work bowl of a food processor fitted with a steel blade. Pulse briefly to blend. Add the 4 ounces chocolate and pulse until it is very finely ground, about 1 minute. (To mix the dough in a bowl with a mixer, chop the 4 ounces of chocolate very finely by hand or in a blender, and proceed by following the instructions for the food processor in this step.)

3 Add the egg whites and almond extract and process or mix until the mixture is well blended and holds together, about 1 minute.

4 Roll out the dough between sheets of wax paper dusted with confectioners' sugar. If the dough is very soft, transfer it to a cookie sheet and chill in the freezer for 10 minutes.

5 Peel off the top layer of wax paper. Use cookie cutters to cut out shapes such as stars, hearts, half-moons, or clover leaves. Transfer to the lined baking sheet.

6 Bake for 10 to 12 minutes, until set but still soft. The cookies will firm up as they cool. Remove the cookie sheet from the oven and transfer to a rack to cool.

7 If desired, dip the cookies in the 3 ounces chocolate, following the chopping, melting, and dipping techniques for chocolate in Chapter 20. Line a cookie sheet with parchment or wax paper. Dip a cookie halfway into the chocolate. Let the excess drip off. Place the cookie on the lined cookie sheet. Store the cookies in an airtight container at room temperature for up to 5 days. Freeze for longer storage.

Per serving: *Calories 53 (From Fat 22); Fat 2g (Saturated 1g); Cholesterol 0mg; Sodium 2mg; Carbohydrate 8g (Dietary Fiber 1g); Protein 1g.*

Spice It Up!

What would life be without a little spice? Personally, I like a lot of spice in my life and in my cookies. I almost always choose a cookie with spice over one without, especially a reduced-fat cookie. The rich, deep flavor of spices can easily make up for the absence of fat. You can choose from a large variety of spices to create wonderful and unique flavors in cookies. Spices also have a way of transporting you to a faraway place because they're different from the everyday flavors you may be used to. Spices come from exotic locations, so if you close your eyes when eating a spice cookie, you may even be able to imagine being in distant lands.

Honey Spice Bars

These cookies are a reduced-fat version of the traditional German honey and spice cookies, Lebkuchen (see Chapter 15), made in a new format — as bars. The flavors deepen and become richer as the cookies age. Although they're delicious the same day they're made, they're even better a few weeks later.

Preparation time: *15 minutes*

Baking time: *20 minutes*

Yield: *2 dozen*

1¾ cups all-purpose flour

½ teaspoon baking powder

½ teaspoon baking soda

⅛ teaspoon salt

1 teaspoon ground cinnamon

½ teaspoon ground cardamom

½ teaspoon ground ginger

½ teaspoon ground cloves

¼ teaspoon ground nutmeg, preferably freshly ground or grated

¼ teaspoon crushed anise seeds

Zest of 1 large lemon, finely minced

1 tablespoon unsalted butter

½ cup honey

¼ cup sugar

¼ cup light brown sugar

½ cup finely ground almonds

1 egg white at room temperature

⅓ cup finely chopped candied orange or lemon peel (optional)

Glaze

½ cup confectioners' sugar, sifted

1 tablespoon fresh lemon juice

1 Preheat the oven to 350°. Coat an 8-inch square baking pan with nonstick cooking spray.

2 Sift together the flour, baking powder, baking soda, salt, cinnamon, cardamom, ginger, cloves, and nutmeg. Toss to blend with the anise seeds and lemon zest.

3 Place the butter, honey, sugar, and brown sugar in a 2-quart heavy-bottomed saucepan. Warm over medium heat until the butter is melted and the sugar is dissolved, about 4 minutes. Transfer to a large mixing bowl.

4 Using a mixer, stir the warm honey mixture. Blend in the ground almonds and then add the flour mixture from Step 2 in three to four stages, stopping to scrape down the sides of the bowl with a rubber spatula after each addition. Blend thoroughly. Add the egg white and blend completely. If desired, add the candied peel and stir in thoroughly.

5 Transfer the mixture to the baking pan. With damp fingertips press the dough evenly into the pan. Bake for 20 minutes, until puffed and golden. Remove the pan from the oven and transfer to a rack to cool for 10 minutes.

6 For the glaze, whisk the confectioners' sugar and lemon juice in a small bowl until smooth. Spread on top of the baked dough while it's warm. Let stand until completely cool. Cut into 1½-inch-x-2-inch bars. Store in an airtight container at room temperature for up to a month.

Per serving: Calories 120 (From Fat 32); Fat 4g (Saturated 1g); Cholesterol 1mg; Sodium 50mg; Carbohydrate 21g (Dietary Fiber 1g); Protein 2g.

Pfeffernuesse (Spice Nuts)

Pepper is the surprise ingredient that gives these medieval German holiday cookies their special flavor. They take their name from the German term for the spice-producing countries of the Far East, Pfefferlander. If you've never tried Pfeffernuesse (FEHF-fyhr-noos), don't be put off by the use of pepper. It enhances the sweet spices in a positive and delicious way.

Preparation time: *45 minutes; includes chilling*

Baking time: *12 minutes*

Yield: *4 dozen*

⅓ cup honey

¼ cup molasses

2 tablespoons (¼ stick) unsalted butter, cut into small pieces

2 tablespoons light brown sugar

2 cups all-purpose flour

½ teaspoon baking powder

½ teaspoon baking soda

½ teaspoon ground allspice

½ teaspoon ground cardamom

½ teaspoon black pepper, preferably freshly ground

½ teaspoon ground nutmeg, preferably freshly grated or ground

¼ teaspoon ground cloves

¼ teaspoon ground ginger

¼ teaspoon crushed anise seeds

¼ teaspoon salt

Confectioners' sugar for garnish

1 Place the honey, molasses, and butter in a 1-quart heavy-bottomed saucepan. Warm over medium heat until the butter is melted. Transfer to a large mixing bowl. Using a mixer, blend the mixture with the brown sugar.

2 Sift together the flour, baking powder, and baking soda. Blend in the allspice, cardamom, black pepper, nutmeg, cloves, ginger, anise seeds, and salt. With the mixer on low speed, add the dry ingredients in three stages to the butter mixture and blend together thoroughly. Cover the bowl tightly with plastic wrap and chill for 30 minutes.

3 Preheat the oven to 350°. Line a cookie sheet with parchment paper. Pinch off walnut-size pieces of the dough and roll into 1-inch balls. Place the balls on the cookie sheet, leaving 1 inch between the cookies. Bake for 12 to 14 minutes, until the cookies are set. Remove the cookie sheet from the oven and transfer the cookies to racks to cool.

4 Dust the cookies lightly with confectioners' sugar. Store in an airtight container at room temperature for up to 2 weeks.

Per serving: Calories 38 (From Fat 5); Fat 1g (Saturated 0g); Cholesterol 1mg; Sodium 30mg; Carbohydrate 8g (Dietary Fiber 0g); Protein 1g.

Cinnamon Stars

These glazed cookies are holiday favorites in all the German-speaking countries. Although they are very delicate and take a bit of time to prepare, they're worth the effort. Because their flavor improves with age, they're a perfect choice to make ahead.

Specialty tools: *1½-inch star-shaped cookie cutter, goosefeather pastry brush*

Preparation time: *3½ hours; includes resting*

Baking time: *15 minutes*

Yield: *6 dozen*

1¾ cup sliced almonds	*Pinch of salt*
2 teaspoons ground cinnamon	*⅛ teaspoon fresh lemon juice*
Zest of 1 large lemon, finely minced	*2½ cups confectioners' sugar, sifted*
2 egg whites at room temperature	*Granulated sugar for rolling the dough*

1 Combine the almonds and cinnamon in the work bowl of a food processor fitted with a steel blade. Pulse to grind the almonds finely. Add the lemon zest and blend briefly. The almonds can also be ground in a blender or in a clean coffee grinder, if a food processor isn't available.

2 Using a hand mixer, make a meringue by whipping the egg whites and salt in a grease-free bowl until the whites are frothy. Add the lemon juice and whip until the whites hold firm peaks, about 3 minutes. Slowly add the confectioners' sugar until well blended. Reserve ⅓ cup of the meringue and cover with a damp paper towel.

3 Blend the ground almond mixture into the rest of the meringue until thoroughly blended and the mixture is a firm dough.

4 Line a cookie sheet with parchment paper. Dust a work surface with granulated sugar and roll out the dough to ¼-inch thick. Use a 1½-inch star-shaped cutter to cut out the cookies. Gather the scraps of dough together, reroll, and cut out additional cookies. Dip the cutter into sugar as needed while cutting out the stars. Transfer to the cookie sheet, leaving 1 inch between the cookies.

5 Use the reserved ⅓ cup meringue to glaze the tops of the stars. Add ½ to 1 teaspoon water to the remaining meringue to liquefy it. Use a goosefeather pastry brush (see Chapter 2) to apply glaze to the top of each star. Let the cookies air-dry at room temperature for 3 hours.

6 Preheat the oven to 300°. Bake for 15 minutes, until set. Remove the cookie sheet from the oven and transfer the cookies to racks to cool. Store in an airtight container at room temperature for up to 1 month.

Per serving: Calories 36 (From Fat 14); Fat 1g (Saturated 0g); Cholesterol 0mg; Sodium 5mg; Carbohydrate 5g (Dietary Fiber 0g); Protein 1g.

Reduced-Fat Ischl Tartlets

This is a reduced-fat version of the Austrian specialty in Chapter 9. They're not really tartlets at all, but delicious sandwich cookies with a bright spot of preserves peeking out from the center.

Specialty tools: *2½-inch diameter daisy petal shape or other fluted-edge cookie cutter and a 1-inch round cutter*

Preparation time: *30 minutes; includes resting*

Baking time: *12 minutes*

Yield: *2 dozen*

½ cup all-purpose flour

⅓ cup cake flour

½ cup sugar

¾ cup finely ground almonds

1 teaspoon ground cinnamon

1 tablespoon unsalted butter

2 ounces lowfat cream cheese

2 tablespoons dried fruit purée

Assembly

½ cup apricot or raspberry preserves

Confectioners' sugar

1 Combine the flour, cake flour, sugar, almonds, and cinnamon in the work bowl of a food processor fitted with a steel blade. Pulse briefly to blend. Cut the butter and cream cheese into small pieces and add to the flour mixture. Pulse until they're cut into tiny pieces. Add the dried fruit purée and process until the mixture forms a ball, about 1 minute. Wrap the dough in plastic and chill for at least 1 hour.

(To blend the dough in a mixing bowl using a mixer, have the butter and cream cheese at room temperature. Beat them together until fluffy, about 1 minute. Add the dried fruit purée and blend well. Combine the flour, cake flour, sugar, almonds, and cinnamon together and toss to blend. Add to the butter mixture in three stages, stopping to scrape down the sides of the bowl after each addition. Blend until smooth and proceed by following the instructions for the food processor.)

2 Preheat the oven to 350°. Line a cookie sheet with parchment paper.

3 Divide the dough in half. Roll out each half between sheets of lightly floured wax paper to a thickness of ⅛ inch. Transfer to a cookie sheet and chill in the freezer for 15 minutes.

4 Peel off the top layer of wax paper. Use a 2½-inch-diameter daisy-petal-shape cookie cutter to cut the dough. In half of the cookies, use a 1-inch round cutter to cut out a hole in the center. Reroll the scraps and cut again. Transfer the cookies to the lined cookie sheet.

5 Bake for 12 minutes, until set. Remove the cookie sheet from the oven and transfer to a rack to cool. Use an offset spatula to release the cookies from the parchment paper when cool. Store unassembled cookies in an airtight container at room temperature for up to 5 days.

6 To assemble the cookies, use a parchment paper pastry bag or a spoon to place a dollop of preserves in the center of the solid cookies. Heavily dust the cookies with the center holes with confectioners' sugar and place these on top of the cookies with the preserves. Store the assembled cookies in a single layer in an airtight container at room temperature for 1 day.

Per serving: Calories 112 (From Fat 49); Fat 5g (Saturated 1g); Cholesterol 3mg; Sodium 10mg; Carbohydrate 15g (Dietary Fiber 1g); Protein 3g.

Spiced Sugar Cookies

These sugar cookies are as delicious as those with more fat. The spices add lots of flavor, so you won't miss the butter. Cake flour gives them a delicate, light texture. These are great for the holidays or anytime. They can be cut into myriad shapes and sizes and decorated in a variety of ways. I especially like to use colored crystal sugar.

Preparation time: *20 minutes*

Baking time: *7 minutes*

Yield: *4 dozen*

⅓ cup sugar

¼ cup light brown sugar

2 tablespoons (¼ stick) unsalted butter, softened

2 tablespoons canola oil

1 egg

1 teaspoon vanilla extract

1¾ cups cake flour

1 teaspoon baking powder

¼ teaspoon salt

1½ teaspoons ground cinnamon

½ teaspoon ground ginger

½ teaspoon ground nutmeg, preferably freshly ground or grated

¼ teaspoon ground cloves

Decoration

2 tablespoons crystal sugar

½ teaspoon powder food color

1 Place an oven rack in the upper third of the oven and preheat the oven to 350°. Line a cookie sheet with parchment paper.

2 Using a mixer, combine the sugar, brown sugar, butter, and canola oil in a large mixing bowl and blend together until well combined. Add the egg and vanilla and continue to mix until thoroughly blended.

3 Sift together the flour, baking powder, salt, cinnamon, ginger, nutmeg, and cloves. Add to the sugar mixture in four stages, stopping to scrape down the sides of the bowl with a rubber spatula after each addition.

4 Roll out the dough between sheets of wax paper dusted with cake flour to a thickness of ⅛ inch. Transfer to a cookie sheet and chill in the refrigerator for 15 minutes. Peel off the top layer of wax paper. Use cookie cutters to cut out shapes. Transfer them to the lined cookie sheet, leaving 1 inch between the cookies.

5 To color the crystal sugar to decorate the cookies, mix it with the powder food coloring until the sugar is evenly colored. Sprinkle the sugar on top of the cookies before baking.

6 Bake for 7 minutes, until set. Remove the cookie sheet from the oven and transfer it to a rack to cool. Store in an airtight container between layers of wax paper at room temperature for up to 5 days. Freeze for longer storage.

Per serving: *Calories 36 (From Fat 11); Fat 1g (Saturated 0g); Cholesterol 6mg; Sodium 22mg; Carbohydrate 6g (Dietary Fiber 0g); Protein 0g.*

Zalettini

These cornmeal cookies are a specialty of Venice, Italy, and can be found in every pastry shop during the winter holiday season. Their name translates as "little yellow diamonds." This reduced-fat version is faithful to the original. For full flavor, use either Monukka or Thompson seedless raisins.

Preparation time: *20 minutes*

Baking time: *15 minutes*

Yield: *2 dozen*

⅓ cup Monukka or Thompson seedless raisins

¼ cup dark rum

¾ cup all-purpose flour

2 tablespoons (¼ stick) unsalted butter, softened

¼ cup sugar

2 tablespoons light olive oil

1 tablespoon light corn syrup

1 egg white at room temperature

¼ teaspoon lemon extract

Pinch of salt

1 teaspoon baking powder

½ cup plus 2 tablespoons fine yellow cornmeal

1 Place the raisins in a small bowl. Heat the rum in a small saucepan over low heat until warm. Pour the warm rum over the raisins. Cover the bowl tightly with plastic wrap and let the raisins soak for at least 30 minutes. Drain the raisins and pat them dry. Toss them with 1 tablespoon of the flour.

2 Preheat the oven to 375°. Line a cookie sheet with parchment paper.

3 Using a mixer, briefly beat the butter in a large mixing bowl. Add the sugar and mix together until smooth. Add the olive oil and corn syrup and blend well. Stir in the egg white and lemon extract and beat well.

4 Sift together the remaining flour, the salt, and the baking powder. Blend this mixture with the cornmeal. Add to the sugar mixture in three stages, mixing well after each addition. Blend in the raisins.

5 Pinch off walnut-size pieces of the dough and roll in your hands into log shapes about 2 inches long, 1 inch wide, and ½ inch thick. Place these on the cookie sheet with 1 inch between them.

6 Bake for 15 minutes, until golden. Remove the cookie sheet from the oven and transfer the cookies to a rack to cool. Store in an airtight container at room temperature for up to 1 week. Freeze for longer storage.

Per serving: *Calories 59 (From Fat 20); Fat 2g (Saturated 1g); Cholesterol 3mg; Sodium 25mg; Carbohydrate 9g (Dietary Fiber 0g); Protein 1g.*

Part VI
Dressing Up Your Cookies

The 5th Wave   By Rich Tennant

"Why do I sense you're upset?
Because you're piping that cookie with
hand grenades instead of rosettes"

In this part . . .

Making your cookies look beautiful is simple. Some easy decorative touches are all you need to add. The recipients of your cookies are certain to appreciate these extra eye-catching details and admire your creative talents. Some creative touches require very little effort, while others can require some practice. Whether it is painting, piping, or dusting, I guide you through the method. I also tell you how to quick-temper chocolate so that you can make your chocolate shine.

Chapter 20

Chocolate Embellishments

In This Chapter

▶ Chopping, melting, and storing chocolate

▶ Using chocolate for dipping

▶ Getting artistic with chocolate

Adding chocolate decorations to your cookies really dresses them up and gives them extra pizzazz. This special touch makes them elegant enough to attend practically any gathering or event and also dresses up any event they attend. Decorating cookies with chocolate is like donning a tuxedo or formal dress to attend a black-tie party. It makes them stand out and be noticed. And, of course, it enhances how they taste. Just about every cookie tastes even better with a little chocolate.

Don't be put off by thinking that decorating with chocolate is difficult. Once you know the tips and techniques covered in this chapter, you'll be a real ace at working with chocolate in no time. You'll know how to choose chocolate and how to treat it to eliminate any problems. There are tips on chopping, melting, and storing chocolate and what to do just in case you do run into trouble. We also talk about how to dip, paint, and write with chocolate so that you can be a chocolate artist.

Anything Tastes Better with Chocolate

The best type of chocolate to use for decorating is the same quality as the chocolate you like to eat plain. It's a good idea to taste chocolate before you use it for decorating to make sure that you like it. Most good-quality chocolate bars work fine for decorating, but be sure that they're plain and not filled or mixed with other ingredients, such as nuts or dried fruit. Personally, I like to use the best-quality chocolate I can find because I figure I'm worth it! Couverture chocolate (see Chapter 3) works very well for decorating, especially for dipping, because it's made for this purpose. Dark chocolate, milk chocolate, and white chocolate are all good to use for decorating. These come in bar or bulk form. No matter which form you buy, you'll have to chop it into small pieces to use. Many store or house brands are much better than you think because they're made by some of the major manufacturers of top-quality chocolate. Taste them and, if you like them, use them.

Use bar chocolate rather than chocolate chips for melting. Chips won't melt completely because they're formulated to retain their shape when baked.

Treating Your Chocolate Like an Honored Guest

This section deals with how to handle, melt, and store chocolate, which can be a bit temperamental if it's not handled with care and respect. However, the rewards of doing so are well worth any effort. You'll have silky smooth, glossy chocolate that will make your cookies look great and, of course, taste terrific.

Chopping chocolate

Chocolate in bars or chunks must be broken or chopped into tiny pieces before it can be melted. If you have small bars, they're easy to break or chop into pieces. Large chunks need to be cut into small pieces first and then chopped into tiny pieces by using a chef's knife with a large blade on a cutting board (see Figure 20-1). Don't work with too much at a time, or you may find yourself chasing chocolate pieces all over the kitchen. Once the chocolate is chopped, transfer it from the cutting board to a bowl or other container, keeping the cutting board free for chopping. Chocolate can be chopped in a food processor, but I don't advise doing this because the machine beats up the chocolate, turning it white. Also, the heat of the motor may melt the chocolate before you're ready. This can be a problem, especially if you're chopping chocolate in advance of when you'll use it.

Chop chocolate and keep it in a tightly sealed container at room temperature. This way you'll be ready for decorating when the mood strikes.

Melting chocolate

Chocolate is delicate and must be melted carefully. It shouldn't be heated over 120 degrees, or it will begin to disintegrate. Don't let chocolate come in direct contact with heat because it burns very easily. The best method for melting chocolate is to do it slowly in the top of a double boiler over warm water, with the burner set on low. If the water in the bottom pot boils, it is too hot and will burn the chocolate. Also, the steam that rises will mix with the chocolate and cause it to thicken or *seize*. The water level in the bottom pot should be shallow and should not touch the bottom of the top pot. Stir the chocolate often as it melts, using a rubber spatula. (See the section "Temper, temper!" later in this chapter for a discussion of tempering.)

1. LARGE CHUNKS OF CHOCOLATE NEED TO BE CUT INTO SMALL PIECES FIRST, THEN USING A CHEF'S KNIFE WITH A LARGE BLADE ON A CUTTING BOARD....

2. .....CHOP THEM INTO TINY PIECES. WORK WITH A SMALL AMOUNT AT A TIME.

3. TRANSFER THE CHOPPED PIECES TO A BOWL. KEEP THE CUTTING BOARD FREE FOR CHOPPING!

KEEP CHOPPING!

Figure 20-1: Chopping chocolate.

Don't use wooden utensils to stir chocolate. They are porous and hold onto other flavors that can taint your chocolate. What if you had used that wooden spoon to stir tomatoes and garlic together for a pasta sauce? I love those flavors, but I don't want to mix them with my chocolate.

Help — my melted chocolate looks like mud!

If your melted chocolate looks like mud, it's because the chocolate has *seized*. Chocolate seizes when a little moisture has mixed with it during melting. The tiniest drop of water or liquid that mixes with chocolate will cause it to stiffen. Also, too much heat causes chocolate to develop lumps.

Chocolate needs to be handled carefully. Be sure to do the following while melting chocolate:

✔ Keep all utensils completely dry.

✔ Make sure that the water level in the bottom of the double boiler is at least an inch from the bottom of the top pot.

✔ Don't allow the water in the bottom pot of the double boiler to boil. Boiling water will turn into steam, which will escape, condense, and mix with the chocolate. Keep the heat under the double boiler low.

✔ Stir the chocolate frequently as it melts.

✔ When the top pot of the double boiler is removed, wipe the bottom and sides very dry so it doesn't carry any stray drops of water that can mix with the chocolate as it's poured out of the pot.

You can melt chocolate in the microwave oven, but you must watch it carefully so that it doesn't burn. Use low power in 15-second intervals. Chocolate in the microwave holds its shape unless it's stirred, so stir the chocolate after every interval to make sure that it's melting.

Storing chocolate

Store chocolate well wrapped in a cool, dry place. Do not, however, store it in the refrigerator because it will pick up moisture that will mix with it when melted.

Chocolate that comes in contact with moisture or becomes too cold during storage develops tiny white or gray sugar crystals on its surface. This is known as *sugar bloom.* It is the result of moisture that condenses on the surface of the chocolate, which draws out sugar that dissolves and leaves crystals after the liquid evaporates. Sugar bloom affects the texture of the chocolate, making it grainy when it melts. As a result, the chocolate is difficult to use for decorating because it will never be smooth and shiny.

If chocolate becomes too warm during storage, some of the cocoa butter may rise to the surface, causing *chocolate bloom,* which is visible as gray or white streaks or dots. This condition doesn't affect the taste of the chocolate but does indicate that the chocolate is out of temper (see the discussion of tempering in the following section). When the chocolate is tempered, the cocoa butter will go back into its emulsion.

Dark chocolate will last for years if properly stored. Milk chocolate and white chocolate contain milk and have a shorter shelf life. They'll last for about a year.

Dipping Cookies in Chocolate

Dipping cookies in chocolate is a great way to decorate them. This section presents tips about quick-tempering chocolate so it will set up quickly and look good. This section also discusses ways to dip various types of cookies.

Temper, temper!

The word *temper* seems to scare a lot of people, but tempering is really not difficult. *Tempering* is the process of stabilizing the crystals in the cocoa butter contained in chocolate so that the chocolate has a smooth, unblemished appearance and produces a sharp snap when broken. Chocolate that will be used for dipping and for decorations must be tempered.

Tempering chocolate involves heating, cooling the chocolate, and heating it again to stabilize the crystals in the cocoa butter. Here's a simplified method for tempering chocolate that's quick and easy:

1. **Chop the chocolate to be tempered into very tiny pieces.**

2. **Place two-thirds of the chocolate in the top of a double boiler over warm water. Stir often with a rubber spatula as the chocolate melts.**

3. **Remove the double boiler from the heat, remove the top pan, and wipe the bottom and sides very dry.**

4. **To cool the chocolate, stir in the remaining chocolate in three batches, making sure that each batch is completely melted before adding the next batch.**

   When all the chocolate has been added, the chocolate should be ready to use.

To test the chocolate, place a dab of chocolate below your lower lip. It should feel comfortable, not too warm or too cool. If it's too warm, stir in a little more finely chopped chocolate and test it again. If it's too cool, place the pan back over the pan of warm water and stir briefly. Check the temperature of the chocolate again to see whether it's warmer, but not too hot. You can use an instant-read thermometer to check the temperature if you want to be exact. The final temperature should be between 89 and 91 degrees for dark chocolate and 85 to 87 degrees for milk and white chocolate.

Once the chocolate is tempered, keep it over the pan of water. Test the water in the bottom pan to make sure that it's no more than a couple of degrees warmer than the chocolate. If it seems too warm, pour some of it out and replace with cool tap water.

Be very careful when testing and adding to the water in the bottom pan of the double boiler that you don't mix any water with the chocolate and cause it to seize.

Dipping techniques

Hold a cookie between your thumb and forefinger and dip each end of finger-shaped cookies in chocolate. For round or square cookies, dip them into chocolate halfway horizontally or on the diagonal.

You can also dip a whole cookie in chocolate. Use a plastic fork and break out the two middle tines. Gently drop the cookie into the tempered chocolate. Use the fork to retrieve it and balance the cookie on the fork. Hold the cookie above the pan of chocolate and let the excess chocolate drip off or gently tap the fork against the side of the pan to remove the excess chocolate. Gently transfer the cookie to a piece of wax paper and carefully slip the fork from under the cookies. Let the chocolate set for 15 minutes at room temperature.

After the cookies are dipped in chocolate, you can dip them into finely chopped or ground nuts or chocolate sprinkles before the chocolate sets up.

Here are some cookies that are great candidates for dipping:

- Mocha Hazelnut Snaps, Almond Butter Cookies, and Sablés (see Chapter 6)
- Almond Coins, Diamond Circles, and Hazelnut Slices (see Chapter 7)
- Classic Scottish Shortbread (see Chapter 8)
- Cocoa Sandwiches and Hazelnut-Almond Sticks (see Chapter 9)
- Cocoa Wafers and Nut Wafers (see Chapter 11)
- Hazelnut Crisscross Cookies, Classic Sugar Cookies, Hazelnut Crescents, various types of biscotti (see Chapter 12)
- Madeleines and variations (see Chapter 13)
- Mandelbrot and variations, and Pizzelle and variations (see Chapter 14)
- Chocolate-Peanut Butter Coins (see Chapter 16)

Be a Chocolate van Gogh (or Renoir, or . . .)

You, too, can become an artist with chocolate once you become familiar with the techniques of chocolate painting, chocolate piping, and dusting and stenciling. These are easy to do, so don't think you can't master them. Like anything else, the more you practice, the better you get. Once you get started and see how much fun it is, you'll find yourself inventing reasons to decorate with chocolate.

To make your chocolate artistry session more fun, set up your work space first and make sure that you have the tools you'll need. Keep a good supply of wax paper and paper towels on hand. Also have a few small (1- and 2-cup size) bowls. If you'll be using two different chocolates (dark and white, for example), you'll need two double boilers or two bowls that fit snugly over the same pan of water. Make sure that your work area is clear and not cluttered and that all your utensils are dry so that you won't have any problems when working with chocolate.

Chocolate painting

Use a natural-bristle pastry brush to paint the entire surface of a cookie with either dark, milk, or white tempered chocolate. (See the section "Temper, temper!" earlier in this chapter). A 1-inch-wide brush works well for this. (See Chapter 2 for more information on pastry brushes.) After the chocolate is applied, let it set at room temperature or place the cookies on a tray or cool baking sheet in the refrigerator to set the chocolate for about 15 minutes.

Melt another batch of contrasting color chocolate in a separate double boiler and temper it. Use a tiny, pointed, natural-bristle brush to apply this chocolate as an accent on top of the first layer of chocolate. You can paint dots, squiggles, swirls, or whatever comes to mind. I like to paint white chocolate dots on top of dark chocolate for a good color contrast. Or you can use colored icing on top of the chocolate.

Use natural-bristle pastry brushes, not nylon bristles, which melt when they come in contact with heat, including warm chocolate. In addition, nylon brushes don't apply the chocolate evenly and tend to leave some of their bristles in the chocolate.

Chocolate touches

A little chocolate goes a long way in dressing up cookies. You can add chocolate touches to your cookies in several ways. Chocolate shavings and curls are very impressive and very easy to do, and they can be made in advance. Chocolate cutouts take a little more work but can also be made in advance and kept in the pantry ready for use. Drizzling chocolate on top of cookies is a great way to add chocolate without going overboard.

To store chocolate shavings, curls, and cutouts, keep them in an airtight container between layers of wax paper in a cool, dry place. They can last for several months, depending on the type of chocolate used to make them.

Chocolate shavings and curls

Use any type of chocolate (white, milk, and dark) to make shavings and curls (see Figure 20-2). Work with at least a ¼-pound bar or block of chocolate. Warm the chocolate in the microwave for a 3-second burst of heat on high to make the chocolate pliable enough to produce curls. Hold the chocolate with a paper towel so that the heat of your hand doesn't melt it. Use a vegetable peeler or a small sharp knife to make the shavings. Working on the thin side of the block or bar, pull the vegetable peeler or knife down — away from yourself — applying pressure to the chocolate, causing it to curl up. You can also use a melon ball scoop to make shavings and curls. To do this, place the chocolate bar or block on a flat surface covered with wax paper and hold it in place with a paper towel. Scrape the melon ball scoop over the surface to make rounded curls and shavings.

@ Making Chocolate Curls @

With a potato peeler....

or

With a french knife...

wedge against a the hard surface like wall!

flat side up!!

On a stable block of chocolate, narrow edge up, push the peeler, using pressure. This will make your curl!!

Using only a small part of the knife (1" to 4" from the point) push away from you to form your curl!

Figure 20-2: Making chocolate curls.

Chocolate cutouts

You can make chocolate cutouts from white, milk, or dark tempered chocolate. You'll need at least a ½ pound of chocolate. Line a baking sheet with wax paper. Pour the tempered chocolate onto the wax paper and, using a spatula, spread it out smoothly and evenly. Lift up opposite corners of the wax paper and shake it gently to eliminate any air bubbles. Place the baking sheet in the refrigerator to set the chocolate, about 15 minutes. Test the chocolate by touching it with a fingertip. If it's too soft, let it stay in the refrigerator for another 5 or 10 minutes. If it's too firm, let it stand at room temperature for 5 to 10 minutes. Use any shape and size cookie cutter to make cutouts. Dip the end of the cutter in warm water, dry it off, and then cut the chocolate.

Chocolate drizzle

Place baked and cooled cookies in a single layer on a cookie sheet lined with wax paper. Dip the tines of a fork in tempered chocolate and then shake the fork from side to side over the cookies, letting the chocolate drop onto them. Dip the fork in chocolate and repeat as often as necessary to obtain the desired effect, but don't drown the cookies in chocolate.

Cookies that are good candidates for chocolate drizzle include most rolled cookies (Chapter 6), refrigerator cookies (Chapter 7), Oatmeal Shortbread Bars (Chapter 8), Shortbread (Chapter 8), most sandwich cookies (Chapter 9), pressed cookies (Chapter 11), hand-formed cookies (Chapter 12), Madeleines (Chapter 13), and some holiday cookies (Chapter 15).

Chocolate piping

You can use chocolate as an accent by piping dots and lines onto cookies or even write names on cookies with chocolate.

Always decorate cookies after they're completely cool. If the cookies are warm, the chocolate will melt on top of them, making them unattractive and unappetizing.

To pipe chocolate, fill a parchment paper pastry cone or a clean plastic squeeze bottle with melted chocolate, snip off a tiny opening at the pointed end with scissors, and *pipe* designs or lines on top of the cookies, or use it to write with. (To find out how to make a parchment pastry cone, see Chapter 9.) Using a parchment paper pastry cone or a plastic squeeze bottle is easier than using a plastic bag or pastry bag because the parchment cone and squeeze bottle are firmer and hold their shapes well. Working with a soft bag that holds a soft material can be frustrating because it's hard to control.

Piping is a technique in which you squeeze frosting, icing, whipped cream, chocolate, jam, or dough from a pastry bag to make shapes or designs. The shape of the pastry tip used determines the design and shape of the piped material. See Chapter 9 for more information on piping and pastry bags.

Chocolate can always be stirred to cool before using it to pipe, and it needs to thicken slightly so it's not too runny to work with. Use tempered chocolate (see "Temper, temper!" earlier in this chapter) for piping. That way, the chocolate is at the correct temperature and texture, making it easy to work with. It also sets ups quickly when tempered.

Dusting and stenciling

Dust (lightly sprinkle) cocoa powder or powdered sugar lightly on top of cookies, as shown in Figure 20-3. A mixture of both cocoa powder and powdered sugar is an interesting contrast. Use cocoa powder to dust one side of a cookie and powdered sugar to dust the other. If you let your imagination go, you'll find lots of creative ways to dress up your cookies with cocoa powder and powdered sugar. Pizzelles (see Chapter 14) are excellent when dusted with powdered sugar. Many sandwich cookies (Chapter 9) are enhanced with a dusting of either powdered sugar or cocoa powder.

Use a small sifter to dust cocoa powder or powdered sugar onto cookies.

Make a stencil out of cardboard or use a small doily as a stencil. Place it over the top of the cookie and dust it with either cocoa powder or powdered sugar (or a combination). To see the design, carefully lift off the stencil so that you don't smudge it.

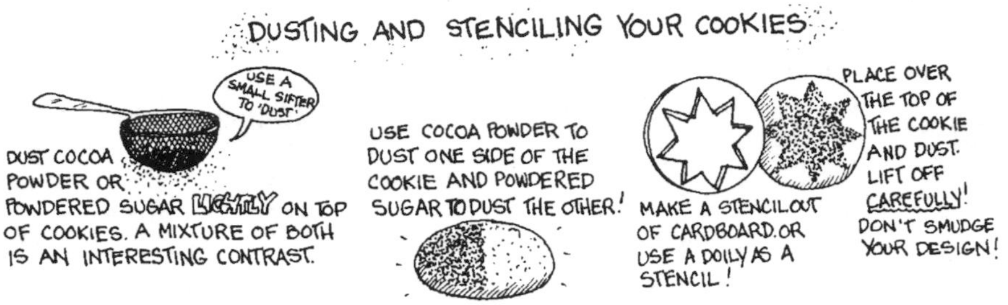

Figure 20-3:
Dusting and
stenciling
your
cookies.

DUSTING AND STENCILING YOUR COOKIES

USE A SMALL SIFTER TO DUST

DUST COCOA POWDER OR POWDERED SUGAR LIGHTLY ON TOP OF COOKIES. A MIXTURE OF BOTH IS AN INTERESTING CONTRAST.

USE COCOA POWDER TO DUST ONE SIDE OF THE COOKIE AND POWDERED SUGAR TO DUST THE OTHER!

MAKE A STENCIL OUT OF CARDBOARD. OR USE A DOILY AS A STENCIL!

PLACE OVER THE TOP OF THE COOKIE AND DUST. LIFT OFF CAREFULLY! DON'T SMUDGE YOUR DESIGN!

Chapter 21

Decoration Sensations

In This Chapter

▶ Topping your cookies with frosting or "paint"

▶ Applying extra-special touches

Recipes in This Chapter

▶ Basic Decorating Icing

▶ Royal Icing

▶ Cookie Paint

*J*azzing up your cookies is easy, whether you're taking them out on the town or showing them off at home. Just a little decoration can make a cookie look real snazzy. There are lots of ways to fancy up your creations with minimal fuss. Let your imagination go, and you'll be really delighted with the results.

Spreading It On

Here's your chance to put the finishing touches on your cookies. Don't be afraid that you'll mess up — it's very easy to finish off your cookies with icings, frostings, and cookie paint. I hear people say, "I'm not the creative type," but you don't have to be to decorate cookies. They almost decorate themselves. It's as simple as one, two, three. First you make up the icings, frostings, or cookie paint that you want to use. Then you color them, and finally, you do your decorating. When it comes to decorating, there are no rules. Go with the flow! Rolled cookies (see Chapter 6) and refrigerator cookies (see Chapter 7) are some of the best candidates for decorating. Many international specialties (see Chapter 14) and holiday cookies (see Chapter 15) are also great to decorate.

Icing and *frosting* are interchangeable terms that mean the same thing. They're both sweet coverings and fillings for cookies, other pastries, and desserts. There are several types of icings and frostings, named primarily by how they're made.

Icings and frostings

A variety of icings can be used to decorate cookies, including fondant, boiled, buttercream, and French buttercream. All these icings have distinctive qualities, but for the purposes of this book, all you really need are the recipes for Basic Decorating Icing and Royal Icing, which appear in this section. If you're in a hurry and need icing, you can use the canned variety found in the baking section of the supermarket. It's not my first choice, but it works. I far prefer to make my own because I know it's fresh and I see what goes into it. Also, it takes less time to make your own icing than it does to go to the store and buy it. Whenever I've used store-bought icing, I find that if any is left over, it doesn't tend to keep well so you may as well toss it out. Enough said!

Basic Decorating Icing

This recipe is quick and easy to prepare. It's a great basic icing that is like a chameleon. It can be colored to add definition and zest to many cookies.

Preparation time: *5 minutes*

1 cup confectioners' sugar, sifted

3 to 4 tablespoons heavy cream or light corn syrup

Combine the confectioners' sugar and cream in a mixing bowl and whisk together until smooth. Thin the icing with water, more cream, or corn syrup as needed. Color for decorating.

Per serving: *Calories 27 (From Fat 0); Fat 0g (Saturated 0g); Cholesterol 0mg; Sodium 2mg; Carbohydrate 7g (Dietary Fiber 0g); Protein 0g.*

Royal Icing

Royal Icing is a versatile decorating icing that dries to a smooth, hard finish. It's great for crisp, clear details. Royal Icing made with meringue powder can be stored in a tightly covered container in the refrigerator for up to 5 days. It can be rebeaten before use. Royal Icing made from egg whites, however, will break down if rebeaten.

You can substitute meringue powder or manufacturer's brand egg white powder for the egg white below. To use meringue powder, substitute 1 tablespoon plus 1 teaspoon meringue powder plus 3 tablespoons water and proceed with the recipe as written. To use manufacturer's brand egg white powder, substitute 2 teaspoons of the powder plus 3 tablespoons water and then proceed with the recipe as written. Each recipe makes about 1¼ cups.

Preparation time: *5 minutes*

1 egg white at room temperature

¼ teaspoon (scant) cream of tartar

2 cups confectioners' sugar, sifted

2 to 3 teaspoons water to adjust consistency

1 Combine all the ingredients in a large mixing bowl. Using a mixer, beat the mixture on medium speed for 5 minutes with a stand mixer or 7 minutes with a hand mixer. If the consistency is too firm, add water to adjust it. Use a few drops of paste food coloring to color the icing as desired.

2 Use the icing immediately. Keep the icing covered with a damp cloth or paper towel when not in use.

Per serving: *Calories 45 (From Fat 12); Fat 1g (Saturated 1g); Cholesterol 5mg; Sodium 1mg; Carbohydrate 8g (Dietary Fiber 0g); Protein 0g.*

Keep the Royal Icing covered at all times with a damp paper towel or cloth because it dries out easily.

To cover a cookie completely with Royal Icing, use a small spatula to apply it. To use Royal Icing for decorative touches, place some in a parchment paper pastry bag fitted with a pastry tip.

Meringue powder is a powdered mixture of dried egg whites, sugar, and edible gum (not chewing gum) used in place of fresh egg whites for icings and decorations.

Cookie paint

Paint your cookies before baking with any color you choose. Cookie paint gives cookies a sheer wash of color. It's different from icing, which is applied to cookies after they're baked and cooled. You can still decorate cookies with icing even if they've been brushed with cookie paint.

Cookie Paint

Cookie paint is really a glaze made with egg yolk that makes the cookie glossy after baking. When you add the coloring to it, use a light hand. This is my favorite recipe for cookie paint.

Specialty tool: *#2 fine-point artist's brush with natural bristles*

Preparation time: *5 minutes*

1 egg yolk

⅛ teaspoon water

Liquid or powder food coloring of choice

1 Combine the egg yolk and water in a small bowl.

2 Add a drop or two of food coloring, if using liquid. Add a pinch if using powder food coloring. Mix thoroughly.

3 Use an artist's brush to apply the paint to the cookies before baking.

Color your cookies

One of the easiest ways to decorate cookies is with tubes of colored frosting. These are available in the baking aisle of supermarkets. Just squeeze the icing from the tube directly onto the cookies to make dots, squiggles, and lines. Often these tubes of icing come with a variety of tips that produce different effects. However, one drawback is that icing tubes tend to dry out when kept for any length of time because of exposure to air. To remedy this, try wrapping the tip of the tube with a damp paper towel and storing it in a plastic bag that zips closed. It's best to use the icing tubes within a couple months after opening them.

Tips for icing cookies

The following tips will help ensure that your icing efforts are a success:

✔ Be sure that cookies are completely cool before applying icing or it will melt.

✔ Test the consistency of the icing. If it's too thick, thin with a few drops of water.

✔ Use a small offset or flexible-blade spatula or a rubber spatula (see Chapter 2) to apply the icing. Push it from the center of the cookie to the edges.

✔ Work quickly so that the icing doesn't dry out and start to set before you're finished.

✔ Keep your spatula clean between applications of icing by dipping it in a cup of warm water. Dry the spatula before putting it back in the container of icing.

✔ Use icing in a parchment paper pastry cone or plastic pastry bag to apply accent colors and designs such as dots, lines, squiggles, and borders. Cleanup is a breeze because these tools are disposable.

Make sure that the icing is completely dry before storing iced cookies. They're best when stored for no more than 2 weeks at room temperature in a tightly sealed container between layers of wax paper. If they're stored for a longer time, the icing can start to soften the cookies.

If you make your own icing or frosting, you'll have to color it. This is easy to do with food coloring. Don't use liquid food coloring. You'll need way too much of it to obtain good color. By the time you've added enough, your icing would be soup. There are two main ways to color icing:

✔ **Paste food coloring:** This coloring comes in small jars in a huge variety of colors. It's very potent, so a tiny bit goes a long way. Start with just a drop or two. Use a toothpick to pick up a tiny bit of color from the jar and transfer it to the icing or frosting. Stir the color in vigorously until the entire batch is colored. You can always add more to deepen the color, but once it's too dark, it's impossible to make it lighter.

✔ **Powder food coloring:** This coloring also comes in small jars in a wide variety of colors. Powder food coloring is also very potent and should be used sparingly. It will last forever if you don't do a lot of baking and decorating. I like to use this to color crystal or regular sugar to sprinkle on top of cookies. Use a toothpick to pick up a few grains and deposit into the material to be colored. Stir or shake it around to coat the items completely. Start with a tiny bit and add more as needed.

Both of these colorings can be found in stores that sell cake-decorating supplies, such as cookware shops and craft stores, and through catalogs. Powder coloring will last practically forever. Paste food coloring will last a long time, but keep the jars tightly sealed so they don't dry out.

If a dark-colored icing tastes bitter, you're most likely tasting the dye in the coloring. Look for taste-free or tasteless paste food coloring, which contain no perceptible dye flavor.

Spread the entire cookie with one color of icing and use another or use chocolate (see Chapter 20) to add special touches. This is a great way to decorate sugar cookies and holiday cookies. You can even write names on the cookies and use them as party favors or place cards. Children love cookies with their names on them.

Jazzing Up Your Cookies

Sometimes the occasion calls for pulling out all the stops when it comes to decorating cookies. The holiday season always calls for a little extra-special touch. Other special events, such as a wedding or baby shower, a graduation celebration, or a milestone birthday, also deserve cookies with out-of-the-ordinary decorations. There are several ways to decorate cookies to give them star quality, such as using candy, fruit, or nut decorations, sprinkles of various varieties, and ribbons.

Candy, fruit, and nut decorations

Use cinnamon Red Hots and candy hearts to press into cookies before they're baked. Raisins and other dried and candied fruits, such as cherries and cranberries, are also fun ways to decorate cookies. Press these into cookies before they're baked or into the icing before it sets. Rolled cookies (see Chapter 6) are some of the best candidates for these types of decorations.

Nuts and seeds, such as sliced almonds, walnut halves, pistachio nuts, pumpkin seeds, and sunflower seeds, make interesting decorations, too. Press them into rolled cookies (see Chapter 6) or refrigerator cookies (see Chapter 7) before baking. Use nuts and seeds to make just about any design you can think of, including flowers, lines, and abstract shapes.

Chocolate coffee beans and chocolate-covered raisins make great easy decorations. Press these into cookies while they're still slightly warm (so the chocolate won't melt) from the oven. Or apply them to icing on cooled cookies.

Candied edible flowers, such as violets and rose petals, add an extra-special touch to cookies, making them very elegant. These decorations, which are reminiscent of Victorian times, can be found in some specialty food shops, cookware shops, and catalogs. Serve cookies decorated with edible flowers at your next afternoon tea party.

All that glitters and sparkles . . .

Some decorations that can be sprinkled or applied to your cookies really jazz them up. You can find these decorations in cake decorating supply stores or in mail-order decorating catalogs. (See Appendix B for ordering information.)

✔ Sprinkles are little balls of sugar that come in an array of colors. They're meant to be sprinkled or scattered over icings applied to baked and cooled cookies. The icing helps hold them in place.

✔ Crystal sugar, also called decorating sugar, consists of large pieces of sugar. You can color crystal sugar with powder food coloring. I like to sprinkle it on cookies or roll cookies in it before baking. The extra crunch is great.

✔ Nonpareils (non PAIR els) are very tiny sugar balls that are available in several different colors.

A little decoration can go a long way. Start with minimal decoration and add more as needed.

Let good taste be your guide. Less really is better. Try to limit yourself to using only one or two colors of icing on a cookie, although three may be okay in some cases. Try to keep the decorations realistic or whimsical. Use subtlety. If you're not sure about adding another color or design, leave it off. Overdecorated cookies aren't appetizing, and no one will want to eat them. That would be too bad because the whole point of making cookies is to eat them and share them.

Metallic-colored decorations are often seen in stores and on cookies in books and magazines, but the U.S. Food and Drug Administration doesn't support their use on edible foods.

Nonedible ribbon decorations

Nothing looks prettier during the holiday season or at a birthday party, than cookies hung by ribbons. They give a very festive feel to the holiday or party celebration. Guests can spend part of the gathering stringing their cookies with ribbons. If you're decorating a Christmas tree, guests can string one for the party tree and one or more to take home to place on their own trees. If it's a birthday or other party, the cookies can be place cards and can be strung as part of the party activities.

Ribbons are beautiful and colorful additions to cookies. Choose a ribbon color that complements the cookies and the season.

You may wish to make ribbon borders for your cookies. To do so, pierce holes around the outer edge of an unbaked cookie at intervals. After baking, pierce the holes again to be sure that they stay open. When the cookies are cool, weave a ribbon through the holes. Don't forget to remove the ribbon before eating the cookies.

To turn your cookies into hanging ornaments, pierce the top of unbaked cookies with a bamboo skewer or the tip of a very sharp knife to make a small hole before baking. Pierce the hole again after baking to make sure that it stays open. After the cookies are cooled, string a colorful ribbon through the hole. Rolled cookies (see Chapter 6) and Speculaas (see Chapter 13) are the best ones to use for ornaments and ribbon borders; you wouldn't want to use bar cookies.

Practice makes perfect, but the main idea is to have fun. Take your time and try out creative cookie decorations when the mood strikes you.

Part VII
The Part of Tens

The 5th Wave   By Rich Tennant

"...because I'm more comfortable using my own tools. Now, how much longer do you want me to sand the cookie batter?"

In this part . . .

This is where you find some great suggestions for making your cookie-making experience even more enjoyable. I offer tips for troubleshooting problems that may arise, and ideas for giving your cookies to others. Whether you want to find out how to keep your cookies from sticking to the cookie sheet or how to pack your scrumptious peanut butter cookies for your son away at college, you can find it in this part. Also, see www.dummies.com/bonus/cookies/ for advice on how to show off your cookies.

Chapter 22

Ten Troubleshooting Tips

Knowing what problems may occur when baking cookies is the best way to prevent them from happening. This chapter tackles the most common cookie baking problems. It shows you what to watch out for and what to be aware of. If you do have trouble, though, try again — after you figure out what caused the problem.

My Cookie Dough Is Too Soft or Sticky When It's Rolled or Pressed

The main cause of soft or sticky cookie dough is that the dough is too warm or it doesn't have enough flour. The butter may have been too soft when it was mixed with the dough, or there's too much liquid in the dough. Maybe the weather is hot and has softened the dough too much while mixing.

Whatever the cause, the solution is to cover the dough tightly with plastic wrap and refrigerate or freeze it until it's firm enough to handle. Divide the dough into quarters and work with only one portion at a time while keeping the other portions cold. Another solution is to stir in one or two more table-spoons of flour to the dough, let it chill for 15 to 30 minutes, and then roll the dough out again. If the dough is still sticky when cold, dust the work surface and the dough lightly with flour. (For more on this topic, see Chapter 6 on rolled cookies and Chapter 11 on pressed cookies.)

My Dough Is Too Crumbly and Cracks When It's Rolled

Dough crumbles and cracks when it doesn't have enough liquid or fat or has too much flour. Another cause of this problem is that the dough is too cold.

The solution for crumbly dough is to add more liquid. If the recipe calls for large eggs and you have used small or medium eggs, add another egg yolk to the dough. Or add 1 to 2 tablespoons of cream, milk, or water to the dough and mix well.

If the dough feels too cold, let it stand at room temperature for 10 to 15 minutes until it becomes more pliable.

Eggs that are too small sometimes contribute to the problem of crumbling. If small or medium eggs are used, they don't have enough liquid for the mixture. (See Chapter 3 for a discussion of eggs.)

Correct measuring of ingredients goes a long way toward preventing problems during baking. Use the scoop-and-sweep method for dry ingredients such as flour. Level off the top of the measuring cups or measuring spoons with a flat blade. Use a liquid measuring cup for liquid ingredients and read it at eye level. You can find information on all these measuring techniques in Chapter 4.

My Cookies Spread Too Much When Baking

Many factors may cause your cookies to spread during baking. The baking sheet may be overgreased, the cookie dough may have been placed on a hot cookie sheet, the unbaked cookies may have been too warm when placed on the cookie sheet, or too much leavening was added when mixing the dough. Cookies will also spread too much if there is too much fat and/or liquid and not enough flour in the dough.

Although lining cookie sheets with parchment paper or another nonstick pan liner is the best way to prepare them, greasing the cookie sheets is okay if you do it sparingly. Too much grease causes the cookies to spread easily. In fact, some cookie recipes call for the sheet to be ungreased.

Parchment paper is one of the world's best inventions. I wouldn't bake cookies without using it to line cookie sheets. Its nonstick surface solves all the problems caused by under- or overgreasing cookie sheets. It also makes cleanup a breeze. If nothing has spilled on the cookie sheets, simply toss out the parchment and return the cookie sheets to the cabinet until the next baking session.

Cookies will start to spread even before reaching the oven if the cookie sheet is too hot. If the cookie sheet has been used to bake one batch, let it cool for 10 to 15 minutes before baking another batch. You can also cool cookie sheets by running them under cold water and then drying them or chilling them quickly in the refrigerator.

If possible, try to have more than one cookie sheet so that you can alternate them. Having three cookie sheets is even better. That way, you can be placing cookies on one while one cookie sheet is in the oven and one cools.

If the cookies have been sitting out at room temperature waiting for a cookie sheet, they may be too soft and warm and will spread too much. Keep waiting cookies in the refrigerator until they're ready to bake.

Measure the baking powder and baking soda accurately. Level off the measuring spoons with a flat blade. Rounded measures yield much more quantity.

Try adding 2 to 4 more tablespoons of flour to the dough and bake a test cookie to see whether it's the right texture and consistency.

My Cookies Are Too Crisp and Dark on the Bottom

There are several possible causes of overly crisp, dark cookies. Perhaps the oven temperature was too hot, or the cookie sheets were too dark or too thin. The cookies may have been baked on the lower rack, too close to the source of heat, or the cookie sheets could have been overgreased.

Keep an oven thermometer in your oven and check it frequently for accuracy. Adjust your temperature down if necessary. It may be time to have your oven calibrated. If you have a gas oven, your local gas company will usually check it for free.

Use shiny, heavy-gauge aluminum cookie sheets. Dark cookie sheets absorb heat quicker than the shiny ones. If you use dark cookie sheets, lower the oven temperature by 25 degrees to prevent overbrowning. If the cookie sheets are too thin, they let too much heat come through. Insulate a thin cookie sheet by lining it with aluminum foil or place a second cookie sheet underneath. You can also use insulated cookie sheets that have a layer of air between two pieces of metal.

Bake cookies on the middle rack or switch the cookie sheets to different oven racks halfway through baking. Grease the pans very lightly or, better yet, use nonstick parchment paper or another nonstick liner to line the cookie sheets.

My Cookies Are Too Dry or Too Moist

Dryness is a result of overbaking. Conversely, cookies that are underbaked are too moist or soft.

Check the cookies for doneness a few minutes before the least amount of baking time given in the recipe. Touch the top of the cookies to check for doneness. If the top springs back or feels firm, they're done.

If the cookies collapse when you touch them, add a couple more minutes of baking time. Check the cookies at 1- or 2-minute intervals so that they don't overbake.

Be sure that your oven is at the correct temperature. You may need to turn the oven down 25 degrees. Keep an oven thermometer in the oven and check it often for accuracy.

My Cookies Break Apart When Moved to a Cooling Rack

Some cookies with a high proportion of fat in the dough are likely candidates for falling apart when moved. The best way to handle this problem is to let the cookies cool on the cookie sheets for a couple minutes before transferring them to a cooling rack.

My Cookies Stick to the Cookie Sheet

You think you've done everything just right when baking a batch of cookies. They look great on the baking sheet, and you can hardly wait to let them cool so you can try one. Bu when you attempt to release the cookies from the cookie sheet, they stick like glue. How disappointing!

Several factors may cause this problem. Either the baking sheet was not prepared properly, or the cookies were allowed to cool on the sheet too long before they were transferred to a cooling rack.

Evenly grease the cookie sheet or use parchment paper to prepare the sheet.

The easiest way to unstick cookies is to return the cookie sheet to the warm oven for 1 to 2 minutes and then immediately transfer them from the cookie sheet to the cooling rack.

My Cookies Bake Unevenly on the Cookie Sheet

Cookie dough that isn't rolled to an equal thickness or shaped uniformly is one cause of uneven baking. Another cause of this problem is hot spots in the oven.

Place cookies that are the same size and thickness on the cookie sheet together. If you're baking more than one cookie sheet at a time, switch the cookie sheets to different oven racks halfway through baking and rotate them from front to back. Also check the oven thermometer for accurate temperature. You may need to adjust the oven temperature by 25 degrees.

My Cookie Dough Sticks to the Mold

When dough sticks to the mold, it means you've used too much fat and too little flour to prepare the cookie mold.

The easiest way to prevent this problem from occurring is to lightly spray the molds with a nonstick combination vegetable oil and flour spray. Or grease the mold with fat (butter) and lightly flour the mold. Tap the mold on the countertop to release excess flour before molding the dough.

My Molded Cookies Lose Their Detail When Baked

If your molded cookies lose some detail during baking, the cookie dough probably had too much leavening, causing the cookies to rise too much and thereby lose their detail. Or perhaps the dough wasn't molded firmly enough to pick up the detail. Another cause, in the case of springele cookies, is that after shaping the cookies may not have been allowed to sit long enough before they were baked (see Chapter 13).

To ensure that you're using the right amount of leavening, measure baking powder and baking soda accurately. Level off the measure with a flat blade. Firmly pack the dough into all the crevices of the mold so it will pick up all the detail. Bake the cookies immediately after molding.

Chapter 23

Ten Tips for Storing and Transporting Your Cookies

*I*f you (and your family and friends) eat all the cookies you make right after they're made, that's great. But most likely you'll want to save a few for later — maybe for the next day or even longer. The main concern you have in this situation is preserving the freshness of your cookies. This is true whether you are keeping them close by, taking them on the road, or sending them around the world. This chapter discusses ways to preserve your cookies so that the very last one tastes as good as the first one.

Keeping the Freshly Baked Taste and Consistency

Freshly baked cookies taste the absolute best! Even if baking and serving cookies immediately isn't possible, it's easy to keep your cookies tasting freshly baked. Most cookies store best in an airtight container at room temperature for up to a week.

Each type of cookie should be stored in a separate container. Don't store crisp cookies with soft cookies, or they'll take on the characteristics of each other. To keep cookies soft, add a slice of apple to the container. Crisp cookies that become limp during storage can be made crisp again by putting them on a baking sheet in the oven at 300 degrees for a few minutes.

Storing Chocolate Cookies

Chocolate is like a sponge and easily picks up other flavors. Store chocolate cookies in an airtight container at room temperature away from any strong-flavored food. You don't want your chocolate cookies to taste like garlic.

Storing Iced or Filled Cookies

Filled and frosted cookies are best stored in a single layer. However, it's not always easy to do that due to lack of space. The next best option is to place two sheets of wax paper between each layer of filled and frosted cookies. Don't stack the cookies more than three layers deep. Chocolate dipped cookies can be stored at room temperature as long as it's not too warm. In hot weather, store them in an airtight container in the refrigerator.

Some filled cookies need to be stored in the refrigerator because of delicate fillings. Keep them in an airtight container so they don't pick up moisture and absorb other flavors in the refrigerator.

Cookie Stacking 101

Shallow containers are best for storing cookies. Using a deep container will tempt you to stack too many layers of cookies.

Stack your cookies no more than three layers deep in the container, with sheets of wax paper between the layers. If cookies are stacked more than three layers high, the ones on the bottom could be crushed.

Don't Put Warm Cookies in Storage

Let cookies cool completely before storing them. If cookies are put away while warm, they'll become too soft and soggy from the steam they produce. The steam will ruin the entire batch of cookies in the container. Let the icing dry completely on decorated and iced cookies before you put them away or they'll stick to each other.

Freezing Cookies

Most cookies freeze well. Place them in airtight containers and heavy-duty freezer bags to keep the moist air from seeping in and ruining them. Place sheets of wax paper between the cookie layers to prevent them from sticking to each other.

Bar cookies can be stored in the freezer in their baking pan when cool, if you don't mind having a baking pan unavailable for use in baking. If the bar cookies are frozen, defrost them in the refrigerator overnight before cutting. Or they can be cut and stored in a separate container with wax paper between them.

Meringue cookies don't freeze very well. They tend to pick up moisture and become soft when frozen and defrosted. Don't freeze sandwich cookies with jam fillings, either. You can freeze the baked cookies for sandwich cookies before putting them together with the fillings.

Taking Cookies on the Road

A plate of cookies is a lovely host or hostess gift when you've been invited to someone's home for dinner. You can be sure that the hosts will enjoy eating them later. Cookies are also great to bring to a potluck gathering. Here, of course, the plate of cookies can be unwrapped and served to everyone. To ensure that your cookies arrive in tip-top condition, here are a few tips to follow:

- ✔ Keep a good supply of sturdy, stylish paper plates and aluminum foil in the pantry so you can always pack cookies to go.
- ✔ Pack similarly flavored cookies on the same plate. If the cookies are too different, they'll end up tasting like each other.
- ✔ Pack a single layer of cookies on one plate. If the cookies are stacked too high, the bottom ones could be crushed.
- ✔ Cover the top of the cookies with a piece of wax paper. Wrap the plate securely in aluminum foil.
- ✔ Place the plate of cookies on a flat surface in the car so they don't get jostled during driving.
- ✔ Try not to place the plate of cookies next to squirming or hungry children (or adults) who might be tempted to taste one or more of them.

 ✔ If the cookies have a delicate filling that requires refrigeration, pack the plate in a cooler with a freezer pack that won't melt into liquid.

 ✔ Instead of bringing the cookies on a plate, transport them in a tightly sealed airtight container, such as the disposable type of plastic containers. Arrange them on a serving plate when you arrive at your destination.

Cookie Exchanges

A cookie exchange is not a place to buy cookies at a discount. A cookie exchange is a place where you get cookies for free, but there is a catch: You need to bring some of your own cookies to exchange for other cookies. Here is how it works. Someone takes the initiative to organize a get-together (oh, let's call it what it is — a party) and invites several people — between six and eight is a good number. Everyone brings a dozen cookies per party guest. For example, if six people, including you, are invited, everyone brings six dozen cookies — one dozen to share at the party with everyone else and one dozen apiece for the other five guests to take home. Each person brings only one type of cookie, which should be one of that person's favorites. The organizer can check with everyone ahead of time to ensure that there will be a diversity of cookies exchanged.

One rule of the cookie exchange is that everyone must reveal where the recipe originated. Having two or three cookie exchanges a year, including a couple around the holiday season, can be a lot of fun. I can guarantee you that you'll be very popular around your neighborhood after a cookie exchange, because you'll surely want to share some of the cookies from the exchange with your neighbors. Or, if you time it right, you can invite all those relatives and friends over for a visit right after a cookie exchange. It's a win, win, win situation.

Have sturdy paper plates and aluminum foil on hand for guests to use to transport their cookies home. Those supplies will prevent the cookies from wandering while in transit.

Cookies Make Great Gifts

Home-baked cookies make great gifts for any occasion — a birthday, anniversary, housewarming party, or just as a thank you to someone who's done you a favor. They make excellent gifts for the holiday season, too. Present them in imaginative containers and wrappings. Colored cellophane and bright bows make fun and colorful wrapping for plates of cookies and can really dress up the presentation. Enclose a card telling the recipients what kinds of cookies they're getting so they won't have to guess at the contents — although the element of surprise may be part of the fun for some people!

Add extras by using a piece of yarn or ribbon to tie on a cookie cutter and the recipe to the gift. Cookies with holes in them can be tied together with colorful ribbons, and individual ones can become tree ornaments. You'll find yourself inventing reasons to give cookies as gifts because it's so much fun to find creative and exciting ways to present them.

Ornament cookies make beautiful gifts that your friends and family will love, but warn them that they're very hard and should not be eaten.

I always keep my eyes open for interesting and unusual tins. You can find them at gift shops, card shops, bookstores, and even flea markets. The tin becomes part of the gift in that it can be reused for holding personal treasures. Antique cookie jars make very special containers, too.

Small bags and boxes, hatboxes, toy pails, bowls, and flowerpots can all be transformed into unique containers for cookies by lining them with tissue paper. Try to match the container to the recipient's personality or lifestyle. Toys also make great containers for kids' cookies. Either wrap the cookies first in an airtight plastic bag or wrap the entire arrangement after the cookies are packed.

Once you get started looking for fun containers and wrappings for cookies, you'll be excited by the myriad possibilities.

Shipping Cookies Out of Town

Once you start giving cookies as gifts, you'll want to send them out of town. They make great gifts for college students during midterms and finals, grandparents, stressed-out friends, and people in the military, just to name a few. There's no reason not to send your cookies as gifts as long as you follow some basic precautions to ensure that they arrive in great shape.

- ✔ Choose cookies that keep well. Here are several good candidates:
  - Biscotti (Chapter 12)
  - Drop cookies (Chapter 5)
  - Refrigerator cookies (Chapter 7)
  - Shortbread (Chapter 8)
  - Hand-formed cookies (Chapter 12)
  - Holiday cookies (Chapter 15)
  - Kids cookies (Chapter 18)

✔ Delicate, easily breakable cookies and those that require refrigeration are bad choices for mail transport.

✔ If you send brownies or other bar cookies, wrap them tightly in plastic before packing them with other cookies. This keeps them from softening the others or making them sticky.

✔ Chocolate-dipped cookies aren't the best candidates for transporting. The chocolate will melt when exposed to too much heat, and it will also crack if it goes through temperature changes. It's hard to know the conditions that cookies will be exposed to while in transit.

✔ Pack cookies in tins sturdy enough to mail.

✔ Pack the tins as tightly as possible without crushing the contents, so the cookies don't rattle around. Fill extra spaces with crumpled wax paper or cellophane.

✔ Pack the tin in another larger container and surround it with lightweight but sturdy packing material. Styrofoam peanuts or bubble wrap are good choices. Popcorn is a good packing material, too. Or try crumpled newspaper or colored tissue paper.

✔ Send the cookies the quickest way possible, either by overnight mail or another type of shipper.

✔ Choose your destinations carefully so that the cookies arrive within a few days. If it takes too long for the package to arrive, the cookies may not taste good and won't be in peak condition. Sending cookies overseas may not be a good idea unless you can be sure that they'll arrive quickly.

✔ Include a note to the recipient about how to store the cookies, although the cookies will probably be eaten so quickly that storing them won't be a problem. Here's an example: "Store these cookies in an airtight container at room temperature for up to two weeks. Enjoy!"

Appendix A

Glossary

This list includes all the terms you need to understand to be successful at baking cookies. Many of the terms are no doubt familiar to you, but some of them may be entering your vocabulary for the first time. Knowing these words makes your cookie-baking experience richer and definitely more fun!

batter: An uncooked mixture of flour, eggs, and a liquid, such as milk, that is the base for some cookie recipes. Sugar and other flavorings are often added. The batter is thin enough to be poured or dropped from a spoon.

beat: To rapidly mix ingredients in a circular motion in order to change their consistency. Beating makes batters smooth and adds volume to egg whites and cream by integrating air into them.

blend: The technique for combining two or more ingredients so that they are smooth and uniform in appearance, texture, and flavor. Blending can be done by hand, using a rubber spatula, whisk, or spoon, or by machine, using a food processor, electric mixer, or blender. *Blend* can also be a noun, meaning a mixture of ingredients.

chill: To put dough or other food in the refrigerator or freezer for a period of time until the food is cold. Chilling changes the texture and makes the food firmer, which makes it easier to handle.

chop: To cut food into small pieces using a chef's knife or another sharp utensil, such as a food processor or blender. The size of the chopped pieces can vary from coarse to very fine, depending on how the ingredient is used in the recipe.

cream: The technique for mixing or beating fat and other ingredients, such as sugar, together until the mixture is so well blended that detecting the individual ingredients is impossible.

dough: An uncooked mixture of flour and liquid that is the basis of most cookie recipes. Dough is thick enough to roll and shape. Stiff doughs contain more dry ingredients in proportion to liquid than do soft doughs.

drain: To pour off excess liquid from a mixture by placing the mixture in a colander or strainer set over a sink. To collect the liquid, place a bowl under the colander.

dredge: To coat the outside of a mixture with another ingredient, such as finely chopped nuts, sugar, cocoa, or flour. Cookie dough shaped into a cylinder can be dredged with sugar by rolling it in the sugar.

drizzle: To lightly, slowly pour a liquid, such as melted chocolate or butter or a sugar glaze, in a very thin, steady stream over the surface of cookies or a plate.

dust: To lightly sprinkle a surface with a fine, powdery ingredient, such as flour, confectioners' sugar, cocoa powder, or finely chopped nuts.

egg wash: A whole egg, egg yolk, or egg white beaten with a little water, milk, or cream that is brushed on top of cookies before baking to give them a glossy surface and aid in browning. Egg wash acts as an anchor for seeds or sugar when they are sprinkled on top and is also used to hold together two pieces of raw dough.

fold: A technique used to combine a light and heavy mixture (beaten egg whites and a batter or custard, for example). Folding maintains the air that has been beaten into the lighter mixture. Place the lighter mixture on top and use a spatula to cut vertically down through the center. Then gently move the spatula along the bottom and bring it over the top in a circular motion. Rotate the mixing bowl a quarter turn in the opposite direction at the same time. Repeat this process several times until the ingredients are blended. Folding should be done rapidly but gently.

garnish: An edible decoration added to food to make it more attractive and appealing. The garnish should be harmonious with the dish. Cookies are often garnished with confectioners' sugar or pearl sugar.

glaze: A thin, shiny coating for cookies. Egg wash, icing, jam, caramel, chocolate, and sugar glazes are all commonly used. Glazes are brushed, drizzled, or poured onto the surface. Occasionally a cookie is dipped into a glaze.

grease: To coat the surface of a baking pan or cookie sheet with fat, such as butter, margarine, or oil, or a nonstick spray to keep the food from sticking during baking.

grind: To transform or reduce food, such as nuts, into tiny pieces. Grinding can be done by machine with a food processor, blender, coffee grinder, or other grinder, or by hand with a mortar and pestle.

mix: To combine ingredients together until they are well integrated and telling one from another is difficult.

pierce: To puncture dough most of the way through. Doing so allows steam to escape while cookies bake and helps the cookies to bake evenly.

pinch: A term that describes the amount of a dry ingredient that can be grasped between the thumb and finger. A pinch is approximately $\frac{1}{16}$ of a teaspoon.

pipe: A technique for forcing frosting, icing, whipped cream, chocolate, jam, or dough from a pastry bag to form specific shapes or decorative designs. The shape of the pastry tip that's used determines the design and shape of the piped material.

preheat: To warm the oven to a specific temperature before baking.

purée: To process food to a smooth consistency. Puréeing is usually accomplished with a food processor or blender.

rest: The period of time during which dough is allowed to stand undisturbed before it's rolled out or baked. Resting lets the gluten relax and makes the dough easier to work with.

ribbon: The consistency of a batter or mixture, such as eggs and sugar, that has been beaten until it is very thick and pale-colored. When the whisk or beater is lifted above the bowl, the batter drops slowly in a ribbonlike pattern. This ribbon holds its shape for a few seconds before it sinks into the mixture.

roll out: The technique of using a rolling pin to flatten out dough to a thin, smooth layer.

scant: A limited amount. A quantity of measure that is slightly less than the full amount.

score: To mark dough lightly so that the lines are visible and can be easily cut through later.

scrape down: To remove dough or batter from the sides of a mixing bowl by using a rubber or plastic spatula or a pastry or dough scraper. The utensil is run around the side of the bowl under the dough or batter, which gathers it up. The dough or batter is added back to the amount in the bowl.

set: To allow an item to stand at room temperature or in the refrigerator or freezer until its consistency is firm or thick.

seize: When a few drops of liquid mix with chocolate as it melts, the chocolate thickens and becomes like mud; this is called *seizing*.

sift: To pass dry ingredients (flour, cocoa powder, confectioners' sugar, and so on) through a fine mesh screen, such as a sifter or strainer. Sifting lightens the ingredients by adding air and breaks up any lumps. Sifting is also used to combine dry ingredients.

simmer: To hold the temperature of a liquid just below the boiling point. Tiny bubbles gently break the surface during simmering.

soften: To bring an ingredient, such as butter or cream cheese, to the temperature at which it becomes pliable. This is sometimes referred to as bringing to room temperature. Softening is done by letting the food stand at room temperature or warming it in a microwave oven or in a double boiler.

sprinkle: To scatter a small amount of an ingredient over the surface of a food, often as a garnish.

stir: The technique for mixing ingredients together in a gentle circular motion until they are thoroughly combined. Stirring is accomplished by using a spoon, spatula, or whisk.

strain: To pass an ingredient through a fine mesh strainer, sieve, or cheesecloth to remove any lumps or other particles and to separate the liquid from the solid.

temper: To stabilize the temperature and consistency of an ingredient, such as the eggs in a custard, by adding a small amount of warm liquid to the eggs before they're cooked. Tempering is also the process of stabilizing the cocoa butter in chocolate so that it maintains an even sheen and texture and so that it will set rapidly. Tempered chocolate is used for dipping, molding, and decorating. There are several methods for tempering chocolate; they all involve heating the chocolate until it is melted, cooling it to a certain temperature, and then slowly raising the temperature to the desired point.

whip: The technique of beating rapidly in a circular motion to incorporate air into a substance such as cream or egg whites. Whipping expands the substance's volume and makes it light and fluffy. Whipping is accomplished either by hand with a whisk or rotary beater or by machine with an electric mixer. Whipping is like stirring that is done rapidly and vigorously.

yield: The amount or quantity of the finished product that a recipe makes.

zest: The colored outer rind of citrus fruit that contains the fruit's sweet flavor and perfume in its essential oils. Zest is removed with a special tool called a zester that separates the zest from the bitter white pith underneath. A vegetable peeler, sharp knife, or grater can also be used to remove zest.

Appendix B

Sources for Ingredients and Equipment

Cookie bakers should have no trouble finding what they need to bake cookies. This chapter presents a list of reliable sources where you can find all the equipment and ingredients you use to bake cookies — and a lot of things that you may not need but are awfully fun to have.

You can order online or obtain a catalog for ordering from a variety of Web sites. One great thing about online shopping is that often you can look at pictures of what you're interested in. If you're not comfortable with the idea of sending your credit card number into cyberspace, most of the sources in this list have toll-free numbers for telephone ordering. And some of them may have a location where you live, so you can see the items up close and personal.

Bridge Kitchenware
214 East 52nd Street
New York, NY 10022
212-274-3435
800-274-3535
www.bridgekitchenware.com

An extensive collection of cookie-baking equipment for home and commercial use, including a variety of cookie sheets and baking sheets.

Beryl's Cake Decorating Equipment
P.O. Box 1584
North Springfield, VA 22151
703-256-6951
800-488-2749
www.beryls.com

A great source for a wide variety of cookie cutters and sets.

Chef's Catalog
3215 Commercial Avenue
Northbrook, IL 60062-1900
800-967-2433
www.chefscatalog.com

A variety of cookie sheets, cookie presses, three-tier baking racks, Neilsen-Massey vanilla extract, and parchment paper.

Dean & DeLuca
560 Broadway
New York, NY 10012
212-431-1691
800-221-7714
www.deandeluca.com

A wide variety of tools, including timers, spice mills, and strainers. Dean & DeLuca also carries Scharffen Berger chocolate, cocoa powder, extracts, and many spices.

J. B. Prince Company
36 East 31st Street
New York, NY 10016
212-683-3553
800-473-0577
www.jbprince.com

Professional-quality baking equipment, including specialty molds, cutters, and knives, mostly imported from Europe.

King Arthur Flour Baker's Catalog
P.O. Box 876
Norwich, VT 05055
800-827-6836
www.kingarthurflour.com

A variety of cookie-baking equipment, including more than 100 cutters, stamps and molds, cookie presses, and ingredients such as extracts, specialty flours, and specialty sugars.

La Cuisine
323 Cameron Street
Alexandria, VA 22314
703-836-4435
800-521-1176
www.lacuisineus.com

A wide variety of cookie-baking equipment, including springerle molds, pastry bags and tips, silicone sheet pan liners, and specialty sugars.

Lamalle Kitchenware
36 West 25th Street
New York, NY 10010
212-242-0750
800-660-0750
www.foodnet.com/epr/sections/writers/trends/lamall.html

A wide variety of molds and specialty tools for cookie baking.

Penzeys Spices
P.O. Box 993
W19362 Apollo Drive
Muskego, WI 53150
800-741-7787
www.penzeys.com

Spices and flavorings, including those that are hard to find. Penzeys also carries spice mills and spice storage containers.

Parrish's Cake Decorating Supplies, Inc.
225 West 16th Street
Gardena, CA 90248-1803
310-324-2253
800-736-8443
www.parrishsmagicline.com/sys-tmpl/door/

A wide variety of cookie cutters, pastry bags and tips, and food coloring.

Sur La Table
1765 Sixth Avenue South
Seattle, WA 93134-1608
800-243-0852
www.surlatable.com

A wide variety of cookie-baking equipment, including mixers, cookie cutters, racks, springerle molds, madeleine plaques, pastry bags and tips, cookie sheets, and cookie presses. Sur La Table also carries a variety of chocolates, including Scharffen Berger and Seattle chocolates. It also carries pure chocolate extract and Neilsen-Massey vanilla.

Sweet Celebrations
P.O. Box 39426
Edina, MN 55439-0426
612-943-1508
800-328-6722
www.maidofscandinavia.com

Specialists in cake-decorating equipment and baking equipment, including cutters, pastry bags and tips, molds, cookie presses, and pizzelle irons. Sweet Celebrations also carries several types of chocolate, including Merckens, Peter's, and Callebaut.

Williams-Sonoma
P.O. Box 7456
San Francisco, CA 94120-7456
415-421-4242
800-541-2233
www.williams-sonoma.com

A wide variety of cookie-baking equipment, including mixers, measuring tools, spatulas, cookie sheets, cookie presses, cookie cutters, parchment paper, and silicon sheet liners. Williams-Sonoma also carries chocolate, including Scharffen Berger, Pernigotti cocoa powder, Neilsen-Massey vanilla, and crystal colored sugar.

Wilton Enterprises, Inc.
240 West 75th Street
Woodridge, IL 60517
630-963- 7100
800-794-5866
www.wilton.com

Copper and other cookie cutters, cookie presses, molds, stamps, giant cookie pans (including heart, teddy bear, flower, and round shapes), and pastry bags and tips.

Appendix C

Metric Conversion Guide

*N**ote:* The recipes in this cookbook were not developed or tested using metric measures. There may be some variation in quality when converting to metric units.

Common Abbreviations

Abbreviation(s)	What It Stands For
C, c	cup
g	gram
kg	kilogram
L, l	liter
lb	pound
mL, ml	milliliter
oz	ounce
pt	pint
t, tsp	teaspoon
T, TB, Tbl, Tbsp	tablespoon

Volume

U.S Units	Canadian Metric	Australian Metric
¼ teaspoon	1 mL	1 ml
½ teaspoon	2 mL	2 ml
1 teaspoon	5 mL	5 ml
1 tablespoon	15 mL	20 ml
¼ cup	50 mL	60 ml
⅓ cup	75 mL	80 ml
½ cup	125 mL	125 ml
⅔ cup	150 mL	170 ml
¾ cup	175 mL	190 ml
1 cup	250 mL	250 ml
1 quart	1 liter	1 liter
1½ quarts	1.5 liters	1.5 liters
2 quarts	2 liters	2 liters
2½ quarts	2.5 liters	2.5 liters
3 quarts	3 liters	3 liters
4 quarts	4 liters	4 liters

Weight

U.S. Units	Canadian Metric	Australian Metric
1 ounce	30 grams	30 grams
2 ounces	55 grams	60 grams
3 ounces	85 grams	90 grams
4 ounces (¼ pound)	115 grams	125 grams
8 ounces (½ pound)	225 grams	225 grams
16 ounces (1 pound)	455 grams	500 grams
1 pound	455 grams	1/2 kilogram

Measurements

Inches	*Centimeters*
½	1.5
1	2.5
2	5.0
3	7.5
4	10.0
5	12.5
6	15.0
7	17.5
8	20.5
9	23.0
10	25.5
11	28.0
12	30.5
13	33.0

Temperature (Degrees)

Fahrenheit	Celsius
32	0
212	100
250	120
275	140
300	150
325	160
350	180
375	190
400	200
425	220
450	230
475	240
500	260

Index

Notes

Notes

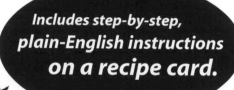

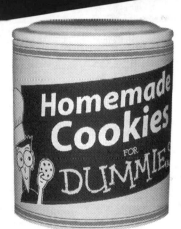

Notes

Notes